THOTH

THE HISTORY OF THE ANCIENT EGYPTIAN GOD OF WISDOM

THOTH

THE HISTORY OF THE ANCIENT EGYPTIAN GOD OF WISDOM

LESLEY JACKSON

Published by Avalonia
Glastonbury, United Kingdom
www.avaloniabooks.co.uk

Published by Avalonia

BM Avalonia, London, WC1N 3XX, England, UK

www.avaloniabooks.co.uk

THOTH: The History of the Ancient Egyptian God of Wisdom

© Lesley Jackson, 2011

First Published by Avalonia 2012

ISBN 978-1-905297-47-4

Typeset and design by Satori

Cover Art "Thoth" by Brian Andrews, 2011
Illustrations by Brian Andrews, 2005, 2011

British Library Cataloguing in Publication Data. A catalogue record for
this book is available from the British Library.

DEDICATION

This book is dedicated to the God of the Scribes,
without whom there would be no books.

And also to Graham, with love and thanks for his support
and steadfast belief in my writing.

BIOGRAPHY

Lesley Jackson has always had an interest in, and a yearning for, the mysterious geographical; be they lost worlds, otherworlds or the sacred places of this world. A career in IT was merely a logical façade. Many years of involvement in the local archaeological society deepened her interest in ancient cultures and their religions.

Since being blessed with early retirement, Lesley had devoted much of her time to researching and writing about early religion and mythology. Ancient Egypt is an enduring passion but other paths are always beckoning from around the misty hills.

She lives in the remote East Riding with a tolerant husband and an ever increasing volume of books and rocks. Any remaining spare time is spent travelling or baking and making chocolates.

TABLE OF CONTENTS

ACKNOWLEDGEMENTS

No study of Egyptian religion would be possible without access to their writings. I am indebted to all of those who have studied these ancient languages and have provided translations for the rest of us to use.

I would like to thank the British Library, the Egyptian Exploration Society and the University of Hull for the use of their libraries.

Quotes are included with permission of the following:

T A Allen *The Book of the Dead or Going Forth by Day* University of Chicago Press 1974.

C J Bleeker *Hathor and Thoth: Two Key Figures of the Ancient Egyptian Religion* E J Brill 1973. © Koninklijke Brill N.V.

J F Borghouts *Ancient Egyptian Magical Texts* E J Brill 1978. © Koninklijke Brill N.V.

R O Faulkner *The Ancient Egyptian Book of the Dead* British Museum Publications 1989. © The Limited Editions Club Inc.

R O Faulkner *The Ancient Egyptian Coffin Texts* Aris & Phillips 2007.

J H Kamstra, H Milde & K Wagtendank (ed.) *Funerary Symbols and Religion. Essays dedicated to Professor MSHG Heerma Van Voss* J H. Kok-Hampden 1988.

K A Kitchen *Ramesside Inscriptions Translated & Annotated. Volume I. Ramesses I, Sethos I and contemporaries.* Blackwell Publishers Ltd 1993. © John Wiley & Sons Ltd.

K A Kitchen *Ramesside Inscriptions Translated & Annotated. Volume II. Ramesses II, Royal Inscriptions.* Blackwell Publishers Ltd 1993. © John Wiley & Sons Ltd.

K A Kitchen *Ramesside Inscriptions Translated and Annotated. Volume III. Ramesses II, his Contemporaries.* Blackwell Publishers Ltd 2000. © John Wiley & Sons Ltd.

K A Kitchen *Ramesside Inscriptions Translated and Annotated Volume IV. Merenptah and the Late Nineteenth Dynasty.* Blackwell Publishers Ltd 2003. © John Wiley & Sons Ltd.

Leonard H. Lesko, *Ancient Egyptian Book of Two Ways.* © 1973 by the Regents of the University of California. University of California Press.

Miriam Lichtheim, *Ancient Egyptian Literature: Volumes I & II.* © 1975 by the Regents of the University of California. Published by the University of California Press.

R Parkinson *Cracking Codes: The Rosetta Stone and Decipherment.* British Museum Press 1999.

W K Simpson, R K Ritner, V A Tobin & E F Wente *The Literature of Ancient Egypt.* Yale University Press 2003.

CHAPTER 1

INTRODUCTION

"Salutation to thee, Thoth. All protection [for me] at dawn."[1]

Thoth is one of the more well known of the Egyptian gods. He is the God of the Scribes, God of the Moon and the Judge who records the verdict at the deceased's judgment. Is this all there is to him, a few pages in every dictionary of Ancient Egyptian Gods?

His name is still with us today; we have the tarot of Thoth, Thoth Publications and Tehuti Knowledge Services to name but a few. In his ibis-headed form Thoth walks the floors of Watkins Books (London) and his ibis is a logo of Ibis Press. To some he is the *'priest from Atlantis'*, to others Hermes Trismegistus, the thrice-great mortal who gave us the wisdom of Hermeticism from Classical Alexandria.

My interest, however, is in Thoth's original form as a god of the Ancient Egyptians, before his metamorphosis in Classical and later periods. I will focus my investigations on what the Egyptians had to say about their god. Over the thousands of years of the Egyptian religion the conception of Thoth, like all the other deities, changed considerably. Different aspects of his character will have been emphasised at different times. His popularity and importance will have fluctuated as society changed and the various cults evolved and

---

[1] *The Wandering of the Soul*, Piankoff, 1972:25, Spell 1092.

interacted with each other. What was true and important to the Egyptians in the early Dynasties will have been very different to those of the Ptolemaic and Roman Periods, yet the common themes and personalities will still be present.

When I first began studying Egyptian religion I kept encountering Thoth and he kept nudging me to find out more about him. As I read more the questions kept on coming. Who is this god and where does he come from? Why is Thoth both an ibis and a baboon? Why does he spend his time sorting out divine problems and recording everything? Who worshipped him and what did he ask of his followers? Was he a bringer of light or the dangerous god of necromancers?

In this book I will attempt an in-depth analysis of the worship and character of Thoth as I delve deeper into these and other questions. It is probably very arrogant to assume that I can describe Thoth as he appeared to the Egyptians but this is what I am attempting to do. No doubt much will be incorrect but I believe that an echo of the old god can find its way through the millennia of changing culture and language and the random selection of surviving evidence, to say nothing of our incorrect interpretations and misunderstandings.

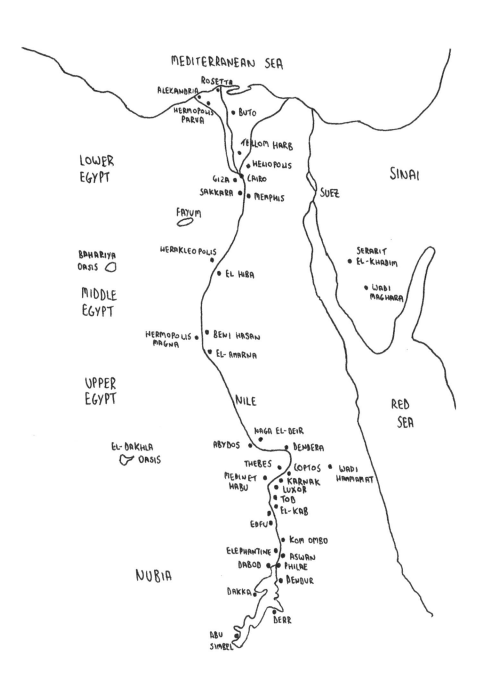

MEDITERRANEAN SEA

ROSETTA
ALEXANDRIA
HERMOPOLIS
PARVA
• BUTO

LOWER
EGYPT

TELLOM HARB
• HELIOPOLIS
GIZA • CAIRO
SAKKARA • MEMPHIS
SUEZ

SINAI

FAYUM

BAHARIYA
OASIS

HERAKLEOPOLIS

SERABIT
• EL-KHADIM

• EL HIBA

• WADI
MAGHARA

MIDDLE
EGYPT

HERMOPOLIS
MAGNA
• BENI HASAN
• EL-AMARNA

UPPER
EGYPT

NILE

RED
SEA

NAGA EL-DEIR

EL-DAKHLA
OASIS

ABYDOS •
• DENDERA

THEBES
MEDINET
HABU
COPTOS • WADI
HAMMAMAT
KARNAK
LUXOR
TOB
EL-KAB

EDFU •

• KOM OMBO

ELEPHANTINE
DABOD •
ASWAN
PHILAE

NUBIA

• DENDUR

DAKKA •

DERR

ABU
SIMBEL

13

CHAPTER 2

THE NAMES OF THOTH

"I know you, and I know your names."[2]

The Importance of Names

Names were very important to the Egyptians because they bestowed identity. A true name expressed the essence of a person, or thing, and connected them to a spiritual reality. To correctly pronounce the name of a person, or thing, was to endow them with existence. If anyone's name was erased so were they. Knowing the proper name of someone, or something, gave you power over them. The funerary texts constantly explain the *'true'* names for this reason.

The Names of Thoth

When written in hieroglyphs, Thoth's name is the figure of an ibis. The direct translation of this seems to be *Dhwtj*, or *Dhwty*. The Egyptians did not write vowels so translators have to guess. Inserting the conventionally accepted vowels gives Djehuti. A few explanations for this name have been made but none are entirely satisfactory. It could mean *'he from Dhwt'*, or Djehut, but there is no reference to a place of this name. Another suggestion is that *dhw* is the oldest name of the ibis and *Dhwtj* means *'he who has the name of an ibis'*. Given

---

2 *The Book of the Dead or Going Forth by Day*, Allen, 1974:64, Spell 71.

the Egyptians fondness for puns and word play it may have derived from *huwtj*, meaning *'messenger'*, from his role as the messenger of Ra. Cryptic names were also used by the Egyptians. These relied on puns and allusions rather than a direct reference to the one being named. One suggestion is that the name Djehuti may derive from *'the crusher'* referring to his role in defeating the enemies of Ra. The fact is we can never know. Thoth's name might be so old that even the priests of the Old Kingdom would not have known its true origin.[3]

Budge uses the name Tehuti and cites the name for the ibis as *tehu*.[4] The use of Tehuti, or Tahuti, rather than Djehuti appears to be solely the result of varying styles of translation at different time periods.

By the end of the New Kingdom Thoth is sometimes called Isdes. This god was originally the judge of the dead, and Lord of the West, and so became associated with Thoth in his afterlife aspects. Both names are used in the *Book of the Dead*; the use of Isdes may be when the afterlife aspects of Thoth are specifically referred to.

Less Elegant Names

All deities had epithets, such as Great One or Golden One, but some of the names used by the Egyptians appear rather impolite by our standards. King Horemheb describes himself as *"rejoicing at Truth like the Beaky one"*.[5] A similar nickname is also used in the *Book of the Dead*. *"O Nosey who came forth from Hermopolis, I have not been rapacious."*[6] This spell is part of the Negative Confession which is recited by the deceased before they are judged. Given the critical importance of this spell, one has to assume that referring to the god who is just about to judge your soul as *'Nosey'* was not in any way considered disrespectful.

Greek Interpretations

The Greeks frequently took an arrogant and condescending attitude to foreign names and on many occasions their interpretations

---

[3] *Hathor and Thoth: Two Key Figures of the Ancient Egyptian Religion*, Bleeker, 1973:106-107.
[4] *The Gods of the Egyptians Vol 1*, Budge, 1969:402.
[5] *The Coronation of King Haremhab*, Gardiner, 1953: 14.
[6] *The Ancient Egyptian Book of the Dead*, Faulkner, 1989:31, Spell 125.

bear little resemblance to the original name. This seems to be true for the name Djehuti, which they translated as Thoth. The Romans also adopted this style and variations used are Theuth, Thoyt, Thot and Thaut. We can only assume that this came about through a mishearing, misinterpretation or contraction of the name Djehuti. Boylan suggests that the name was pronounced De-howti or Te-howti.[7] If the '*t*' or '*d*' was pronounced as '*th*' it is possible to see Thoth as a contraction of the name. Such speculation is of limited use as we will never know how the Egyptians pronounced this or any other word.

We tend to follow the Greek and Roman authors and so most of the Egyptian deities are known to us by their classical names. Over time academic interpretations change and the spelling of the Egyptian names can vary depending on the period that the translated source document is from, such as the use of Re rather than Ra. Some are consistent in their spelling and Thoth is one.

The Greeks associated Thoth with their god Hermes and often called him Hermes Trismegistus, three times great, taking one of Thoth's epithets. The Romans equated him with Mercury and also gave him the epithet *Ter Maximus*. This will be covered further in chapter 14.

The Epithets of Thoth

The gods were said to be '*rich in names*' and Thoth is no exception. At the back of his book Boylan lists the epithets of Thoth. As these cover about twenty pages, including the associated hieroglyphs, they are not reproduced here. Many of the more common epithets have been cited throughout this book. The following is a selection of some of the others:

- Bull of the Two Truths[8]

- Chiefest of the Gods[9]

- Counter of the Stars[10]

---

[7] *Thoth Or The Hermes Of Egypt*, Boylan, 1922:5.
[8] *The Papyrus of Khnememhab in University College, London*, Shorter, 1937:36.
[9] *The Ancient Egyptian Coffin Texts Vol 1*, Faulkner, 2007:280, Spell 345.

- Expert One[11]

- Giver of Old Age[12]

- Great Bull[13]

- Him of Many Names[14]

- Lord of All[15]

- Lord of God's Words[16]

- Maker of Everlasting[17]

- Master of Papyrus[18]

- Thoth the Mysterious[19]

- Thoth the Wise[20]

A deity will sometimes take another's name, which is done to emphasise a specific aspect of that deity. The phrase *"in this my name of"* occurs many times throughout the various texts. In his declamation from Spell 182, of the *Book of the Dead*, Thoth says *"I have opened beautiful things in this my name of Wep-wawet, Opener of the Ways"*. Wepwawet was the jackal god who helped the deceased. This puts the emphasis on Thoth's role as guide of the vindicated dead as he leads them to the rewards of the afterlife.[21]

What's in a Name?

A name can mean everything, yet nothing. Given the Egyptians' respect for the power of true names it is no surprise that the deities had many names and that the important ones were kept secret even from the other deities. *"Oh you eight gods there who came forth from*

---

[10] *The Gods of the Egyptians Vol 1*. Budge, 1969:400.
[11] *Thoth Or The Hermes Of Egypt*, Boylan, 1922:103.
[12] Petrie Museum, London. Basalt fragment from the Ptolemaic Period.
[13] *The Ancient Egyptian Coffin Texts Vol 3*, Faulkner, 2007:14, Spell 824.
[14] *Egyptian Magic*, Budge, 1971:32.
[15] *The Ancient Egyptian Coffin Texts Vol 2*, Faulkner, 2007:170, Spell 565.
[16] *Cracking Codes: The Rosetta Stone and Decipherment*, Parkinson, 1999:143.
[17] *Ramesside Inscriptions Translated & Annotated. Vol III*. Kitchen, 2000:452.
[18] *Egyptian Magic*, Budge, 1971:128.
[19] *The Book of the Dead or Going Forth by Day*, Allen, 1974:93, Spell 116.
[20] *The Book of the Dead or Going Forth by Day*, Allen, 1974:10, Spell 8a.
[21] *The Wisdom of Ancient Egypt*, Kaster, 1993:75, Spell 182.

Nun...as for their true name, it is a fact that it is not known."[22] The stele of Amenemhat at Abydos has this to say about the names and forms of god: *"Many are (your) names, sacred (your) kheperu-transformations, secret (your) iru-forms in the temples."*[23]

Despite all that is said about the importance of names and ensuring the correct pronunciation, it probably doesn't matter what name we use. Mispronouncing or using the incorrect name of your deity is not viewed as a sin. They always know who calls them.

---

[22] *Ancient Egyptian Magical Texts*, Borghouts, 1978:36.
[23] *The Gods of Egypt*, Traunecker, 2001:42.

CHAPTER 3

SYMBOLISM

"Venerate God on your road, whatever form He may take."[24]

Introduction to Iconography

In the minds of explorers and conquerors, from the Greeks and Romans to the Victorians, the Egyptians were a strange, ignorant people who worshipped animals and half-human creatures and their reactions ranged from puzzled amusement to downright contempt. The Egyptians knew that their hybrid and animal depictions weren't what their deities really looked like. They understood that the divine is unknowable and beyond our comprehension, indeed they describe their deities as hidden and mysterious, but they wanted a way of representing them. In addition, for a polytheist society it is essential to be able to distinguish between deities and iconography and symbols facilitate this. Each god and goddess had to be immediately recognisable to their followers, so how could the deities be best represented? The Egyptians attached great spiritual significance to their environment and most of the creatures and natural forces spoke of a connection to the sacred spiritual world. It was logical for them to portray their deities using creatures taken from the natural world. Divine nature was fluid. They believed that each deity could manifest

---

[24] *The Living Wisdom of Ancient Egypt*, Jacq, 1999:44, *Merikare*.

in any form they chose and that they were able to do this simultaneously. Thus, any number of creatures could portray the same deity whilst the same creature could portray any number of deities.

The Egyptian religion, as we recognize it, developed from the earliest beliefs of the native people and it is probable that these were shamanic in origin. When in trance states humans tend to encounter animals and hybrid-animals who are viewed as either deities or guides. The concept of deities assuming animal forms would thus have been present from the birth of their religion.

The depicted forms of the deities had two main purposes. They were a symbol to identify the deity, or a specific attribute of them, and at a deeper level they were to remind people of something intangible and to speak to the soul. This is just as true of the classical religions, and of Christianity, all of which are steeped in symbolism had the detractors of the Egyptian religion only paused to reflect on this. The *'Lamb of God'* is a recognised Christian symbol yet any Christian would be incredulous at the suggestion that they worshipped a sheep.

The Iconography of Thoth

Thoth can be portrayed in four ways: as an ibis, an ibis-headed man, a baboon or a baboon-headed man. His most common depiction is as an ibis-headed man then as a baboon. He can appear in two different forms in the same illustration. For example, in some depictions of the Weighing of the Heart, in the *Book of the Dead*, Thoth is portrayed both as a baboon adjusting the balance and as an ibis-headed man recording the verdict. Each image alludes to a different aspect of him. As with any deity is not possible to show the true nature of Thoth, as nothing can encompass or comprehend him, so this variable iconography was considered the best way of illustrating the intangible.

Silver was strongly associated with the moon, as it is in Western culture, and with ritual purity. It had to be imported so it was considered a prestigious metal; the bones of the deities were said to be made of silver.[25] Despite this strong lunar association silver isn't

---

[25] *Precious-Metal Polychromy in Egypt in the Time of Tutankhamun*, Schorsch, 2001:55-57.

always used in images of Thoth. Gold may have been considered more appropriate for divine images as it is as imperishable as the deity it portrays. The flesh of deities was believed to be made from gold so a gold statue was considered a better reflection of the divine. Some statues of Thoth will have been partially gilded with silver. A serpentine statue of the baboon form of Thoth, from the 25th Dynasty, has the face inlaid with silver which will have helped to emphasise Thoth's lunar aspects.[26]

The Ibis

The sacred ibis (*Threskiornis aethiopicus*) is the ibis form of Thoth. (In older texts it is sometimes called *Ibis religiosa*.) It has distinctive black and white plumage and a curved bill. This bird is closely associated with Thoth and, as far as we know, with no other deity. An ibis hieroglyph is immediately distinguishable as Thoth. In the Old Kingdom Thoth's name was indicated by an ibis on a perch rather than being fully written.

Could it have been the sight of ibises perching on boundary markers of fields and settlements that provided the inspiration for this? It would suggest an immediate link to Thoth in his role as regulator and lawgiver for, no doubt, land and boundary disputes would have been as common in Egypt as anywhere else. *"Great God of primeval times...who hands over houses and establishes temples, who makes known the gods and what is theirs...the lands and their boundaries and fields likewise."*[27]

By the Middle Kingdom Thoth's name is sometimes spelt in full but his ibis hieroglyph still predominates. Boylan suggests that the ibis form of Thoth is the earliest representation of him.[28] There are more portrayals of Thoth in ibis form in the earlier periods, by the late New Kingdom and beyond he is more often portrayed in baboon form. As early as the end of the 4th millennium BCE the ibis ensign is used in religious processions. The ibis form appears on slate palettes of the Predynastic period and is on the *'Battlefield palette'* (a cosmetic palette) although it is not proven that this ibis form is definitely

---

[26] *Symbol and Magic in Egyptian Art*, Wilkinson, 1994:99.
[27] *Some Remarks on the Mysterious Language of the Baboons*, Velde, 1988:133.
[28] *Thoth Or The Hermes Of Egypt*, Boylan, 1922:76.

associated with Thoth.[29] The ibis appears on the standard of the 15th nome of Lower Egypt, at Hermopolis Parva, the centre of Thoth's cult in the Delta region.

Birds frequently have divine associations because they can fly. In many cultures they are considered messengers of the deities and they fly to the *'great beyond'* to bring back wisdom. To the Egyptians wetland birds were also associated with creation. They believed that the ordered universe rose out of the watery chaos of the *Nun*, often symbolised by swampland, so birds of the wetlands held special significance. But how did this particular bird come to represent Thoth? Thoth was known as the messenger of Ra and the Egyptians loved puns. The fact that *hbj*, the word for *'ibis'*, was similar to *h3b*, the word for *'messenger'*, would have been seen as evidence of Thoth's connection to this species.[30]

One suggestion is that the sacred ibis is a lunar symbol; its thin, curved beak representing the crescent moon and its black and white plumage symbolising the phases of the moon. Classical authors drew an immediate connection between the ibis and the moon and the lunar symbolism of the ibis was commented on by a number of writers. However, the Classical writers made many observations about many things but not all of them can be considered experts or even reliable observers. Aelian, for example, who wrote in the early 3rd century CE never left Italy. All his work is based on hearsay and other people's accounts.

Plutarch said, *"By the relative position of its legs to one another, and [of these] to its beak, it forms an equilateral triangle; and yet again, the variegation and admixture of its black with its white feathers suggest the gibbous moon".*[31] The flight of the ibis was said to be dignified and poised, mimicking the path of the moon across the sky. Perhaps flocks of ibises returning to roost at sunset suggested a relationship with the rising moon. Aelian made a number of observations about the ibis. *"It knows when the moon is waxing and when waning...The bird is sacred to the moon. At any rate it hatches its eggs in the same number of days that the goddess takes to wax and to*

---

29 *Hieroglyphics: The writings of Ancient Egypt*, Betro, 1996:76.
30 *Hathor and Thoth: Two Key Figures of the Ancient Egyptian Religion*, Bleeker, 1973:106.
31 *Plutarch: Concerning The Mysteries Of Isis And Osiris*, Mead, 2002:249.

wane, and never leaves Egypt".[32] During a lunar eclipse *"it closes its eyes until the goddess shines out again"*.[33] (To the Greeks and Romans the moon was always a goddess.)

The Egyptians held cleanliness and purity in high regard especially in relation to religious and spiritual matters. Thoth himself was deemed to have laid down the principles that they followed. Plutarch again; *"As for the ibis, while killing the death-dealing of the reptiles, it was the first to teach them the use of medicinal evacuation, when they observed it being thus rinsed out and purged by itself"*.[34] Aelian also says *"the priests of Egypt do not purify themselves with water of every kind...but only with that from which they believe an Ibis has drunk. For they know full well that this bird would never drink water that was dirty or that had been tainted"*.[35] Strabo, writing about 7 CE, was less complimentary about the hygiene of the ibis. *"Every cross-road in Alexandria is full of them...The bird is useful because it singles out every animal and the refuse in the meat-shops"*.[36] He goes on to say that it is considered unclean for this reason, which is in complete contrast to the comments of Plutarch. Urban scavengers are seldom viewed in a good light despite the refuse collection task they perform.

Thoth is associated with protection from snakes (see chapter 8) as is the ibis. Herodotus writes about the protective nature of the ibis. *"There is a place in Arabia more or less opposite the city of Buto...On my arrival I saw their skeletons in incalculable numbers...it is said that when the winged snakes fly to Egypt from Arabia in spring, the ibises meet them at the entrance to the pass and do not let them get through, but kill them. According to the Arabians, this service is the reason for the great reverence with which the ibis is regarded in Egypt, and the Egyptians themselves admit the truth of what they say."*[37] Aelian records that *"the Egyptians maintain that all snakes dread the feathers of the ibis"*.[38]

---

[32] *On the Characteristics of Animals Vol 1*, Aelian, trans. Schofield, 1957:133-135.
[33] *On the Characteristics of Animals Vol 1*, Aelian, trans. Schofield, 1957:325.
[34] *Plutarch: Concerning The Mysteries Of Isis And Osiris*, Mead, 2002:249.
[35] *On the Characteristics of Animals Vol 2*, Aelian, trans. Schofield, 1957:161.
[36] *Geography Vol VIII*, Strabo, trans. Jones, 1932:151.
[37] *The Histories*. Herodotus, trans. Salincourt, 2003:124.
[38] *On the Characteristics of Animals Vol 1*, Aelian, trans. Scholfield, 1957:59.

Maybe to some the sacred ibis gave an impression of intelligence not normally associated with birds, hence it could represent the wisdom aspects of Thoth.[39] Admittedly I do not know much about the natural history of the ibis but this seems unlikely. A few species of birds are deemed more intelligent than others, but the ibis does not appear on this list.

Horemheb says of himself *"all his plans were as the gait of the Ibis"*.[40] Meaning, perhaps, that they were measured and purposeful and always achieved their objective. On reflection this is no worse a description than some of the political and marketing jargon in use today.

The cubit was the basic unit of measurement for the ancient world and was considered to be of divine origin. It was based on the length of a man's forearm; the royal cubit being about 52cm. Who else but Thoth, the recorder and measurer of creation, could have given this unit of measurement? Aelian said of the ibis *"I have heard further that its stride when walking measures a cubit"*. Aelian also noted the following connection between the ibis and Thoth. *"When it buries its neck and head between its breast-feathers, it imitates the shape of the heart...It is said to be beloved of Hermes the father of speech because its appearance resembles the nature of speech: thus, the black wing-feathers might be compared to speech suppressed and turned inwards, the white to speech brought out, now audible."*[41]

The habits of the sacred ibis do reflect some of this lore. Ibises associate with humans and they will roost in villages in close proximity to the inhabitants. They spend a lot of time cleaning their plumage and bathing in shallow water. Ibises will also fly from their foraging grounds to find freshwater ponds to drink from. Unlike many gregarious birds, ibises don't vocalise a lot. Maybe this gave the impression of silent wisdom as opposed to superficial chatter.[42] Sadly, the sacred ibis is no longer found in Egypt. It was relatively common until about 1800. Like much of Egypt's once abundant bird

---

[39] *Hathor and Thoth: Two Key Figures of the Ancient Egyptian Religion,* Bleeker, 1973:110.
[40] *The Coronation of King Haremhab,* Gardiner, 1953:14.
[41] *On the Characteristics of Animals Vol 2,* Aelian, trans. Scholfield, 1957:325.
[42] *Handbook of the Birds of the World Vol 1,* Elliott & Sargatal (eds), 1992:476-477.

population they have vanished, due to development, hunting and the draining of wetlands.

While the Classical writers commented upon the habits of the ibis the Egyptians recorded nothing about them. Either they thought it irrelevant, as only the religious symbolism was worthy of note, or else nothing has survived. The *Onomasticon of Amenope* is a dictionary, but it also acts as a guide to some of the religious symbolism. It has the following to say about the hieroglyph of the ibis. *"Everything is perceived through him ... It is the ancient one, who emerged from the box. It is the palette...Everything in this land is perceived through the treatises and the utensils, which came into existence through him. It is his finger.. Thot[h], the chief of the marvels in the house of clothing, who regulates the entire land."*[43] (The House of Clothing may refer to Thoth's afterlife aspects as shrouds and mummy bandages were an essential part of the funerary rituals.) When the Egyptians looked at the ibis they saw not only a bird but a link to Thoth, a reminder of the God who created the world with his words, regulated creation and who gave them the gift of writing.

A shrine in Thebes, dating to the Ptolemaic Period, has a text of dedication which says that Thoth descended on the temple each night in the form of an ibis and left every morning.[44] This temple was used as a shrine for night oracles, which were based on dreams received whilst sleeping at the temple. Many temples functioned in this way, but one visited by the ibis of Thoth would have been regarded as being especially potent.

The ibis form of Thoth is shown standing or sitting, never flying for some reason. Perhaps a flying bird would suggest a solar or sky connection which Thoth does not have. It seems to be used in general contexts where there is no lunar or scribal connection, it is rarely used in the afterworld judgement scenes. If the ibis is used to depict Thoth's name it is shown as perched on a standard. The ibis emblem for Thoth was always used in temple processions. Stelae have been found showing ibis receiving offerings or worship.

---

[43] *Ancient Egyptian Science - A Source Book Vol 1*, Clagett, 1989:240-241.
[44] *Thoth Or The Hermes Of Egypt*, Boylan, 1922:168.

From the Predynastic Period there is a marble unguent vessel for offerings, now in the Berlin Museum, which is in the form of an ibis.[45] In the Late and Ptolemaic Periods statues of ibises occur. These appear to be designed for devotional offerings, rather than for personal use, as they have been found alongside sacrificed ibis. They are made either of wood, bronze or a combination of both and are shown seated or standing. One from the Late Period, now in the Hildesheim Museum (Germany), is of wood and bronze and portrays a walking ibis.[46] From Hermopolis there are a number of ibis statues dating to the Late Period. One shows a scribe and an ibis, and another shows an ibis on a plinth in front of the kneeling goddess Maat (the goddess personifying truth and justice).[47]

A few amulets for personal use have been found but these are sparse compared to the other forms of Thoth. The ibis is not an easy form to sculpt nor is it an ideal shape for an amulet which would get considerable wear. From the Late Period there is an amulet of turquoise and dark blue faience. The ibis has its bill resting on the feather of Maat.[48]

The Ibis-Headed Man

Many of the Egyptians deities are portrayed with an animal head and Thoth is no exception. It may be that the portrayal of animal headed deities evolved from illustrations of their priests who wore a mask depicting the animal form of the deity. Masks are commonly used in religious ritual and drama. They remove both the participant and the observer from the normal world and allow the priest or priestess to more easily assume the persona of the deity. On a practical note it is easier to portray a human figure carrying out human tasks, rather than an animal, which produces a more aesthetic painting or sculpture.

Thoth is normally portrayed as an ibis-headed man when he is shown doing something or when he makes pronouncements. He is also shown receiving worship and offerings in his ibis-headed form. As

---

[45] *Sacred Luxuries,* Manniche, 1999:42.
[46] *The Complete Gods and Goddesses of Ancient Egypt,* Wilkinson, 2003:216.
[47] *The Animal World of the Pharaohs,* Houlihan, 1996:161.
[48] *The British Museum Dictionary of Ancient Egypt,* Shaw & Nicholson, 2008:278.

the Divine Scribe Thoth is frequently shown carrying the scribal palette and reed and he is often caught in the act of writing. When without his scribal equipment Thoth often carries a *was*-sceptre (a sceptre with a curved head that symbolises divine power) or the *ankh* (the symbol of life).

In paintings and reliefs his ibis head is shown in profile and he usually wears a black tripartite wig or a wig-cover - the *nemes* headdress. This is common to all animal headed deities. It shows divinity and is more aesthetically pleasing in a composite figure. Often Thoth is without a headdress but sometimes he wears a crown or a lunar crown when his lunar aspect is emphasised. The lunar crown consists of a crescent new moon that supports a disc symbolising the full moon. Thoth wears a kilt, sometimes with a long animal tail. A white sash, worn diagonally across his chest, indicates the role of a lector priest; one who created and recited the rituals. He wears bracelets on the wrists and upper arms and a heavy collar necklace is common. Thoth is unshod in almost all contexts as are the other deities. This may reflect the fact that shoes were not normally worn in sacred places.

Most statues of the ibis-headed Thoth are clothed. The Petrie Museum (London) has one where the figure is naked. This is a 12cm, green faience piece from the 27th Dynasty. Here he is shown walking forwards and is empty handed and bare headed. The representation is not clear. It doesn't appear to be related to sexuality or fertility and Thoth has no known aspects in these areas. Possibly it has afterlife connotations of being stripped of all symbolism and accomplishments to be left only with the essential self. Or it may relate to creation mythology where Thoth appears from nothing and so is shown without clothing and regalia.

According to Wilkinson there is one context where Thoth is portrayed as a naked man wearing only jackal-headed shoes.[49] He suggests that this portrays Thoth as the Hermopolitan creator god (see chapter 12), but Hornung suggests that the jackal-headed shoes connect Thoth with Wepwawet, the jackal god who was known as *"the Opener of the Ways"*.[50] This title is sometimes used when referring to

---

[49] *The Complete Gods and Goddesses of Ancient Egypt*, Wilkinson, 2003:217.
[50] *The Secret Lore of Egypt and its Impact on the West*, Hornung, 2001:66.

Thoth in his role as guide of the vindicated dead as he leads them to the rewards of the afterlife.

Sometimes the ibis-headed man is shown squatting, with his knees drawn up to his chest, and draped in a white cloth as if mummified. Such portrayals are probably intended to indicate that the deities' forms are indeterminate and undifferentiated. One illustration in the *Book of the Dead*, for the spell of Knowing the Souls of Hermopolis, is of three ibis-headed men depicted in this manner.[51]

Many scenes portray Thoth interacting with the other deities. In the temple of Sety I, at Abydos, a relief shows an ibis-headed Thoth reviving Osiris by holding an *ankh* to his face.[52] At the cult chapel of Amenhotep, at Saqqara, an ibis-headed Thoth stands before Osiris with his palette and reed as if ready to record the god's words or to report something to him.[53] Other illustrations show Thoth attending the sun god Ra (or one his other solar forms) either enthroned or, more frequently, in his solar or night barque. Thoth is shown either steering the ship or just standing in it.

On reliefs and coffins Thoth is shown being attended to by both kings and the non-royal deceased and also performing rituals for them. The deceased are also depicted worshiping and making offerings to Thoth who often sits on a throne to receive them. He is also present as a protector of, and mourner for, the deceased. On a relief at the Temple of Ramesses II an enthroned Thoth writes with a brush, he is assisted by Ramesses who holds his water pot and writing kit.[54] In one illustration from the *Book of the Dead*, Here-Ubekhet the Chantress of Amun kneels before Thoth who pours a purifying stream of divine water, shown as a stream of *ankhs*, over her.[55] The most iconic portrayal of Thoth is in the Weighing of the Heart illustration from the *Book of the Dead*. Here he holds a scribal palette and reed ready to announce the verdict to Osiris and to record it.

On a relief at the Temple of Ramesses II, Thoth is shown taking part in a purification ritual with Horus, Seth and the falcon god

---

[51] *The Ancient Egyptian Book of the Dead*, Faulkner, 1989:109, Spell 114.
[52] *The Hieroglyphs of Ancient Egypt*, Dodson, 2001:99.
[53] *The Complete Gods and Goddesses of Ancient Egypt*, Wilkinson, 2003:65.
[54] *The Complete Gods and Goddesses of Ancient Egypt*, Wilkinson, 2003:215.
[55] *Egyptian Drawings*, Peck, 1978:92-93.

Dunanwi each personifying the cardinal points.[56] The cardinal points were represented in different ways and did not appear to have had specific guardian deities, though on a number of occasions Thoth is aligned to the north. The north wind was seen as beneficial and life giving by the Egyptians in contrast to the desiccating, hot south wind. In one illustration from the *Book of the Dead* four ibis-headed men stand ready to open the four doors, which block the four winds, and give the deceased entry to the afterworld.[57] Although he is illustrated in the spell, Thoth is not one the deities invoked regarding the four winds.

Statues of the ibis-headed Thoth are reasonably common in all periods and the quality of both material and craftsmanship varies considerably. The statues tend to take one of two forms. They can be similar to the depictions in paintings and reliefs and in these Thoth carries either a palette and reed or a *was*-sceptre. In the other form he is shown striding and looking forwards holding his hands by his sides. Many of the statues are small, about 15cm or so, and were likely to have been made for personal devotions. From the Late Period there is a wooden statue of an ibis-headed man striding forwards. The ibis head is made of bronze and the statue retains traces of gilt and resinous coating. It is now in the Metropolitan Museum (New York).[58] A bronze statue from the Late Period portrays Thoth and the Hermopolitan Ogdoad (see chapter 12 for further details). An ibis-headed man sits enthroned in front of the four pairs of divinities of the Ogdoad. A small baboon squats on one arm of the throne.[59]

Amulets were designed both for wearing on their own or as part of a bead necklace. A number of amulets of an ibis-headed Thoth have been found, some of which hold the sacred *wedjat* Eye (see chapter 4 for further details). The British Museum has a gold amulet of an ibis-headed Thoth holding the *wedjat* Eye dating to the 10th century BCE.[60] An ibis-headed Thoth appears on an elaborate gold pectoral belonging to Tutankhamun. A scarab supports a *wedjat* Eye surmounted by the moon. On its disc the king is flanked by Thoth and

[56] *The Complete Gods and Goddesses of Ancient Egypt*, Wilkinson, 2003:217.
[57] *The Ancient Egyptian Book of the Dead*, Faulkner, 1989:159, Spell 161.
[58] *Hieroglyphs and the Afterlife in Ancient Egypt*, Foreman & Quirke, 1996:6-7.
[59] *Divinity and Deities in Ancient Egypt*, Silverman, 1991:35.
[60] *Magic in Ancient Egypt*, Pinch, 2006:27.

Ra-Horakhty (a fusion of Horus and Ra).[61] The ibis-headed Thoth is also inscribed on many scarabs.

The Baboon

The dog-headed baboon (*Papio cynocephalus*) is the baboon used to portray Thoth. It has a dog-like muzzle and a thick, shaggy mane. There is no evidence to show that baboons were indigenous to Egypt, although the environment in Predynastic Egypt would have supported them.[62] Throughout their history the Egyptians imported baboons from southern countries such as Ethiopia and the Sudan. Baboons were kept in the temples and all species of baboons and monkeys were kept as pets. During the Old and Middle Kingdom they were second in popularity to dogs. Whether their association with Thoth was a factor in this it is impossible to guess at. Probably it wasn't, people just enjoyed their antics. There are numerous depictions of baboons in paintings, and on friezes, often in humorous situations. They swing on the ropes of boats and on other animals' necks and sit wearing jewels and clothes. They are shown on leads being exercised; one is even depicted apprehending a thief in the market.

There have been many debates as to why a baboon was chosen to represent Thoth. It is likely that the baboon was considered a sacred animal when the Egyptian religion was first developing and there are many archaic representations of such creatures. They are prominent on the reliefs on the step pyramid of Djoser, dating from the 3rd Dynasty, and a number of small statuettes of baboons have been found from this period. A baboon god was worshipped in Hermopolis in the Late Predynastic period, about 3000 BCE. He was *"Hedj-wer - the Great White One"*, also called *"Hedjwerew - the Whitest of the Great Ones"*. A large alabaster statue of a squatting baboon from this period is now in the Egyptian Museum (Berlin).[63] As Hermopolis became the cult centre of Thoth it is likely that the baboon form of Thoth evolved from this baboon god.

While Classical writers had a lot to say about the ibis they wrote surprisingly little of relevance about the baboon, possibly it wasn't

---

[61] *The Treasures of Ancient Egypt from the Egyptian Museum in Cairo*, Bomgioanni & Croce (ed), 2003:327.
[62] *The Animal World of the Pharaohs*, Houlihan, 1996:95.
[63] *Ancient Egyptian Religion*, Cerny, 1952:21.

considered as sacred as the ibis by the Greco-Roman Period. Some of them believed that the behaviour of baboons was influenced by the phases of the moon and so was linked to Thoth in his lunar aspect. Did the Egyptians see the shape of a baboon where we see the *'man in the moon'*? Another suggestion is that it was the dexterity of the baboons' hands, similar to our own, and its behaviour and cunning intelligence, mimicking that of humans, which provided the connection.

The baboon is associated with speech. At sunrise and sunset they became restive and noisy and were said to be worshiping Ra. *"The baboons that announce Re when this great god is to be born again about the sixth hour in the Netherworld...they dance for him, they jump gaily for him, they sing for him."*[64] Their actions were compared to religious ecstasy during worship. By the New Kingdom it was believed that baboons used divine speech and that some priests could understand it. An initiate would have been proud to be able to say that they knew the *"speech of the baboons and the ibises"*.[65] Knowledge of divine speech could give access to the hidden mysteries. *"The king N. knows this secret language that is spoken by the Souls of the East."*[66] (The Souls of the East are the baboons.) It was during this period that the use of the classical Middle Egyptian language for official documents was finally abandoned; from then on it was only used for ritual purposes. By the Late Period it is unlikely that any lay person could understand the archaic speech used by the priests, it would have been as incomprehensible as the noises made by baboons. For a comparison with the evolution of the English language, consider how the Anglo-Saxon of a mere thousand years ago now has to be taught as a foreign language.

In modern society the baboon, like all monkeys, is not highly regarded and is often seen as a figure of fun or as a caricature of a human. It is seldom viewed as attractive and is often considered aggressive and greedy. To the Egyptians the baboon form of Thoth was handsome. A hymn to Thoth, from the *Papyrus Anastasi*, offers praises to Thoth *"holy baboon with shining mane, of pleasing aspect,*

---

64 *Some Remarks on the Mysterious Language of the Baboons*, Velde, 1988:130.
65 *The Ancient Egyptian Book of Thoth*, Jasnow & Zauzich, 2005:453.
66 *Some Remarks on the Mysterious Language of the Baboons*, Velde, 1988:134.

gentle, charming, loved by all.[67] Even though we may struggle to see such creatures in this way some of the huge statues of baboons do have a remarkable presence and dignity.

Baboons, even when domesticated, are often aggressive. The image of a baboon is used as a determinative (a sign which gives the meaning of the word but which isn't part of the pronunciation) in writing the phrase '*to be furious*'.[68] This aggressive side of the baboon is in direct contrast to the personality of Thoth who does not show uncontrolled aggression even when dealing with enemies and hostile forces.

Baboons are also connected with Ra, allegedly from the way they greet the rising sun. Solar baboons, in contrast to the baboon form of Thoth, often have their arms raised in adoration towards the sun. Thoth himself has a close and loyal relationship with Ra (see chapter 11) which might be relevant to his baboon symbolism.

Occasionally the baboon sign is used for Thoth's name, but it appears that the ibis expressed the essential character of Thoth better than the baboon did.

As "*the great Baboon*"[69] Thoth is depicted in baboon form in both lunar and scribal contexts. The baboon has a thick mane and is shown seated with his legs drawn up to his body and his paws on his knees. The statues are life-like and imitate the pose of a sitting baboon. Sometimes the baboon will wear a lunar crown, which symbolises the phases of the moon.

The baboon form of Thoth is usually portrayed observing an action, as do the inquisitive baboons. In the Weighing of the Heart illustrations a small baboon often sits on top of the balance.[70] Having made sure that the balance is '*true*' he then observes the proceedings to make sure they are carried out fairly, in accordance with the principals of *maat*. A few representations show the baboon accepting offerings. On a votive stele from the Late Period, now in the Petrie Museum (London), the baboon form of Thoth holds the ostrich feather symbol of Maat. Its dedication is to "*Thoth, Lord of Hermopolis*". In a

---

[67] *Hymns, Prayers and Songs*, Foster, 1995:146, *Hymn to Thoth*.
[68] *Hieroglyphics: The writings of Ancient Egypt*, Betro, 1996:102.
[69] *An Ancient Egyptian Book of Hours*, Faulkner, 1958:25.
[70] *The Egyptian Book of the Dead*, Faulkner & Goelet, 2008, plate 3.

temple decoration Nectanebo I offers *maat*, in the form of a small statue of the goddess, to the baboon form of Thoth who wears a lunar crown and is seated on a plinth.[71]

Although the baboon form is closely associated with scribes, it is not normally shown writing or carrying scribal equipment. It is usually only the ibis-headed form of Thoth who is depicted this way. The baboon form of Thoth generally watches, or supervises, the scribe who is the one depicted, not surprisingly, in the act of writing. One exception is in the illustration of the Negative Confession, from the *Book of the Dead*, on the *Papyrus of Nakht*.[72] Here the baboon holds a scribal palette and, with Maat, observes the deceased who addresses the forty two Assessors.

There are many examples of the baboon form of Thoth. The following is a selection of some of the different representations and sizes from all periods.

Amenhotep III, in the 18th Dynasty, set up huge quartzite statues of squatting baboons at Thoth's main cult centre of Hermopolis.[73] They stand 4.5m high, excluding the plinth, and weigh about 35 tons. Two of these are still standing. At the other end of the scale numerous small statues and figurines of the baboon form of Thoth have been found and these seem to be the most popular depiction of Thoth for use in domestic worship and veneration.

Statues of squatting baboons have been found from the Archaic Period, these are without the heavy mane that the later ones possess. These are likely to be devotional offerings as they were found in temple precincts. Manchester Museum has a small faience baboon, about 10cm high, dating to the Early Dynastic period before 3,100 BCE, from Hierakonpolis. A travertine statuette of a baboon, dating from 1st Dynasty around 3,000 BCE, is the earliest known monumental sculpture of an animal.[74]

Statues of scribes and baboons were particularly popular during the reign of Amenhotep III. A common form was of a scribe sitting in the traditional cross-legged position while the baboon form of Thoth,

---

[71] *Decoding Egyptian Hieroglyphs,* McDermott, 2001:114.
[72] *The Ancient Egyptian Book of the Dead,* Faulkner, 1989:28, Spell 125.
[73] *The Animal World of the Pharaohs,* Houlihan, 1996:179.
[74] *The British Museum Dictionary of Ancient Egypt,* Shaw & Nicholson, 2008:333.

wearing a lunar crown, looks down on him from a pedestal. Is Thoth inspiring and guiding the scribe or checking that his words are accurate and true? Such statues can be seen in the Cairo Museum and the Louvre Museum (Paris). There is a beautiful scribe and baboon statue from the 18th Dynasty, of the scribe Nebmerutef, now held in the Louvre Museum (Paris). It is small, about 20cm high, and carved from schist and it gives an air of elegant serenity. Nebmerutef was a high ranking priest and scribe of Amenhotep III. The scroll on his knees shows the *menhed* hieroglyph, which was used in the word *sesh* denoting *'writing'* and *'scribe'*. This hieroglyph portrays the scribal equipment of a palette, water pot and pen holder. On the offering table between the scribe and the baboon the hieroglyphs express Nebmerutef's hope that he will be able to partake of offerings made to Thoth in the afterlife.[75] In other scribe and baboon compositions the baboon sits on the shoulders of a scribe. One such example is in the Ashmolean Museum (Oxford).

Many of the baboon figurines are very small, ranging from about 2cm to 15cm in height. They vary in both the quality of the material used and the quality of the craftsmanship, an illustration of the wide social range of Thoth's worshippers. The Petrie Museum (London) has an interesting figurine modelled in faience. The detailed carving is particularly fine and the sculptor has captured a lovely expression on the animal's face. There is a blue glazed terracotta figurine of a baboon, decorated with gold and silver, in the Louvre Museum (Paris). Two small figurines from Manchester Museum have a slightly different pose. One in bronze, dating to 360 BCE, portrays a baboon standing with a human posture wearing a pectoral necklace. The other, a glazed piece dating to around 600 BCE, shows a squatting baboon draped in a white cloth.

Baboons also appear on jewellery. One of the gold pectorals of Tutankhamun depicts a solar barque carrying a scarab with the sun disc. It is flanked by two baboons wearing lunar crowns.[76] Amulets of baboons are frequently found and were thought to have been worn predominantly by scribes. They are designed to be worn either on their own or as part of a bead necklace. These amulets are up to 3cm long and occur with and without the lunar crown. From a New

---

[75] *The Hidden Life of Ancient Egypt*, Gibson, 2009:108-110.
[76] *The Animal World of the Pharaohs*, Houlihan, 1996:150-151.

Kingdom cemetery in Sesebi, in the Sudan, came a little green feldspar pendant of beautiful workmanship showing the baboon form of Thoth with a lunar crown.[77]

Baboon statues and figurines are common but they were not all directly related to Thoth; other gods, such as the moon god Khonsu, also had a baboon form. Without the lunar crown only the context and inscriptions can indicate whether the statue refers to the baboon form of Thoth, or to one of his sacred animals, rather than to another deity. In addition, baboons were also popular pets and an easy animal to show in various poses. For example, the Metropolitan Museum (New York) has a marble ointment jar in the form of a baboon holding a jar, dating to the 12th or 13th Dynasty. There is also an ointment bowl in blue marble which has two baboons carved in relief, which dates to the 15th to 17th Dynasty.[78] There is no reason to link these artefacts specifically to Thoth.

The Baboon-headed Man

For some reason Thoth is seldom depicted as a man with a baboon's head. He is portrayed in this way in some illustrations of the *Book of the Amduat* (see chapter 11). In the tomb of Sety I there is a baboon-headed man, who holds an ibis on his hand.[79] Recent excavations at Luxor have discovered a statue of Thoth in his baboon-headed form (see chapter 13).

The Sacred Animals of Thoth

As mentioned previously, the Egyptians sought the divine in nature and considered many animals to be sacred. These animals were not worshipped but were believed to be held in special regard by the deities and so were treated accordingly in religious ceremonies. Being a divine symbol, or favourite, did not guarantee an easy life for the animal. Sacred wild animals were still hunted and sacred domesticated animals were still used for food, as beasts of burden and so forth as in any other community.

---

[77] *Preliminary Report on the Excavations at Sesebi, Northern Province, Anglo-Egyptian Sudan, 1936-37,* Blackman, 1937:151.
[78] *Sacred Luxuries,* Manniche, 1999:70-71.
[79] *Hathor and Thoth: Two Key Figures of the Ancient Egyptian Religion,* Bleeker, 1973:109.

Sacrificial Offerings

Mummified sacred animals have been found from all periods. Some may have been sacrificed others embalmed when they died naturally. By the time we get to the end of the Late Dynastic and into the Ptolemaic Period there is large scale breeding of sacred animals for cult celebrations. They were considered suitable offerings to the deities, and were associated with oracles, so were kept in sanctuaries attached to temples. Ibises are by far the most plentiful as they were the easiest to breed. A block relief from a New Kingdom tomb (now in the Museo Archeologico, Florence) shows a man feeding ibises in an open poultry shed.[80] These were sacred birds raised for temple use. There are much lower numbers of baboon mummies because they were more expensive; they had to be imported and were slower and harder to breed compared to the ibis.

At the entrance to some of the catacombs were a series of small niches which had contained wooden shrines holding mummified baboons. There is a statue of Thoth, as a squatting baboon with a lunar crown, in his chapel in the catacombs of Tuna el-Gebel where several million ibises have been found.[81] At Saqqara an estimated four million ibises have been found each mummified and placed in a pottery jar. Four hundred baboons were also buried in the catacombs.

A wide variety of ibis mummies have been excavated. Many had elaborately embroidered, or appliquéd, designs such as a seated ibis-headed man, an ibis on a lotus and a baboon. The head of one mummified ibis had been outlined in gold leaf, on another the body was modelled in a limestone paste. A large number were in pots of unbaked clay. In one area the mummified ibises were placed without pots. This may have been the cheaper option for poorer pilgrims or the practice at certain periods. There were bundles containing the remains of younger birds, feathers or bones, and pottery vases containing ibis eggs. Sometimes eggs were wrapped in linen and buried under the bodies of scarab beetles.[82]

These mummies were sold to pilgrims as offerings to the deities. Gullible pilgrims were an easy target for the less scrupulous officials.

---

[80] *The Animal World of the Pharaohs,* Houlihan, 1996:158.
[81] *Cults, Caches and Catacombs,* Nicholson, 2009:33-37.
[82] *Preliminary Report on the Excavations at North Saqqara 1964-5,* Emery, 1965:4-6.

From the archive of Hor there is an ostracan (a piece of pot or stone used as a writing surface) stating the regulations of the catacombs and the rule of one *'god'* per vessel. This wasn't always adhered to, there were a number of empty pots or some containing multiple birds. These sacred animals were not always well looked after. The archive of Hor has a petition which complains that the feeding of the sacred ibis had been neglected and that the birds were starving.[83] Of some thirty-five baboons examined from Tuna el-Gebel most were in poor health.

For some reason the practice of sacrificing sacred animals increased rapidly at the end of the Late Period and it reached horrific proportions in the Ptolemaic Period. The extent of this massacre is distressing and perplexing especially when, according to Herodotus, *"for killing an ibis or a hawk, whether deliberately or not, the penalty is inevitably death"*. He also reports that dead ibises were taken to Hermopolis.[84] So why were sacred animals slaughtered in such numbers? Were the Egyptians losing their respect for the natural world? The period at which these mass sacrifices occurred was a time of great uncertainty and change. The old religion, with all its learning and rituals, was dying out. Temples were neglected and underfunded and priests poorly trained. Was individual piety being replaced by superstition? A series of foreign invasions may have been seen as the deities' displeasure and a sign that they were demanding ever more offerings. It is likely that these, and other, factors combined to produce a system that encouraged superstition and gave a lucrative income to those involved. Oracles were associated with sacrificed sacred animals and they formed the focus of popular worship at this time.

Conclusion

The origins of all sacred symbols are now lost to us and their meanings have changed considerably over time. We will never know why the Egyptians chose the symbols they did to depict their deities. By the time the Greeks were learning about the Egyptian religion it is suspected that even the priests themselves were not sure about much of their once great religion. Those that did have genuine understanding would surely have been reluctant to pass on such

---

[83] *Cults, Caches and Catacombs*, Nicholson, 2009:37.
[84] *The Histories*, Herodotus, trans. Selincourt, 2003:122.

sacred knowledge to the Greek invaders. We do know that the Egyptians loved puns and word play and this would have had a major impact on the evolution of the symbolism.

As with all sacred and spiritual matters it is better not to over analyse the symbols but to accept them and let them speak to our souls as they were intended to do. Why shouldn't we just accept the Egyptians' interpretation? The ibis came into being when Ra asked Thoth to dispatch a message. The baboon form of Thoth was created by Ra to form the moon so that people would not have to be afraid of the dark.

CHAPTER 4

LUNAR ASPECTS

"What is there in thee, Moon! that thou shouldst move my heart so potently?"[85]

The Aspects of the Divine

We like to classify our deities and give them job titles: God of War, Goddess of Wisdom and so on, but in reality we cannot even classify ourselves with one epithet so how can a deity be described in such terms? Their roles can only give an indication of part of a complex character. Deities are impossible to know or define; their aspects give us a rough approximation of one of the facets of their character. Yet within this image we may glimpse a signature of the nature of our deity. The older and more important the deity the more complex their character is likely to be and the aspects will often merge into each other or contradict. In addition, the Egyptians saw no problem with having different deities share the same roles, all were participants in the mysterious energy of creation. For them life was so rich, complex and mysterious that contradictions were only to be expected.

"The conception of god which we encounter here is fluid, unfinished, changeable...It is evidently unnatural for Egyptian gods to

---

85 *Selected Poems*, Keats, 1976:161, Endymion: Book Three.

be strictly defined. Their being remains a fluid state."[86] This and the following chapters look at the major aspects of Thoth and how they flow into and influence each other.

Lunar Aspect

The lunar aspect was an important part of Thoth's personality from his earliest origins, both as a moon god and god of the moon. He wears a lunar crown on his head to show his close association with the moon.

To the Western mind the moon is a wanderer. It is vague, inconsistent and unstable and the full moon is said to cause lunacy. All these negative characteristics were labelled 'feminine', hence the moon is feminine and thus has a goddess. Ancient religion was not always so definite. Even in the West some relics of the lunar gods survive. We have the 'man in the moon' and in the Teutonic languages the word for moon is a masculine noun. The Egyptians had lunar gods as did some of their neighbours. The Assyrian, Babylonian and Sumerian religions all had a lunar god, Sin, as well as lunar goddesses. Isis has a strong lunar association but this only developed in the Late and Ptolemaic Periods when she became the prime goddess. The Egyptians regarded the moon in a completely different light to Western Europeans. The wax and wane of the moon acted as the metronome that regulated time and it brought the gift of light in the night. The full moon was a moment of triumph representing the uniting of the sun and moon and the restoration of the Sacred Eye, which brought light back into the night sky.

Plutarch has the following to say about the attributes of the moon compared to the sun. *"And they have a myth that Heracles is settled in the Sun and accompanies him in his revolutions, while Hermes does the same for the Moon. For the [revolutions] of the Moon resemble the works of reason (logos) and super-abundant wisdom, while those of the Sun are like penetrating strokes [given] with force and power."*[87]

---

[86] *Conceptions of God in Ancient Egypt*, Hornung, 1996:99.
[87] *Plutarch: Concerning the Mysteries of Isis and Osiris*, Mead, 2002:222.

The Moon

A large number of stelae from the New Kingdom are dedicated to Thoth in his lunar aspect referring to him as *"Moon-Thoth"*, *"Lunar-Thoth"* and *"Lord of Heaven"*. He may have had a greater association with the moon at this period or it may be just a reflection of what has survived from each period. Later epithets include *"Beautiful one of the night"*, *"brightly shining"*, *"Silver Sun"*[88] and *"Silver Aten"*.[89] (Aten being a form of Ra.) Tjunuroy, a director of works at Deir el-Medina, refers to Thoth as *"O Sole One, who rises as the Moon"*.[90] A stele of Pashed, Draftsman in the Palace of Truth, shows an ibis-headed Thoth seated between two goddesses with stars. The inscription reads, *"Giving praise to Moon-Thoth, paying homage to the stars of heaven"*.[91] Other lunar quotes are; *"When Thoth and the stars are invisible"* and *"Hail O Lunar-Thoth who enlightenest the Duat in the necropolis!"*[92]

In a reflection of the perpetual waxing and waning of the moon, he is *"Thoth, born regularly"*.[93] Thoth is *"Moon in the night, ruler of the stars, who distinguishes seasons months and years: he cometh ever-living, rising and setting"*.[94] It is he who controls the workings of the sky. *"The King is Thoth in authority over the sky."*[95]

One hymn, from the stele of Horemheb, addresses Thoth as *"the moon, beautiful in its rising, lord of bright appearings who illuminates the gods"*.[96] Spell 152 of the *Coffin Texts* addresses Thoth as: *"O you Sole One who rises in the moon, O you Sole One who shines in the moon"*.[97] Spell 156 of the *Coffin Texts* ends *"What is small in the full month and great in the half-month, that is Thoth"*.[98]

From the Roman Period we have: *"Thoth in Hermonthis, moon resplendent in the heavens"*.[99] The following may also refer to the

---

[88] *Thoth Or The Hermes Of Egypt,* Boylan, 1922:64-65.
[89] *The Complete Gods and Goddesses of Ancient Egypt,* Wilkinson, 2003:216.
[90] *Ramesside Inscriptions Translated & Annotated. Vol III.* Kitchen, 2000:345.
[91] *Ramesside Inscriptions Translated & Annotated. Vol III.* Kitchen, 2000:442
[92] *Thoth Or The Hermes Of Egypt,* Boylan, 1922:63-64.
[93] *The Book of the Dead or Going Forth by Day,* Allen, 1974:103, Spell 127.
[94] *Thoth Or The Hermes Of Egypt,* Boylan, 1922:83.
[95] *The Ancient Egyptian Pyramid Texts,* Faulkner, 2007:303, Utterance 694.
[96] *A Statue of Horemhab Before His Accession,* Winlock, 1924:3.
[97] *The Ancient Egyptian Coffin Texts Vol 1,* Faulkner, 2007:131. Spell 152.
[98] *The Ancient Egyptian Coffin Texts Vol 1,* Faulkner, 2007:134. Spell 156.
[99] *Thoth Or The Hermes Of Egypt,* Boylan, 1922:64.

moon: *"my messenger appears, Thoth is on high"*[100] and *"the Judge awakes; Thoth rises high"*.[101] Thoth can also be referred to as Isdes when his lunar aspect is being emphasised. *"I know the souls of the new moon: they are Osiris, Anubis and Isdes."*[102] In many of the funerary texts there is reference to Thoth travelling the sky and to the night barque. Both the sun and the moon, with their associated deities, were believed to sail across the sky in boats in a reflection of the importance of the Nile as a means of transport. *"I travel about the sky like Thoth."*[103]

Lunar deities were always important and tended to have a special position in many pantheons. Thoth is no exception. He is often equated to Ra as a Night Sun and acts as his deputy, seated at his right hand in the position of honour. *"I am this Re who shines by night"*[104] and *"Thoth, the herald of Re in the sky"*.[105] The *Book of the Heavenly Cow* explains how Thoth became the lunar deputy of the sun god. Ra says *"'Besides, I shall cause you to encompass both the heavens with your perfection and with your brightness'. And so the Moon of Thoth came into being."*[106]

The 15th nome of Upper Egypt, which is strongly associated with Thoth, is the Hare nome. It is tempting to link the hare to the lunar aspect of Thoth as there is a strong link in Celtic mythology. However, the hare is the sacred animal of the nome goddess Wenet, who has no apparent lunar aspects.

The Guardian of the Moon

The sun and moon were considered the Eyes of Heaven by the Egyptians. They were not deities in themselves, merely composed of divine substance and so needed a divine guardian at times. In this context the moon was considered the Left Eye of Horus and Thoth was

---

[100] *The Ancient Egyptian Coffin Texts Vol 1*, Faulkner, 2007:148. Spell 173.
[101] *The Book of the Dead or Going Forth by Day*, Allen, 1974:187. Spell 178f.
[102] *The Ancient Egyptian Coffin Texts Vol 1*, Faulkner, 2007:134. Spell 155.
[103] *The Ancient Egyptian Coffin Texts Vol 1*, Faulkner, 2007:172. Spell 216.
[104] *The Ancient Egyptian Book of the Dead*, Faulkner, 1989:200. Spell 131.
[105] *The Book of the Dead or Going Forth by Day*, Allen, 1974:177. Spell 169i.
[106] *The Literature of Ancient Egypt*, Simpson et al. 2003:295. *The Book of the Heavenly Cow*, trans. Wente.

its guardian. "*Thoth who possesses the Sacred Eye.*"[107] The sun was the Right Eye of either Horus or Ra.

The moon is constantly waxing and waning and this represents its destruction by the forces of chaos and darkness and its restoration by Thoth acting as the force of light and order. The Left Eye of Horus was wounded, or plucked out, in a battle with the chaos god Seth (this is given in further detail in chapter 11). Plutarch reports, "*And they say that Typhon at one time strikes the Eye of Horus, and at another takes it out and swallows it. By 'striking' they refer enigmatically to the monthly diminution of the moon*".[108] (The Greeks equated Seth with their god Typhon.) It is Thoth who finds, restores and heals the injured Eye. He '*makes new*' the damaged Eye. "*It is I who bring the Sacred Eye, having saved it from him who would conquer it*"[109] and "*This is Thoth who is in the sky; the Eye of Horus is on his hands in the Mansion of the Moon*".[110]

Tjunuroy aligns himself with Thoth in this inscription from his tomb. "*I open Hermopolis which Thoth the excellent had sealed before me...I am the Moon among the gods, I have not failed to stand up for you, Horus.*"[111]

In another myth Thoth searches for the scattered pieces of the Eye, he counts them and then makes the Eye whole. From the Middle Kingdom onwards Thoth is shown holding out the whole Eye represented by the *wedjat* Eye. It is offered either to Ra or to Horus, who in his turn offers it to Osiris. It is this offering by Thoth which becomes the precedent for all offerings to the deities.

The illustration of the *wedjat* Eye combines a human eye and eyebrow with the facial markings of a falcon (the bird associated with Horus). The six parts of the Eye were used to write fractions in the hieroglyphic script when recording grain measures. They were also used to work out the relative proportions of drugs in medicines linking them to Thoth's healing aspect. The parts represent the fractions from ½ to 1/64. When these are summed they give a total of 63/64, which is short of the unity of one. It is said that only Thoth can supply the

---

[107] *An Ancient Egyptian Book of Hours*, Faulkner, 1958:14.
[108] *Plutarch: Concerning The Mysteries Of Isis And Osiris*, Mead, 2002:233.
[109] *The Ancient Egyptian Coffin Texts Vol 3*, Faulkner, 2007:152. Spell 1094.
[110] *The Ancient Egyptian Coffin Texts Vol 3*, Faulkner, 2007:152. Spell 1096.
[111] *Ramesside Inscriptions Translated & Annotated. Vol III*. Kitchen, 2000:345.

last 1/64th. Using magic he creates the missing part and restores the wholeness of one. "*I have found it complete, fully numbered and intact.*"[112] In his guardian role we have Thoth as he "*who seeks the wedjat-eye for its lord*", he "*who makes full the eye*" and "*who brings back the Eye*".[113] His role in restoring the Eye of Horus makes Thoth a specialist in the treatment of eye diseases (see chapter 9). The left Eye of Horus, which was wounded by Seth, is restored in parallel with the moon's waxing from new to full.

The rising full moon is illustrated in the Sokaris chapel at Dendera. An ibis-headed Thoth, assisted by Shu (the god of sunlight and dry air), holds the Restored Eye in a net. Two ibises stand beneath the net.[114] The moon's cycle is fourteen days waxing and fourteen waning and this is illustrated in a number of temples. The ascendant phase of the moon is represented by fourteen steps, of unequal height, on which fourteen gods stand. Thoth stands on the top of the flight of stairs facing the ascending gods. He holds out the healthy Eye.[115] The full moon is particularly associated with Thoth in relation to his role as protector of the moon and the Eye. The new moon, which was considered the first of the month, was also sacred to him. Festivals were held in his honour at new and full moons. "*I am one who celebrates exactly every monthly festival and half-monthly festival; the Eye of Horus which my hand holds goes round about for me in the suite of Thoth.*"[116]

To the Egyptians the full moon was a period for rejoicing as the Eye, and the moon, had been restored to its true nature. There doesn't seem to be anything linking a full moon to the negative attributes it has in the West in the form of instability and madness or to creatures such as werewolves. This is probably because Thoth, its major deity, didn't have any negative attributes. A number of astrological ceilings in tombs show how important the Egyptians considered the moment of opposition of the sun and moon; the rise of the full moon as the sun sets. The following description of a ceiling is from Deir el-Hagar, Dakhla Oasis. The ceiling dates to the 2nd century CE and portrays the waxing of the moon. Sixteen gods face a disc holding the *wedjat*

---

112 *The Ancient Egyptian Coffin Texts Vol 1*, Faulkner, 2007:193. Spell 249.
113 *Thoth Or The Hermes Of Egypt*, Boylan, 1922:72-73.
114 *The Egyptian Calendar A Work For Eternity*, Bomhard, 1999:81.
115 *The Egyptian Calendar A Work For Eternity*, Bomhard, 1999:79.
116 *The Ancient Egyptian Book of the Dead*, Faulkner, 1989:140. Spell 149.

Eye, which represents the full moon. The sun and moon are shown united at the moment of opposition. Two figures stand in a boat holding hands, the one on the left carries the sun disc and the one on the right the moon disc. Next to this image a child carrying the sun disc sits in one boat that faces a second carrying a baboon holding the moon disc. The moment of opposition is described as *"the uniting of the two bulls"*.[117] The sun and moon are considered to be of equal status. A similar ceiling is found in the Sokaris chapel at Dendera. The text reads *"for the left eye receives its light from the right one as they reunite on the day of the two bulls"*.[118]

The lunar eclipse is portrayed as yet another battle between Horus and Seth in which Seth, in his black pig form, swallows the Left Eye. Thoth forces him to disgorge it thus returning the moon to the sky. Plutarch reports, *"There are some, however, who call the shadow of the earth into which they think the moon falls and is eclipsed, Typhon"*.[119] There are many references to this; *"Seth will swallow the Eye of Horus for himself"*[120] and *"I give you the lesser Eye of Horus, of which Seth ate"*.[121] Aelian reports that *"the Egyptians are convinced that the Sow is an abomination to the sun and the moon"*.[122]

Thoth is also associated with the stars as they are seen together in the night sky. A stele, now in the Hanover Museum, depicts the adoration of the stars. An ibis-headed Thoth is flanked by two unnamed goddesses who wear a star on their heads. The text refers to Thoth as *"bull among the stars"* and the deceased prays to Thoth as the moon and the stars in the sky.[123]

The Reckoner of Time

His lunar aspect gives Thoth an obvious link to timekeeping and to the calendar, but his wisdom and scribal aspects (covered in chapter 5) are as important given the long and careful observation and recording that is needed to develop an accurate calendar. He is *"Thoth*

---

[117] *The Astronomical Ceiling of Deir el-Haggar in the Dakhleh Oasis*, Kaper, 1995:190-193
[118] *The Egyptian Calendar A Work For Eternity*, Bomhard, 1999:80.
[119] *Plutarch: Concerning The Mysteries Of Isis And Osiris*, Mead, 2002:224.
[120] *The Ancient Egyptian Coffin Texts Vol 2*, Faulkner, 2007:190. Spell 587.
[121] *The Ancient Egyptian Coffin Texts Vol 3*, Faulkner, 2007:70. Spell 935.
[122] *On the Characteristics of Animals Vol 2*, Aelian, trans. Scholfield, 1957:307.
[123] *The Secret Lore of Egypt. Its Impact on the West*, Hornung, 2001:27.

who reckons time"[124] and he shares the role of *"Divine Tutor of Time and Calendar"* with his consort Seshat.[125] (See chapter 11.)

The moon provided the first method of measuring time periods longer than a day. Its regular waxing and waning are so obvious compared with the more accurate measurements needed for the solar year. From the lunar cycles came the calendar which fixed the dates of the Egyptians' religious and civil festivals and ordered their lives. Thoth is the one who invented this essential, sacred lunar calendar. Thoth is the moon in its association with time; both as the image of eternal time and of time with its regular changes. Thoth is thus outside time as *"Creator of Everlastingness"* and *"Maker of Eternity"*.[126] At the same time he is within time acting to regulate creation. In this aspect he is *"lord of time"* and *"determiner of time"*. The calendar he created came from outside the time it regulates making it sacred in origin as well as sacred when applied to religious festivals. Thoth *"divides seasons, months, and years, who increaseth time and multiplieth years, who maketh record of kingship for the Ruler of the Two Lands. Thousands are at his disposal: tens of thousands in his right hand"*.[127] With Seshat he counts the *"years back into the past, and forward into the future"*.[128]

To such a highly centralised and bureaucratic civilization such as Egypt an accurate calendar was essential. The Greeks were said to have been very impressed by the precision of the Egyptian calendar. *"It is due to these priests also that people reckon the days, not by the moon, but by the sun, adding to the twelve months of thirty days each five days each year...They attribute to Hermes all wisdom of this particular kind."*[129]

The lunar calendar will never align with the solar calendar as it gives a year of 360 days. Both calendars have to be synchronised and Thoth is credited with aligning them. Five extra days were needed to realign the lunar and solar calendars. These intercalary days were called the epagamonal days by the Greeks and their story is recounted by Plutarch. Nut and Geb (the sky goddess and earth god) had been

---

[124] *An Ancient Egyptian Book of Hours*, Faulkner, 1958:15.
[125] *The Egyptian Calendar A Work For Eternity*, Bomhard, 1999:4.
[126] *The Gods of the Egyptians Vol 1*, Budge, 1969:412.
[127] *Thoth Or The Hermes Of Egypt*, Boylan, 1922:84.
[128] *The Egyptian Calendar A Work For Eternity*, Bomhard, 1999:XI.
[129] *Geography Vol. VIII*, Strabo, trans. Jones, 1932:125.

separated by Shu on the order of Ra who was unhappy at their being lovers. When Nut became pregnant Ra was furious and decreed that she could not give birth on any day or night of the year. Thoth took pity on her plight. He played a game of draughts with the moon and won 1/70th of each day which gave him enough light to create five extra days. These became sacred days, days out of time, and were added onto the end of the year. During these days Nut gave birth to her five children: Osiris, Horus the Elder, Seth, Isis and Nephthys. These days were considered unlucky as the children of Nut were born on them. Although popular deities, with the exception of Seth, their actions caused upset and strife. It is worth noting that the end of the Egyptian year was at the height of summer and so was a time of pestilence and illness.

An inscription in the Ramesseum at Karnak shows the astronomical cycles. The vertical axis shows Sirius as the pivotal moment which begins and ends each year. The axis is supported by the baboon form of Thoth who symbolises the precision and durability of the calendar. He is seated on a djed-pillar, a symbol of Osiris and eternity.[130]

The *Cairo Calendar*, dating to the 19th Dynasty, starts *"Here begins the beginning of infinity and the end of eternity"* and, naturally, it was *"compiled by the Majesty of Thoth"* and found *"in the library in the rear-house of the Ennead"*.[131] (The Ennead is the Council of deities.)

The first month of the year is called *Dhwty*, or *Thoth*, in recognition of his calendar. Images of Thoth often adorned timekeeping instruments. There are two water-clocks, one of limestone the other of alabaster, which have the baboon form of Thoth above the drip hole.[132] A water-clock from Karnak, dating to 1300 BCE, has a spout in the form of a squatting baboon. Above the spout is a register containing twelve gods representing the months. As well as providing a drip hole the baboon also shows the thirteenth intercalculated month.[133] An ivory sundial, dating from the 13th

[130] *The Egyptian Calendar A Work For Eternity*, Bomhard, 1999:84-85.
[131] *Village Life in Ancient Egypt: Laundry Lists and Love Songs*, McDowell, 1999:113-114.
[132] *Bibliography 1916-1917: Ancient Egypt*, Griffith, 1917:273.
[133] *Timekeeping in Ancient Egypt*, Wernick, 2009:31.

century BCE, is inscribed on one side with a boat whose occupants are worshiping Thoth.[134]

In the Myth of Horus at Edfu there is a long recitation regarding the division of time which adds nothing to the story but illustrates the importance of reckoning time. *"Seth hath been judged in the Tribunal of Re and Thoth saith: A happy day, O Horus...A happy day on this day which is divided by its minutes! A happy day on this night which is divided by its hours! A happy day in this month which is divided by its fifteenth-day feast! A happy day in this year which is divided by its months!"*[135]

Destiny

As a regulator of time *"Thoth who travels eternity"*[136] is also responsible for the destiny and the life-span of people and deities. *"A reckoner of time for gods and men."*[137] In the *Book of the Dead*, Atum (a creator god) complains to Thoth about the Children of Nut. They have disturbed the other deities with their constant quarrels and have caused divisions amongst them and Atum is getting tired of the tumult. He tells Thoth to *"Shorten their years, cut short their months"*.[138]

Thoth is *"reckoner of years"* as he records the passing of time and also assigns the length of the king's reign, a task also associated with Seshat. On a relief in the Ramesseum at Thebes they are shown writing the length of the king's reign on the leaves of the *ished* tree. *"I write thee years without number"* and *"I write for thee a mighty kingdom"*.[139]

The birthing bricks used by a mother when she delivered her child were of ritual significance. They were personified as the goddess Meskhent who protects the newborn. Thoth, sometimes with Seshat, inscribed a person's fate on these bricks. There is mention of *"the end

---

134 *Primitive Methods of Measuring Time: With Special Reference to Egypt*, Sloley, 1931: 173.
135 *The Myth of Horus at Edfu: II.C*, Blackman & Fairman, 1943:5
136 *The Ancient Egyptian Book of the Dead*, Faulkner, 1989:132. Spell 140.
137 *Thoth Or The Hermes Of Egypt*, Boylan, 1922:85.
138 *The Ancient Egyptian Book of the Dead*, Faulkner, 1989:175. Spell 175.
139 *Thoth Or The Hermes Of Egypt*, Boylan, 1922:85.

of his life that Thoth had written for him upon his brick of birth".[140] Because he had foretold everyone's destiny Thoth knew the future and so could say, *"I am Thoth who foretells the morrow and foresees the future".*[141]

The Mansion of the Moon

The vindicated dead had a choice of destinations in the afterlife. (This is covered in more detail in chapter 6.) *"As for anyone who is in his suite, he will live forever among the suite of Thoth."*[142] Those who went to Thoth became a spirit in the Night, or Lunar, Barque or the Mansion of the Moon.

The Watching Moon

As the moon, Thoth is always watchful and so aware of crime. *"It is the Moon who declares his crime"* and *"He will be caught by the might of the Moon".*[143] Thoth is also prepared to act as a witness to deeds: *"The Mansion of the Moon is a witness".*[144]

Other Egyptian Lunar Deities

Although its principal deity, Thoth was not alone in his association with the moon. The god Iah personified the moon, his name equating to that of the moon, but he seems to have had very little status. He was a relatively early god but was most popular after the end of the Middle Kingdom, during the Hyksos period, as the Hyksos rulers equated him with their moon god, Sin. From then onwards Iah's popularity declined and there is little evidence for his cult after the 18th Dynasty, although there are amulets and statues of him. He has similar lunar attributes to Thoth. A statuette from the Late Period shows Iah in human form, with a beard to show his divinity, wearing the lunar crown. He holds a plaque inscribed with

---

[140] *Magical Bricks and the Bricks of Birth,* Roth & Roehrig, 2002:137.
[141] *The Ancient Egyptian Book of the Dead,* Faulkner, 1989:181. Spell 182.
[142] *The Ancient Egyptian Coffin Texts Vol 3,* Faulkner, 2007:153. Spell 1098.
[143] *Ancient Egyptian Literature Vol 2,* Lichtheim, 2006:150-151. *The Instruction of Amenemope.*
[144] *The Ancient Egyptian Coffin Texts Vol 3,* Faulkner, 2007:152. Spell 1094.

the *wedjat* Eye.[145] Sometimes he was merged with Thoth and is shown as an ibis-headed man.[146]

A much more important lunar god was Khonsu (or Chons). His name derives from *khenes* meaning *"he who traverses [the sky]"*.[147] Khonsu was originally an unpleasant and bloodthirsty god who feasted on the hearts of the dead. *"I will appear as Khons who lives on hearts."*[148] In the *Pyramid Texts* he helped the king hunt and kill lesser deities so that the king could absorb their strength. Khonsu also had a baboon form who was feared as the Keeper of the Books of the Year. These held the names of those who would die that year. At times Khonsu seems to be the lunar equivalent of the Angry Eye of Ra. It is little wonder that Thoth was the preferred lunar god at that time.

By the New Kingdom Khonsu had transformed into the benign young son of Amun and Mut, as part of the powerful Theban Triad. (Amun was a creator god, often combined with Ra, and Mut the preeminent goddess of Thebes.) In the Fayum region Khonsu was regarded as the son of the goddess Hathor and the crocodile god Sobek. He is often portrayed as a youth wearing a side-lock of hair. By this period people appealed to him as a healing god. A 4th century BCE story tells how a statue of Khonsu was sent to a princess in Bakhtan, where the god successfully exorcised the evil spirit she was possessed by. It is not clear how or why this transformation of Khonsu occurred, but it does demonstrate that as deities can be demonised (such as Seth) they can also be rehabilitated.

Khonsu does possess some similar traits to Thoth because of the lunar connection. People appealed to *"Khonsu the merciful"* to alter their fate as he was considered a reckoner of peoples' life-span.[149] In the *Coffin Texts* there are references to Khonsu as a messenger and scribe, and at times he seems to be equated with the afterworld aspects of Thoth. Despite these similarities Khonsu cannot be viewed as a form of Thoth, many of the Egyptian deities shared characteristics.

---

[145] *The British Museum Book of Ancient Egypt*, Quirke & Spencer (eds), 1992:65.
[146] *The Complete Gods and Goddesses of Ancient Egypt*, Wilkinson, 2003:111.
[147] *The Complete Gods and Goddesses of Ancient Egypt*, Wilkinson, 2003:113.
[148] *The Ancient Egyptian Coffin Texts Vol 1*, Faulkner, 2007:229. Spell 311.
[149] *Egyptian Mythology*, Pinch, 2002:155.

As mentioned previously, when Isis became a major goddess she was associated with the moon. The cat goddess Bastet (Bast) also had lunar associations as the Eye of the Moon. These are both later developments when the concept of a lunar goddess, rather than a god, became dominant in the Ptolemaic Period in line with the conqueror's beliefs.

CHAPTER 5

THE WISE GOD

"His flint has struck the spark of speech from spirit's tinder."[150]

The Wisdom God

Thoth is perhaps best known for his role as God of the Scribes, and Scribe of the Gods, but this is only part of his character as a wisdom god. Thoth's wisdom is seen as innate; he does not have to seek out knowledge because he is already omniscient and is the repository of all knowledge and reason. He is understanding personified, the *"one who knows"*,[151] because of this Thoth had the ultimate gnosis which raised him above the other deities. He was the *"Mysterious"* and the *"Unknown"*.[152] Thoth could be thought of as the creative intelligence of the divine mind, the Greek concept of the Logos, and he is referred to as the *"Heart and Tongue of Atum"*.[153] In this context it is Thoth who takes the creative desires of the Creator and turns them into reality.

Thoth was considered to have given the Egyptians their culture. A civilization's culture was of supreme importance to them and was considered a divine gift rather than an evolving human invention.

[150] *Poems*, Lewis, 1964:12. *The Planets.*
[151] *Thoth Or The Hermes Of Egypt*, Boylan, 1922:99.
[152] *Ancient Egyptian Religion*, Cerny, 1952:60.
[153] *Myth and Ritual in the Ancient Near East*, James, 1958:151.

Through his wisdom, and love of Maat (see chapter 7), Thoth is able to sustain the cosmic order and administer creation. It is Thoth *"who guides sky and earth and nether world"*.[154]

The deceased hopes to emulate his wisdom. *"There is nothing which I do not know of what Thoth does not know, there is nothing which I do not know of what Thoth knows, and there is nothing which I do not know in my abode."*[155] Thoth's wisdom is all encompassing *"There is nothing done without your knowing"*[156] and *"With the knowledge of everything that happens"*.[157] Of all the deities it was Thoth who best personified wisdom; he was *"the sage at the heart of the Ennead"*.[158]

The kings and officials were eager to compare themselves to the deities. Whether they tried as hard to emulate their best qualities is open to question. Ramesses III said of himself *"his majesty was as discerning and shrewd as Thoth"*.[159] The leader of an expedition to Wadi Hammamat, in the 11th Dynasty, calls himself *"more intelligent than Thoth"*.[160] A rather rash boast one suspects.

His wisdom and skill with words and speech also makes Thoth a great judge (see chapter 7) and magician (see chapter 8).

Sacred Sounds

Sound, in the form of the spoken word, was considered extremely important and powerful by the Egyptians. Thoth was the *"Lord of Divine Words"*.[161] Creation happened because he spoke the divine words and their sound crystallised into matter. (See also chapter 12.) The divine word was considered immanent in all things, hence the Egyptians' love of puns and multiple layers of meaning. They believed that if two words sounded the same then there was some connection, however hidden, between the two objects or actions referenced. It was as if the Creator had left a trail of clues that people could follow if only they put enough thought and effort into the task. We are often too

---

[154] *The Book of the Dead or Going Forth by Day*, Allen, 1974:197. Spell 182.
[155] *The Ancient Egyptian Coffin Texts Vol 2*, Faulkner, 2007:79. Spell 443.
[156] *Hymns, Prayers and Songs*, Foster, 1995:112. *Hymn to Thoth.*
[157] *The Living Wisdom of Ancient Egypt*, Jacq, 1999:42. *Petosiris.*
[158] *The Living Wisdom of Ancient Egypt*, Jacq, 1999:68. *Statue of Horemheb.*
[159] *The Libyans and the End of the Egyptian Empire*, Wilson, 1935:76.
[160] *The Secret Lore of Egypt. Its Impact on the West*, Hornung, 2001:5.
[161] *Egyptian Magic*, Budge. 1971:128.

saturated by words, written and spoken, to appreciate their potency. Language is not just a way of referring to an object, or action, for our own convenience when we want to communicate with each other. As an echo of the energy which created the world correctly spoken and written words had immense power and Thoth was Lord of these Words.

The Egyptians gave the description of the hieroglyph *hwy*, speech, as follows. *"That is, speaking; that is, the throat from which every sound comes forth as words; that is, Thoth when he comes forth from the throat of Re."*[162]

The power of words is also reflected in their effectiveness at being obeyed and what Thoth said happened as he desired, *"I am Thoth...and all that comes from my mouth comes into being"*.[163] The kings and officials were keen to associate themselves with this power. Merenptah, in the *Papyrus Anastasi*, said that his words were as effective as Thoth's whose *"act cannot be brought to naught"*.[164]

Thoth gave humanity speech differentiating them from the animals. *"Who gave (us) the language and the scripture."*[165] One of his epithets is *"who hath given words and script"*.[166] He also created and separated the languages. Different languages must have been viewed as enriching rather than an obstacle to communication, unlike the biblical story of the Tower of Babel where it is seen as divine retribution. *"Hail to thee, Moon-Thoth, who made different the tongue of one country from another"*[167] and *"O Thoth, who separated languages from land to land"*.[168] Because he understands all languages Thoth is *"Lord of Foreign Lands"*.[169]

When you have different languages you need an interpreter. In the *Book of the Dead* Thoth is described as an interpreter; some versions use the term *'dragoman'* which was the modern Egyptian term for a

---

162 *The Semitic Root Hwy in Ugaritic and Derived Stems*, Ward, 1969:266.
163 *Some Remarks on the Mysterious Language of the Baboons*, Velde, 1988:143.
164 *The Ancient Egyptian Book of the Dead*, Faulkner, 1989:181. Spell 182.
165 *Hathor and Thoth: Two Key Figures of the Ancient Egyptian Religion*, Bleeker, 1973:1.
166 *Thoth Or The Hermes Of Egypt*, Boylan, 1922:95.
167 *Thoth as Creator of Languages*, Cerny, 1948:121.
168 *The Gods of Egypt*, Traunecker, 2001:39.
169 *Thoth Or The Hermes Of Egypt*, Boylan, 1922:189.

guide and interpreter. Thoth the Interpreter meets the deceased before they enter the Judgement Hall. The need for an interpreter might suggest that foreigners were also accepted in the afterworld, though there is no direct reference to this. A more likely explanation of this title is that it is Thoth's role to help the deceased understand the mysteries of the afterworld. He is *"master of the mysteries which are in heaven and earth"*.[170] Thoth as the source of magic words, and the magical power of words, is further discussed in chapter 8.

In the temple of Horus, at Edfu, there is a relief showing Horus holding a harpoon and rope in his right hand, accompanied by Isis. Thoth stands in front of them and recites from a scroll. *"Utterance by Thoth, twice great, lord of Hermopolis, him with the honeyed tongue, skilled in speech, who heralded the going of Horus to launch his war-galley, who overthrew his enemies with his utterances."*[171]

A very useful spell for the living, as well as the dead, comes from spell 90 in the *Book of the Dead*. It is a spell for ensuring that your speech will be relevant and wise rather than foolish nonsense. Thoth is not mentioned in the spell, but in the illustration the deceased Horemheb holds out a scroll to an ibis-headed Thoth who holds an *ankh* and *was*-sceptre.[172] This spell will ensure that your words will be worthy of speaking to the Greatest of Utterance and the True of Voice. A *Coffin Text* spell assures the deceased that *"your tongue is Thoth"*[173] which will enable them to pronounce the spells correctly.

Speech does not have to be magical to be effective. The correctly chosen words can pacify and comfort. Thoth drives away depression and despair caused by the presence of evil. It is he *"who soothes the heart of the gods by his words"*.[174]

Sacred Words

It is hard for us to comprehend what respect writing was given in this scholarly and bureaucratic but largely illiterate society. Thoth invented writing as a gift to mankind. He is particularly associated

---

[170] *Some Remarks on the Mysterious Language of the Baboons,* Velde, 1988:133.
[171] *The Myth of Horus at Edfu (Continued): II.C,* Blackman & Fairman, 1943:3.
[172] *The Ancient Egyptian Book of the Dead,* Faulkner, 1989:85, 87. Spell 90.
[173] *The Ancient Egyptian Coffin Texts Vol 2,* Faulkner, 2007:293. Spell 761.
[174] *Thoth Or The Hermes Of Egypt,* Boylan, 1922:128.

with hieroglyphics, *mdw ntr* - the sacred words of the gods. The *"Lord of the hieroglyphs"*[175] was also associated with the sacred literature which was written using them and so is the *"Lord of writing"*.[176]

In Greek *'heiros'* means *'sacred'* and *'glypho', 'carvings'.* Hieroglyphs were considered a potent script because they linked the heard sound and the perceived meaning. Through their complexity many layers of meaning could be transmitted and recorded. In comparison our script is more practical, and easier to learn, but it cannot contain the nuances that the hieroglyphs could and it operates on one level only. Poetry can take our language deeper but there is still no image to talk to the soul or to relay secret teachings. To the Egyptians the overall aesthetic effect was just as important as the elegance of the words and the best scribes aimed to achieve balance and symmetry in their writings.

The written word was powerful for a word could manifest and gain life energy. Hieroglyphs of dangerous creatures were mutilated in an attempt to limit their potency. In the temples the hieroglyphs, along with the reliefs, were brought to life by magic so that the rituals and myths which they represented would continue forever.

The Ancient Egyptian language is a sophisticated and multi-layered language, its richness does make it harder for us to translate. Even when poetry is translated from one living European language to another closely related one it loses some of its potency and meaning. The translators of hieroglyphics have an immense and complicated task, yet it is still possible for the beauty and wisdom of the Egyptians' words to shine through the translations.

Jean-Francois Champollion (1790-1832), when trying to decipher hieroglyphics, managed to translate the name Ramesses in a cartouche. A second cartouche contained similar hieroglyphs and also one of an ibis. Champollion knew from Classical sources that this bird was a representative of Thoth and so he was able to translate the name Thutmose, born of Thoth. Once he realised that hieroglyphics contained both phonetic symbols and logograms (symbols which represent whole words) he knew that he had found the key.[177] It is

---

[175] *Ramesside Inscriptions Translated and Annotated. Vol III.* Kitchen, 2000:12.
[176] *An Ancient Egyptian Book of Hours*, Faulkner, 1958:14.
[177] *Cracking Codes: The Rosetta Stone and Decipherment*, Parkinson, 1999:35.

elegantly fitting that the god who gave the Egyptians hieroglyphics should provide us with the key to deciphering them.

Thoth, the *"lord of Sacred Writing"*, was often referred to during the act of writing especially when using hieroglyphs.[178] *"Who puts it in writing in the characters of Thoth."*[179] The written word was considered very important, in many of the myths and spells the action or order is recorded giving it more weight and permanence. *"I am Thoth...whose reed (pen) has protected the Lord of the Universe."*[180] Writing is also magical in that it conveys words, and thoughts, through time and space and records them for thousands of years. The fact that we study and reproduce texts that are now up to 5,000 years old would have appeared magical, as well as gratifying, to their authors. The Egyptians held the written word in great esteem. *"Might I let you love the books more than your mother, might I let you see their beauty."*[181] Writing was widespread covering all aspects of life from the sacred to the bureaucratic. There are over 110,000 objects in the British Museum's Ancient Egyptian collection and about one third of these contain text inscriptions.[182]

Writing should be useful as well as elegant and aesthetically pleasing and so Thoth was associated with literature and was the *"Lord of Books"*.[183] Thoth was also a divine author and there are many references to the *Book of Thoth*. All sacred writings were attributed to Thoth so it is perhaps inevitable that the authors gifted authorship to him. Clement of Alexandria (160-215 CE) said that Thoth had written forty two books of secret wisdom which contained all the knowledge that humanity needed. Forty two was a significant number for the Egyptians, hence there were forty two nomes in Egypt and the same number of deities in the Judgement Hall. This number expressed some divine or cosmic truth and so forty two books were needed to hold all this knowledge and to convey the completeness of Thoth's wisdom. From Clement's description, confirmed by catalogues from temple libraries, we know that these covered all aspects of religion,

---

[178] *Some Graffiti from the Reign of Hatshepsut*, Wente, 1984:48.
[179] *Hymns, Prayers and Songs*, Foster, 1995:77. *The Leiden Hymns.*
[180] *The Book of the Dead or Going Forth by Day*, Allen, 1974:196. Spell 182a.
[181] *The Rainbow. A Collection of Studies in the Science of Religion*, Bleeker, 1975:97.
[182] *Cracking Codes: The Rosetta Stone and Decipherment*, Parkinson, 1999:12.
[183] *Thoth Or The Hermes Of Egypt*, Boylan, 1922:99.

royal history, astrology, geography, law and medicine. Some of this learning was considered occult, or secret, knowledge and could be revealed only to those who wouldn't misuse its power. It was also knowledge that the deities needed. There is reference to Hathor *"bearing the script of the divine words, the book of Thoth"*.[184]

In spell 146 in the *Book of the Dead* the deceased have to pass through a series of doorways. The goddess guarding the 19th portal was a *"possessor of power, (namely) the writings of Thoth himself"*.[185]

On a relief from the temple of Edfu, Ptolemy X offers a scribal palette and inkwell to Thoth, Seshat and seven falcon-headed gods. These are *"the Utterances"* who personify the written word. The accompanying text describes them.

"These mighty ones created writing in the beginning

in order to establish heaven and earth in their moment

...lords of the act of acting exactly,

a mooring post for those who travel on mud,

craftsmen of knowledge,

leaders of teaching."

It concludes

"A wonder of their excelling fingers,

so that friends can communicate when the sea is between them,

and one man can hear another without seeing him!"[186]

To this we can add the almost miraculous '*and those who find this writing thousands of years later can still hear their words*'.

Scribe and Messenger of the Gods

It would appear that most of the Egyptian deities were either illiterate or they preferred to rely on a scribe. Thoth was the scribe of the Ennead and in the myths was forever writing down what Ra said.

---

184 *The Ancient Egyptian Book of the Dead*, Faulkner, 1989:70. Spell 68.
185 *The Book of the Dead or Going Forth by Day*, Allen, 1974:135. Spell 146t.
186 *Cracking Codes: The Rosetta Stone and Decipherment*, Parkinson, 1999:193-194.

He recorded the deities' words and was responsible for all the divine record keeping and accounts. A relief from the temple of Ramesses II, in Abydos, shows an enthroned Thoth in the act of writing. The inscription reads *"for recitation by Thoth, Lord of Khmunu, the scribe, '[may there be] to you joy in your mansion".*[187] One of Thoth's duties was to record everything that happened and report it to Ra each morning. The introductory hymn to Ra in the *Book of the Dead* says *"may Thoth and Maat write to you daily".*[188] In the Contendings of Horus and Seth, Thoth is constantly being asked to write and read letters. (See chapter 11.)

Not surprisingly Thoth is frequently shown holding a scribal palette and reed or is pictured in the act of writing. In a vignette from the Ramesside Period (1305-1080 BCE) an ibis-headed Thoth advances towards an enthroned Ra-Horakhty. In this fine drawing Thoth holds his scribal palette in one hand and appears caught in the act of dipping his reed into one of the two ink containers. His title is given as *"lord of divine speech"*[189] and there are many references to *"in Thoth's writing, by his own fingers".*[190]

Thoth is also credited with teaching Isis who states *"and I was taught by Hermes, and with Hermes I devised letters, both the sacred and the demotic, that all might not be written with the same".*[191]

God of the Scribes

It is no surprise that Thoth was to be found in the *"hall of writing".*[192] Egypt was a well controlled bureaucracy which relied on large numbers of civil servants to run it. This, combined with the control that the scribe had over words of power, made him an important member of society. The scribal profession was open to any boys who showed the necessary talent though it must have been easier for those with rich or professional parents to enter the scribal schools.

---

[187] *Understanding Hieroglyphics: a Quick and Simple Guide,* Wilson,1993:97.
[188] *The Ancient Egyptian Book of the Dead,* Faulkner, 1989:27. *Hymn to Re.*
[189] *Egyptian Drawings,* Peck, 1978:125.
[190] *Ramesside Inscriptions Translated and Annotated Vol IV.* Kitchen, 2003:24. *Festal Song of Thoth.*
[191] *Hymns to Isis in Her Temple at Philae,* Zabkar, 1988:140. *The Aretalogy of Kyme.*
[192] *Ancient Egyptian Science - A Source Book Vol 1,* Clagett, 1989:35.

There were no official female scribes that we are aware of, though some women would have been literate. Daughters of royalty were often educated, there are references to tutors to the royal princesses. A few elite women are shown with writing equipment under their chairs and there are some palettes which are inscribed for women. The administrative title of *sesh-sehemet*, *'female scribe'*, occurs in the Middle Kingdom but it is not clear if this refers to a professional scribe.[193] There are records of a few high ranking female administrators; an example from the Middle Kingdom is Lady Tchat, Treasurer and Keeper of the Property. In the New Kingdom we have a letter written to Esamenope, scribe of the necropolis, by his wife Henuttawy regarding a shortfall in grain shipments.[194] Ostraca from Deir el-Medina suggest that some ordinary women had basic literacy. The ostraca show notes and lists likely to have been written by women such as laundry lists and dressmaking advice.

Pupils learnt by the rather dull method of endlessly copying texts and there are several examples of doodles by bored pupils. The *Papyrus Lansing* is a copy of a teaching text. In the middle of an eulogy about his teacher the pupil, Wenemdiamen, has drawn a picture of a disreputable looking baboon. This is probably a caricature of his teacher, sadly for us the teacher's reaction is not recorded. The word for scribe was sometimes written cryptographically using the sign of a baboon so he may have got away with it. Wenemdiamen also drew two sketches of Thoth, one as a baboon with a lunar disc holding his writing kit and the other as a squatting ibis-headed Thoth holding a large *ankh*.[195] The pupils wrote endless letters as part of their training. The *Papyrus Lansing* extols the virtues of "*[this] noble [profession] 'follower of Thoth' they nickname him that practiseth it*". It tells the pupil to avoid drinking and dancing and to "*spend the whole day writing with thy fingers, and read by night*". It then goes on to tell the pupils how awful the other professions are compared to that of a scribe. "*If thou hast any sense, be a scribe.*"[196]

---

[193] *The Life of Meresamun,* Teeter & Johnson (eds), 2009:58.
[194] *Daughters of Isis,* Tyldesley, 1995:121, 125.
[195] *Cracking Codes: The Rosetta Stone and Decipherment,* Parkinson, 1999:133, 150.
[196] *Papyrus Lansing: A Translation With Notes,* Blackman & Peet, 1925:285, 270.

Like virtually all cultures the Egyptians believed in beating education and wisdom into the reluctant or less able. *"Thoth has placed the stick on earth in order to teach the fool by it."*[197]

Thoth is seen as the recorder of everything. *"Thoth who reckons all things".*[198] From the *Hood Papyrus* the reader is told to instruct his pupils about everything *"that Ptah created and Thoth has registered".*[199] The *Onomasticon of Amenope* is a word list, equivalent in concept to our encyclopaedia, which gives an index of everything that you need to know. It starts *"Beginning of the Teaching for making intelligent, instructing the ignorant, and for knowing all that is - what Ptah fashioned and Thoth copied down: heaven in all its constellations, earth and all that is in it"*. It then lists constellations, different types of land and weather and so on.[200]

Like any scribe *"Thoth the book-scribe"*[201] is frequently shown with his writing kit or reference made to it. Writing kits were high status objects, the kings had their own writing kits whether they needed to use them or not. The kit consisted of a palette, a bowl for water, a flint blade for cutting pens, spare blocks of ink and an eraser of either soft leather or sandstone. The kit was kept in a drawstring bag. The palette was a narrow rectangular piece of wood with a central slot to keep the reed pens in. Blocks of red and black ink were held in two depressions at one end. More elaborate versions of palettes had sliding panels and were inlaid with ivory.[202] A number of terms were used to refer to the palette, one of which was the *"arm of the baboon".*[203]

Frequently palettes were inscribed with their owner's name and an invocation to Thoth. The following are two of the inscriptions to *"Thoth of the palette"*[204] from palettes in the British Museum (London). *"An offering which the King gives to Thoth, Lord of Hieroglyphs: that he may grant knowledge of the writings that came forth from him and*

---

[197] *Ancient Egyptian Literature Vol 3*, Lichtheim, 2006:192.
[198] *An Ancient Egyptian Book of Hours*, Faulkner, 1958:15.
[199] *A New Duplicate of the Hood Papyrus*, Glanville, 1926:171.
[200] *Cracking Codes: The Rosetta Stone and Decipherment*, Parkinson, 1999:61.
[201] *An Ancient Egyptian Book of Hours*, Faulkner, 1958:15.
[202] *Understanding Hieroglyphics: a Quick and Simple Guide*, Wilson, 1993:97-99.
[203] *Some Ptolemaic Spielerei with scribal palettes*, Meyer, 2004:222.
[204] *An Ancient Egyptian Book of Hours*, Faulkner, 1958:15.

understanding of the hieroglyphs" and *"An offering which the King gives to Thoth, Lord of Eshmun, and Seshat lady of writings".*[205]

The scribes in the Houses of Life, attached to major temples, were considered to be under the special supervision of Thoth. The House of Life was more than a library or scriptorium, it was a centre of learning. Thoth supervised the scriptoria and libraries attached to temples as well as the acquiring and using of such knowledge. As expected Thoth has a strong link with libraries, one epithet from Ptolemaic times is the *"dweller in the Library".*[206] All written documents fall under his care. He is *"Thoth in the House of Books"* and *"Thoth pre-eminent in the Mansion of Books".*[207] In the temple of Isis at Philae, as no doubt in other temples, a statue of Thoth in his baboon form guarded the temple archives because he was responsible for all *"the sacred books in the house of life".*[208] He was the *"Scribe of records who protects the scrolls"*[209] and that *"excellent scribe"* and the *"scribe of accounts".*[210]

To all scribes, indeed anyone connected with writing and learning in any form, Thoth was their god, their patron and their protector and held in very high esteem. Before starting work every scribe and scholar would make a libation to Thoth; a drop of water from the pot in which they dipped their brushes. *"As for any scribe who shall write with this waterpot, and shall make libation with it ... (then) Thoth and Seshat shall favour him, and Sight-and-Hearing, Thoth Lord of Hieroglyphs, shall instruct /bear witness to/ him."* Another variation of this inscription reads *"Thoth...shall be loving (?) to him".*[211] Thoth also took an interest in his worshippers' careers judging by the hymns asking for success and thanking him for it. He *"gave offices to whom he loved".*[212]

During the Hyksos Period the foreign rulers were keen to associate themselves with Egypt's religion and learning. One scribe inscribed on

---

[205] *Scribes' Palettes in the British Museum. Part 1*, Glanville, 1932:57-60.
[206] *Thoth Or The Hermes Of Egypt*, Boylan, 1922:99.
[207] *An Ancient Egyptian Book of Hours*, Faulkner, 1958:14.
[208] *The Routledge Dictionary of Egyptian Gods and Goddesses*, Hart, 2005:158.
[209] *Hymns, Prayers and Songs*, Foster, 1995:112. *Hymn to Thoth.*
[210] *Ancient Egyptian Religion*, Cerny, 1952:60-61.
[211] *Ramesside Inscriptions Translated and Annotated. Vol III.* Kitchen, 2000:25.
[212] *Ancient Egyptian Religion*, Cerny, 1952:60.

his writing palette "*one of those whom Thoth himself has instructed*".[213] King Apepi said he was "*a scribe of Ra, taught by Thoth himself ... [blessed] with numerous deeds on the day when he reads faithfully all the difficult passages in the writings, as flows the Nile*".[214]

Scribes had high status and many officials had portraits, or statues, showing themselves as scribes. Amenhotep, a high official of Amenhotep III, was responsible for the most extensive building program in Egypt and he had himself portrayed as a scribe. The inscription below his statue tells of his desire to "*go out and be united with the stars*".[215]

Accuracy was essential, though not always achieved. From the stele of Petehornebkhem comes this plea:

"*O craftsmen of Thoth,*

entire teams of the Ibis,

who travel guided by the heart,

...who look at these inscriptions

- fix your heart on the contents,

without neglecting special phrases! Copy the texts!

Be firm in its utterance, to perfection!"[216]

In the *Book of Thoth*, the initiate is warned "*do not permit the coming into being of an incompetent man as a servant of the Demotic script...Be engaged (?) with all types of difficult passages*".[217] Not all scribes lived up to the exacting standards of their god no matter what they claimed. The scribe Khamwese ended his copy of the *Story of the Shipwrecked Sailor* with a description of himself as, amongst other things, "*the servant of his lord, the scribe who rendered account (?), skilled in the art of Thoth*". Gardiner, the translator of many copies of this story, says "*Our gratitude to the scribe Khamwese is tempered*

---

[213] *Egyptian Religion*, Morenz, 1992:64.
[214] *Osiris*, Mojsov, 2005:55.
[215] *Decoding Egyptian Hieroglyphs*, McDermott, 2001:17.
[216] *Cracking Codes: The Rosetta Stone and Decipherment*, Parkinson, 1999:6.
[217] *The Ancient Egyptian Book of Thoth*, Jasnow & Zauzich, 2005:450.

with the regret that he did not use more care in the copying of his originals".[218]

Thoth will also protect his scribes. *"May no part of me be without God. May Thoth the God of Knowledge protect me."*[219] The *Tale of the Two Brothers* was written by a scribe named Ennana in the 19th Dynasty. It concludes with the warning *"Whoever maligns this book, Thoth will contend with him"*.[220] A good warning for book critics! From the *Papyrus Sallier* comes the threat *"as for him who shall speak against this doctrine of the scribe Amenkhau, to him shall Thoth be an adversary (when) in the condition of death"*.[221]

Thoth is ever watchful to make sure that the scribes do not abuse his gift. The *Instructions of Amenope* warn the scribes against misusing their skills.

"Do well that thou mayest reach what I (?) am;

do not ink a pen to do an injury.

The beak of the Ibis is the finger of the scribe;

beware of disturbing it.

The Ape dwelleth in the House of Khmun;

(but) his eye travels round the Two Lands."[222]

Secret Wisdom

Plenty of knowledge is secret and is hidden so only those worthy, or clever, enough can find it. There are many references to the secret knowledge of Thoth. He is referred to as the *"Silent One"*.[223] Wisdom was considered to be a gift from Thoth. Words bestow knowledge which in turn gives power. Although Thoth knows all there is to know, not all of his knowledge is available to humans or even to all of the deities. To have knowledge of everything would be to have the

---

[218] *New Literary Works from Ancient Egypt*, Gardiner, 1914:21.
[219] *The Living Wisdom of Ancient Egypt*, Jacq, 1999:45. *The Second Book of Breath.*
[220] *Ancient Egyptian Literature Volume 2*, Lichtheim, 2006:210. *Two Brothers.*
[221] *The Origin of Certain Coptic Grammatical Elements*, Gardiner, 1930:224.
[222] *The Teaching of Amenophis the Son of Kalakh. Papyrus BM. 10474*, Griffith, 1926:214.
[223] *Ancient Egyptian Religion*, Cerny, 1952:60.

universal power of the Lord of Creation. "*I descended to earth with the secrets of "what belongs to the horizon.*"[224] Thoth knew what lay in the hearts of men and gods. "*He knows what is in the heart*" and "*thou lookest into hearts*".[225] From the *Hymn to Thoth*, on the statue of Horemheb, he is described as having access to the afterlife "*Knowing all those there, and who records them, each according to his name*".[226] No-one escaped his scrutiny. "*The knowing one who doth search out the hidden things of the body*" because Thoth was "*he that lookest through bodies, and testeth hearts*".[227]

The best wisdom is, naturally, secret; "*the holiness of God is secret*" and "*Thoth is inside the secrets*".[228] As are its teachers "*Thoth is in the secret places*".[229] He was the "*Possessor of the secrets that are in heaven and on earth*".[230] To those found to be worthy Thoth would impart some of his secret wisdom. In the spell for Knowing the Souls of Hermopolis the deceased state that they were given the information by the *sem*-priest and confirm that they haven't repeated it to anyone, deity or human.[231] The illustration for this spell shows three squatting ibis-headed gods. On his stele Chief Priest Rudjahau says "*I am a knower of things, one guided by Thoth, close-mouthed [on] temple secrets*".[232]

As well as referring to the afterlife the following inscription of Neferronpet-Kenro, a Treasury Scribe, may also allude to the gaining of wisdom or spiritual awakening. "*Your eyes are opened [...] by Thoth.*"[233]

---

[224] *Egyptian Religion*, Morenz, 1992:33.
[225] *Thoth Or The Hermes Of Egypt*, Boylan, 1922:101.
[226] *Hymns, Prayers and Songs*, Foster, 1995:112. *Hymn to Thoth.*
[227] *Thoth Or The Hermes Of Egypt*, Boylan, 1922:101.
[228] *The Ancient Egyptian Book of Two Ways*, Lesko, 1977:102-103. Spell 1099.
[229] *The Ancient Egyptian Book of the Dead*, Faulkner, 1989:119. Spell 130.
[230] *Hathor and Thoth: Two Key Figures of the Ancient Egyptian Religion*, Bleeker, 1973:1.
[231] *The Ancient Egyptian Book of the Dead*, Faulkner, 1989:112-113. Spell 114.
[232] *Ancient Egyptian Autobiographies*, Lichtheim, 1988:71.
[233] *Ramesside Inscriptions. Translated and Annotated. Vol III.* Kitchen, 2000:237.

The Book of Thoth

There are many references to a *'Book of Thoth'* and there are surviving parts of a *Book of Thoth* dating to the 1st and 2nd centuries CE. The original age of the book is not known and it will have had a number of sources. It is believed to go back to the Ptolemaic Period and incorporates sections which are even older. Like the Hermetic treatises discussed in chapter 14, the *Book of Thoth* is presented as a dialogue between Thoth and his pupil. Thoth is referred to as *"the-one-who-praises-knowledge"* and *"the-one-of-Heseret"*.[234] Heseret was Thoth's sacred precinct in Hermopolis. The book's aim is to instruct the initiate in a wide range of scribal, scholarly and theological knowledge. It does cover the more mundane knowledge, such as geography, as all learning was considered a sacred act. Because such knowledge was sacred it was hidden from ordinary people and the teachings in the *Book of Thoth* are obscure and veiled in symbolism and multiple layers of meaning.

The training of the scribe becomes a metaphor for the spiritual path which is also illustrated by reference to the journey through the afterlife. Writing is shown as both a symbolic and a creative act and the act of writing and the writing kit all allude to secret knowledge and the gaining of wisdom. *"Come that I may instruct you concerning...the writing which Thoth gave to the hand of his disciple."*[235]

The House of Life becomes a symbolic place, reflecting concepts such as the divine mind and the afterlife. It is described as being in the *"darkness of twilight"*.[236] Secret knowledge is hidden and must be searched for away from all earthly distractions. It is also a reference to the illuminating wisdom of Thoth which will be available, like the moon in the night sky, to all who are hard working and worthy. *"As for his (the god's) beloved, he being in complete darkness, the teaching/teacher will light for him a torch."*[237]

The path is not for the faint hearted, requiring serious study and commitment. The disciples know that they must *"bow the shoulder under the papyrus roll of the great god"*.[238] But the true seeker is

234 *The Ancient Egyptian Book of Thoth*, Jasnow & Zauzich, 2005:447.
235 *The Ancient Egyptian Book of Thoth*, Jasnow & Zauzich, 2005:449.
236 *The Ancient Egyptian Book of Thoth*, Jasnow & Zauzich, 2005:35.
237 *The Ancient Egyptian Book of Thoth*, Jasnow & Zauzich, 2005:5.
238 *The Ancient Egyptian Book of Thoth*, Jasnow & Zauzich, 2005:252.

focused on enlightenment and aims to understand more about this god *"who has ordered the earth with his scribal palette"*. Then the disciple can be with Thoth and praise him. *"May I see the darkness as a servant of Isten."*[239] Isten is an epithet of Thoth and appears to be a variation of Isdes. (See chapter 2.)

Lord of Ritual

Because he is all knowing, Thoth understands exactly what rituals are required and what pleases the various deities. Sety I said of himself *"Now, His Majesty sought out beneficial deeds (to do) for the father of all the gods (and for) the Tribunal upon the waterflood, his mind being adept like Thoth in searching out their preferences"*.[240] Thoth was thus responsible for all temple ceremonies. Ritual was used to connect the mundane material world to the divine spiritual world. The focus, often a consecrated statue, was considered to be an object that straddled both worlds and which was able to act as a conduit through which divine power could enter the mundane world.

The Mendes stele tells how the king venerated the gods *"according to what was found in the writings of Thoth"*. One hymn to Thoth describes him as *"He who...makes the temples to prosper, who founds shrines, and makes the gods to know what is needful"*. (Namely to receive sacrifice and ritual.) When Thoth uttered words they had great power. *"It is your messengers who bring him: it is the Divine words that cause him to ascend."*[241] Thoth's divine words are recreated by ritual and liturgy in particular by the speaking of magical incantations.

As *"Lord of ritual"*,[242] Thoth is the Master of Ceremonies who leads and oversees all rituals. He is frequently depicted as a lector priest, identified by a white sash worn diagonally across the chest. The chief lector priest, or the king, would assume the role of Thoth during the ceremony. Lector priests were responsible for the preservation and the development of rituals and were referred to as *"scribes of the House of Life"*, or as *hierogrammateis* by the Greeks - those who write in sacred script.[243]

---

[239] *The Ancient Egyptian Book of Thoth*, Jasnow & Zauzich, 2005:451-452.
[240] *Ramesside Inscriptions Translated & Annotated. Vol I.* Kitchen, 1993:75.
[241] *Thoth Or The Hermes Of Egypt*, Boylan, 1922:95.
[242] *Thoth Or The Hermes Of Egypt*, Boylan, 1922:146.
[243] *The Priests of Ancient Egypt*, Sauneron, 2000:61.

On a relief from the Temple of Horus, at Edfu, we learn that *"Thoth the Great One reads the festival ritual for him"*.[244] It also states that the king *"directs the ceremonial like the Lord of the hdn-plant"*.[245] Despite being all-knowing Thoth still uses books. *"Thoth has gone forth in his brightness with his ritual-book in [his] hands"*[246] and *"It is Thoth who has brought a lector who reads it when walking on the morning of the 'prt-jar"*.[247]

Thoth also gave instructions regarding the materials to be used during the rituals. The Dendera inscriptions inform us that the ointments and incense were made according to the order of Thoth and accompanied by the recitation of his formulae. *"According to the writings of Thoth which are in the library."*[248] Thoth was responsible for all offerings because of his first offering, that of the restored Eye of Horus. *"I am Thoth, a possessor of offerings to Osiris and a possessor of offerings to myself."*[249] 'I give so you may give back' was a common reasoning behind offerings to the deities. *"An offering which the king gives, (to) Thoth, Lord of hieroglyphs, True Scribe of the Great Conclave of Gods, that he may give me food-offerings in the necropolis."*[250]

A spell was recited to ensure that the offerings were *"enduring forever; (as) endures the name [of] Thoth in Hermopolis, enduring forever"*.[251] In the Middle Kingdom offerings to the dead were made *"according to this script of the Divine words which Thoth himself hath made"*. In the texts of Deir el-Bersha the offering is made *"according to the hymn of glorification of divine words which Thoth hath made"*.[252] Thoth oversaw the offerings. *"Thoth is in charge of what is carried out for me; his festival-offerings are on his hands, he grants my power."*[253]

[244] *The Temple of Edfu*, Kurth, 2004:58.
[245] *The Consecration of an Egyptian Temple according to the Use of Edfu*, Blackman & Fairman, 1946:79.
[246] *The Ancient Egyptian Coffin Texts Vol 3*, Faulkner, 2007:97. Spell 987.
[247] *The Ancient Egyptian Coffin Texts Vol 2*, Faulkner, 2007:191. Spell 590.
[248] *Thoth Or The Hermes Of Egypt*, Boylan, 1922:96.
[249] *The Ancient Egyptian Coffin Texts Vol 3*, Faulkner, 2007:165, Spell 1124.
[250] *Ramesside Inscriptions Translated and Annotated. Vol III.* Kitchen, 2000:85.
[251] *Certain Reliefs at Karnak & Medinet Habu & the Ritual of Amenophis I (Concluded)*, Nelson, 1949:327.
[252] *Thoth Or The Hermes Of Egypt*, Boylan, 1922:92.
[253] *The Ancient Egyptian Coffin Texts Vol 1*, Faulkner, 2007:243. Spell 317.

Ritual food offerings were "*prepared for you in accordance with the writing which Thoth made for Osiris in the scriptorium of the god*".[254] Offerings were made to the deceased because Osiris received offerings. "*I am he who is at the hand of Thoth, I am he who cooks a hnmt-cake for Osiris among those who make offerings.*"[255] From the Temple of Horus, at Edfu, the text reads "*Be satisfied and worshipful, O Living Falcon...through the offerings which this thy son bringeth thee...this thy Thoth, this thy Abundance upon earth*".[256]

Thoth was always prominent in royal and court ceremonies, where a priest would take his role. Amongst other things Thoth was responsible for giving the royal name, determining the length of the reign and foretelling feasts and victories. "*Thoth, Lord of Hermopolis, who presents abundant jubilees.*"[257] During the coronation ceremony the king was crowned in an act which symbolically united the two lands of Egypt. This was originally carried out by Horus and Seth, but Thoth takes Seth's place in some of the later texts.

Much of the mystery play of the accession of Senusret I has been preserved. Many of the words are spoken by a lector priest taking the role of Thoth. As the king is crowned Thoth says "*Take thou thine Eye, whole, to thy face*", the Eye being symbolised by the crown. Thoth also authorises the ceremony "*that means Thoth lets the gods be in attendance upon Horus*" ensuring its legitimacy and giving divine approval.[258]

The sarcophagus of Queen Hatshepsut describes her as "*honoured before Thoth, the great wife of the king,*" and a relief in her tomb shows Thoth announcing her accession to the Ennead.[259] Egypt's kings ruled by divine right and each king was assumed to be the actual son of Ra, or Amun. This theory is first documented in about 1600 BCE. Queen Hatshepsut deliberately emphasised her divine inheritance to strengthen her claim to the throne. Her conception is depicted at her mortuary temple at Deir el-Bahri. The relief shows the ibis-headed

---

[254] *The Ancient Egyptian Coffin Texts Vol 3,* Faulkner, 2007:54. Spell 894.
[255] *The Ancient Egyptian Coffin Texts Vol 3,* Faulkner, 2007:136. Spell 1047.
[256] *The King of Egypt's Grace before Meat,* Blackman, 1945:60.
[257] *Ramesside Inscriptions Translated and Annotated Vol IV.* Kitchen, 2003:22. *Festal Song of Thoth.*
[258] *Kingship and the Gods,* Frankfort, 1948:131.
[259] *A Tomb Prepared for Queen Hatshepsuit and Other Recent Discoveries at Thebes,* Carter, 1917:117.

Thoth escorting Amun into Queen Ahmose's bedroom.[260] The text describes the events. Amun tells Thoth of his intention to father Hatshepsut. Thoth replies *"this princess of whom you have spoken, Queen Aahmes is her name...and thou mayest then go!"*[261] Thoth's involvement gives a witness to the divine succession. He also authorises Amun to visit the Queen. This may emphasise the legitimacy of the visit but you can't help wondering if Thoth is also ensuring that the gods are not using divine succession as an excuse for sexual gratification, like the Greek god Zeus would have done. After the Queen has conceived Thoth visits her again, like the Archangel Gabriel, to inform her of the titles of her divine child.

An important annual ritual in every temple was bringing in the New Year, when the temple was purified and rededicated. In the *"spell for illuminating (or pervading) the house"* the priests brought in the temple torch which ushered in the New Year and symbolised both the day and the night when Thoth's moon illuminated the darkness as the torch illuminated the temple. *"This House is illuminated (or pervaded) by Amun, Lord of the Thrones of the Two Lands, when it (i.e. the torch) inaugurates a good year together with Re, when it brings the light together with Thoth...likewise [by] Thoth, Lord of Hermopolis, when it inaugurates a good year."*[262]

Other Wisdom Associations

Thoth is *"skilled in knowledge"* so is considered the patron of all areas of learning and knowledge. Said to have invented astronomy, mathematics, medicine and many other sciences Thoth was the *"great and august Baboon"*.[263] The stele of Vizier Rahotep states that he is *"skilled without my equal, one capable in all the works of the Fulfiller, Thoth"*.[264]

Science and knowledge were considered to be closely intertwined with religion. The modern antagonistic attitude of these disciplines would have appeared unbelievable to the Egyptians. They used sacred

[260] *Ancient Egypt*, Oakes & Gahlin, 2004:346-347.
[261] *The Wisdom of Ancient Egypt*, Kaster, 1993:119-120.
[262] *Certain Reliefs at Karnak & Medinet Habu & the Ritual of Amenophis I (Concluded)*, Nelson, 1949:339-341.
[263] *Ancient Egyptian Religion*, Cerny, 1952:60.
[264] *Ramesside Inscriptions Translated & Annotated. Vol III.* Kitchen, 2000:36.

myths to express both the unknowable and scientific truths. If you studied how things worked then you were studying the divine. Strabo reported that *"the priests devoted themselves both to philosophy and to astronomy"* and also that they *"rather meticulously record in their sacred books, and thus store away, all facts that reveal any curious information"*.[265] It was Thoth who imparted all wisdom and learning. *"Thoth gives words and script: he makes the books, he gives success to the learned and to the physicians in his train."*[266]

The architect Imhotep was responsible for Djoser's step pyramid at Saqqara and was said to be the author of works on medicine and temple design. One of the few Egyptians to be deified after his death Imhotep was considered the most learned pupil of Thoth.

In Conclusion

A summary of Thoth's wisdom aspect is given in the *Hymn to Thoth*, from the statue of Horemheb. *"Who openest the place of the gods, who knowest the mysteries, who established their utterances, who distinguishes (one) report from another...skilful in the boat of Millions of years."*[267]

Such all penetrating wisdom should be frightening, but there is little hint of fear when the Egyptians write about Thoth. Their hymns to him show only adoration and awe. As Thoth knows everything he knows individual weaknesses and understands failings. Any retribution he gives is acknowledged as deserved. He may be wisest and all knowing but he is also kind and protective.

---

[265] *Geography Vol VIII*, Strabo, tr. Jones, 1932:9,19.
[266] *Thoth Or The Hermes Of Egypt*, Boylan, 1922:131.
[267] *A Statue of Horemhab Before His Accession*, Winlock, 1924:3.

CHAPTER 6

IN THE AFTERLIFE

"The soul goes to the place it knows; it does not stray on its road of yesterday."[268]

Introduction

Thoth might not have been the day to day god of the ordinary people but all would meet him, and need his help, in the afterlife. His role there reflects his relationship with Osiris and Ra. What he did for Osiris he does for the deceased. (See chapter 11 for further details.) On an inscription in the Temple of Ramesses II, at Abydos, he is called *"Thoth of the westerners"*, westerners being a euphemism for the deceased.[269]

As a lunar god Thoth also has a link to the afterlife, he guides the moon through its phases which is easily associated with the cycles of birth and death. As the moon brings light into the darkness of night so Thoth brings his guiding light into the darkness of the afterlife. His role as magician is also critical, the deceased cannot pass through the perils of the afterworld without using spells.

---

268 *Ancient Egyptian Cosmogonies and Cosmology*, Lesko, 1991:103.
269 *Thoth Or The Hermes Of Egypt*, Boylan, 1922:140.

Funerary Texts

All funerary texts were seen as the work of Thoth and it is from them that we get much of our information about Egyptian religion. These texts range from the earliest *Pyramid Texts*, from about 2,350 BCE, into the Ptolemaic Period and consist of writing and inscriptions on pyramid chamber walls, papyrus, sarcophagus, coffins and amulets. They do not form a coherent sacred text and are often inconsistent and contradictory. To the Egyptians religion was an intuitive part of their culture; they did not need a teaching text. The funerary texts were a collection of spells that helped the deceased navigate the afterworld, merge with deities and re-enact sacred myths as well as reaching their desired destination. In many spells the deceased assume the role of a deity, not because they think that they are worthy but because they need to assume the attributes of that deity to empower themselves. The afterlife was full of dangers and difficulties, as was life; only with the help of spells and a guide and protector could the deceased survive the journey. The goal for the deceased was to become an *akh,* a transfigured spirit.

The *Pyramid Texts* occur towards the end of the Old Kingdom and were reserved for royalty. We do not know what ordinary people expected in the afterlife but kings expected to become gods. It is likely that spells were recited at non-royal burials, the length and type reflecting the status and wealth of the deceased. The priests who carried out the rituals for the king were likely to have wanted something similar for themselves even if it was carried out more discreetly.

A slightly more democratic afterlife came in the Middle Kingdom with the *Coffin Texts,* so named because most of them are found on coffins. These spells were available to anyone who could afford them, now it was no longer just the kings who could strive to become an Osiris and be reborn as an imperishable star. The circumpolar stars appeared never to set and thus symbolised eternity; it was believed that the vindicated dead became one of these stars. The greatest proportion of *Coffin Texts* comes from Deir el-Bersha, the necropolis of Hermopolis. Many of these coffins are of the highest workmanship as are the texts, appropriately enough for the cult centre of the God of the Scribes. The rulers and officials of this nome refer to themselves as the *"genuine son of Thoth"*.[270] A distinct sub-set of the *Coffin Texts* is the *Book of Two Ways*, named for the map of the afterworld that accompanies it. It is believed that the priests of Thoth conceived of and developed this work. Thoth is more prominent in the *Book of Two Ways* especially those from his cult centre of Hermopolis. The *Coffin Texts* are the least well studied of the funerary texts. They are very difficult to interpret and are often poorly preserved.

The *Coffin Texts* were the antecedent to the better known *Book of the Dead*, called the *Book of Coming Forth by Day* by the Egyptians. Introduced just prior to the New Kingdom, the *Book of the Dead* consisted of about two hundred spells usually written on papyrus. About half of the spells came from the preceding funerary texts. Although more people were buried with the *Book of the Dead* it was still under ten per cent of the population who could afford such a text. Papyrus was very expensive as was the production of such an elaborate document. One copy of the *Book of the Dead* was written on a shroud. It was obviously not written by a skilled scribe as it was full of repetition and errors.[271] Despite that, it must have been considered better than nothing, at least it gave the deceased something to help them deal with the perils of the afterlife.

The *Book of the Dead* began to be superseded by various documents relating to the Opening of the Mouth for Breathing. These date from the 4th century BCE to the 2nd century CE. They served as a letter of recommendation, giving protection and access to the afterworld, as well as a rite that would reanimate the deceased. *"The letter of breathing of Thoth is your protection. You cannot be turned back from the hall of Osiris."*[272]

All funerary texts had the same aim; to restore the deceased to life and to allow them to be integrated with the blessed spirits and even the deities themselves. Thoth was considered to be the author of all funerary work and so a number of spells claim direct authorship. The important spell 30B in the *Book of the Dead,* for not letting your heart oppose you during your judgement, was said to have been written by Thoth and found in Hermopolis under one of his statues. Another very

---

270 *The Secret Lore of Egypt. Its Impact on the West,* Hornung. 2001:5.
271 *Journey Through the Afterlife. Ancient Egyptian Book of the Dead,* Taylor (ed). 2010:62.
272 *Traversing Eternity,* Smith. 2009:429.

useful spell from the *Book of the Dead* is for *"Knowing all the chapters of going forth by day"*. This was also *"found in Hermopolis on a brick of the ore of Upper Egypt, written on real lapis lazuli"* under a statue of Thoth.[273] Another spell was found by the king's son, Hardedef, in the temple of Wenet the Hare goddess of Hermopolis. From the Ptolemaic Period there is the *Book of Breathings*, of which it was said *"[Thoth] has written for you with his own fingers the Book of Breathings"*.[274]

The funerary texts were considered an essential prerequisite for survival in the afterlife. *"Thoth has made you a (Liturgy of) Opening the Mouth for Breathing. He has made you a (Book of) Going Forth by Day. You will take them to your house of re[juvenation]."*[275] Even in these later periods not everyone could afford to be buried with these essential guidebooks. One can only hope that the deities were understanding and accommodating to the poorer people who would have made up the vast proportion of the deceased.

Mortuary Role

Prayers were addressed to Thoth for a pleasant burial, preferably after a long and fulfilling life. A stele of Ramose, a royal scribe from Deir el-Medina, shows a man kneeling before a table of offerings and a baboon with a lunar crown. The text reads *"Giving praise to Thoth, Lord of Hermopolis, paying homage to the Master of hieroglyphs;- that he may give to me a goodly burial after old age, on the mighty West of Thebes"*.[276]

The jackal god Anubis is the Lord of the Mortuary Rituals but in many places he is viewed as interchangeable with Thoth. After the body of Osiris had been torn apart by Seth it was reassembled and preserved by Thoth and Anubis and so they will be available to help all the deceased in the same manner. As Thoth's spells and amulets prevented Seth from destroying the body of Osiris for a second time so they will protect the mummies of the deceased. The Ptolemaic *Book of Glorifying the Spirit* contained *"words to be recited over a figure of Thoth standing upright, a writing palette in his hands"*.[277]

---

[273] *The Egyptian Book of the Dead*, Faulkner & Goelet. 2008:106-7. Spell 64.
[274] *Egyptian Religion*, Morenz. 1992:219.
[275] *The Liturgy of Opening the Mouth for Breathing*, Smith. 1993:30.
[276] *Ramesside Inscriptions Translated & Annotated. Vol III*. Kitchen. 2000:424.
[277] *Traversing Eternity*, Smith. 2009:461.

The preservation of the physical body, by mummification, and the reassembly of the various components of the body in the afterlife was considered an essential first step on the journey through the afterworld. A whole body was a prerequisite for eternal life. The deceased plead for Thoth to recreate their body. *"O Thoth, reassemble me, that what is on me may cease to be."*[278] The Egyptians believed that every person consisted of several distinct components. These were: the physical body (the *khat*), the shadow (the reflection of the body), the *ba* (similar in concept to what we term the soul), the *ka* (the life force) and the *akh* (the celestial subtle body). A separate component, but equally critical to a person's survival after death, was the person's true name - the *ren*. It was not only the physical body but all these components that had to be reassembled. For such a critical and complex task who but Thoth, the Restorer of the Eye and the *"Sound of Hand,"* could be relied upon?[279]

Ra was thought to be washed each day by Thoth and Horus, in the Marsh of Reeds, before he rose in the morning. In a reflection of heaven the king was thus washed by priests assuming the role of Thoth and Horus. This was done before he entered the temple to officiate in the House of the Morning and also when he died before his ascent to heaven. There are many illustrations of this in temple reliefs. The water the priests used was identified with Elephantine, the traditional source of the Nile. In the *Pyramid Texts* there are references to Thoth helping wash the deceased. Purity, important in life, was essential to pass into the afterworld and the *"Lord of Purification...who created purification"* was there to assist the deceased purify themselves both physically and spiritually.[280]

The opening of the mouth ceremony was critical as it enabled the deceased to speak. Without a voice how could they have recited the spells and answered the questions on their journey through the afterworld? The mummy's mouth was *'opened'* with iron instruments which were made out of *'celestial iron'* - iron which came from meteorites. Iron does not occur naturally in Egypt and was rare until the Roman Period hence its suitability as a ritual item. Thoth enables the deceased to speak again. *"May your mouth be split open by Thoth*

---

[278] *The Ancient Egyptian Pyramid Texts,* Faulkner. 2007:149. Utterance 448.
[279] *Thoth Or The Hermes Of Egypt,* Boylan. 1922:158.
[280] *Thoth Or The Hermes Of Egypt,* Boylan. 1922:188,198.

with this wondrous book of his wherewith he split open the mouth of the gods. He speaks and splits open the mouth of N that he may speak."[281] Seth was blamed for the loss of speech. "*Thoth comes fully equipped with magic; he looses Seth's bonds that gag my mouth.*"[282] The use of iron instruments to '*open the mouth*' was probably deliberate, iron was found in the desert which was the domain of Seth and he was known as the Lord of Metals. Iron was referred to as the '*bones of Seth*' and so would have been viewed as imbued with his power. What better material to use against Seth and who better than the Lord of Words to call upon to help? "*O Isdes, give speech to N.*"[283]

Thoth then returns life to the deceased. This is shown as his handing them a "*papyrus-amulet of feldspar which Thoth's arm supports. Injury [is] its abomination. If it stays sound, I stay sound; if it stays uninjured, I stay uninjured*".[284] The green papyrus symbolised the renewal of life, green was the colour of life as it was the colour of growing vegetation. Revived and revitalised the deceased can begin their journey. "*I am Thoth, the heart of Re. You will go forth from the darkness for love of the light.*"[285]

Thoth was also asked to protect the tomb and its contents, as in these Old Kingdom inscriptions which warn any infiltrator or robber. "*The god will judge it against him*" or, more graphically, "*Thoth will wring his neck like a duck*".[286] The Vizier Rahotep had the following text on his sarcophagus. "*Words spoken by Thoth. Re lives, the tortoise dies; safe is he who is in the sarcophagus.*"[287] (The tortoise, a form of the chaos serpent Apophis, was one of the enemies of Ra.)

The mummies and coffins of the deceased were decorated with all the important deities and symbols. In the Greco-Roman period tombs at Bahariya some of the mummies have images of Osiris, Horus, Anubis, Thoth and Maat painted directly onto the body. One mummy has a gilded chest plate, which has moulded images of Thoth as a squatting ibis who holds the ostrich feather of Maat in his claws.[288] In

---

[281] *The Ancient Egyptian Coffin Texts Vol 1*, Faulkner. 2007:184. Spell 231.
[282] *The Book of the Dead or Going Forth by Day*, Allen. 1974:36. Spell 23.
[283] *The Ancient Egyptian Coffin Texts Vol 1*, Faulkner. 2007:17. Spell 27.
[284] *The Book of the Dead or Going Forth by Day*, Allen. 1974:156. Spell 160.
[285] *The Liturgy of Opening the Mouth for Breathing*, Smith. 1993:32.
[286] *The Egyptian Book of the Dead*, Faulkner & Goelet. 2008:153.
[287] *Ramesside Inscriptions Translated & Annotated. Vol III.* Kitchen. 2000:40.
[288] *Valley of the Golden Mummies*, Hawass. 2000:57-58,67-68.

the 26th Dynasty tomb of Zed-Amun-Efankh images of Thoth appear frequently and include many lunar symbols. It is thought that this is a reflection of a strong lunar cult in the area of Bahariya Oasis.[289]

Psychopomp

The way through the afterworld is dangerous, even when armed with a book of spells; the deceased need divine assistance, a psychopomp, to guide and help them through the afterworld. Sometimes this help is direct at other times the deceased are provided with the necessary knowledge. Despite the assured assistance of a guide the deceased have to do the hard work themselves and they often identify themselves with the deities and their sacred tasks. As Thoth assisted Osiris in the afterworld so he is willing to help all those who ask for his aid at this perilous time. *"Thoth will make clean for you the fair paths of the West (which lead) to Osiris."*[290]

The first stage is to get across the Winding Waterway to the afterworld. In a reflection of the geography of Egypt the Milky Way was seen as a celestial river. During the conflict between Horus and Seth the deities were believed to have escaped the uproar and chaos and travelled on the wings of Thoth to the far side of the Winding Waterway. The Eye of Horus also escaped over the Winding Waterway to protect itself.[291] The deceased must follow the same route. After both placating and threatening the celestial ferryman the deceased have complete faith that Thoth will assist them even if the ferryman won't. If the ferryman lets them down they just have to leap onto Thoth's wing and he will fly them over the Winding Waterway. During the Ptolemaic Period the dead were still believed to fly to heaven on the wings of Thoth. It was he who could open the doors of earth and gates of heaven. *"A hand is extended to you by Thoth."* [292] Whatever happens the deceased can be sure of Thoth's assistance. *"Do I forget the outer chamber of Thoth, does he forget the wish of the dead until my soul and my shade pass by it?"* [293]

---

[289] *Valley of the Golden Mummies*, Hawass. 2000:186.
[290] *The Ancient Egyptian Coffin Texts Vol 1*, Faulkner. 2007:281. Spell 346.
[291] *The Ancient Egyptian Pyramid Texts*, Faulkner. 2007:116. Utterance 359.
[292] *The Ancient Egyptian Coffin Texts Vol 1*, Faulkner. 2007:15. Spell 24.
[293] *The Ancient Egyptian Coffin Texts Vol 1*, Faulkner. 2007:97. Spell 98.

One thing that the deceased needs is knowledge that is not in the funerary spells. No matter how clever the magicians and priests are they have limited knowledge especially about the afterlife. Thoth will initiate the deceased in the "*secrets of the night*", namely the afterlife.[294]

In spell 5 of the *Book of the Dead*, the deceased state that they have been to Hermopolis and have been initiated into the secrets of the baboons.[295] No doubt most of them wouldn't have been, but spells should never be taken literally.

The Ptolemaic *Document for Breathing* acted as a letter of authority enabling the deceased to pass through the afterworld. The following is from the *Document for Breathing* for the noblewoman Tentdjemet. "*I am the ibis, black-headed, white-bodied, blue-backed. I am he before whom the decree is issued at Iunu, for his voice to be heard in the place Secret of Plans. Turn to me, O doorkeepers of the West, O guardians of the Underworld, let me come and go.*"[296]

Spells may be useful, but what you really want is a strong, reliable protector when you have to face the demons of the afterworld. The deceased are protected both by Thoth, "*the arm of Thoth [is about you(?)]*",[297] and some of the other deities. "*Anubis and Thoth guard me.*"[298] In a reference to the full moon, which illuminates the night and makes travel safer, the deceased are confident that "*Thoth crosses the sky in my presence, and I pass safely*".[299] In a spell for passing by the demons the deceased state that they are a "*companion of Thoth*" so "*the protection of Thoth is my protection from you*".[300] The deceased frequently associate themselves with Osiris, and most references to Osiris are actually to the deceased. Osiris was the one who was first reborn, a prototype for life after death, and all other deceased are following his experience aided and protected by Thoth.

---

[294] *Hathor and Thoth: Two Key Figures of the Ancient Egyptian Religion*, Bleeker. 1973:147.
[295] *The Ancient Egyptian Book of the Dead*, Faulkner. 1989:36. Spell 5.
[296] *Hieroglyphs and the Afterlife in Ancient Egypt*, Foreman & Quirke. 1996:171.
[297] *The Ancient Egyptian Pyramid Texts*, Faulkner. 2007:237. Utterance 583.
[298] *The Ancient Egyptian Coffin Texts Vol 1*, Faulkner. 2007:104. Spell 107.
[299] *The Ancient Egyptian Coffin Texts Vol 3*, Faulkner. 2007:134. Spell 1042.
[300] *The Ancient Egyptian Coffin Texts Vol 3*, Faulkner. 2007:144. Spell 1071.

At other times the deceased can assume the power of Thoth and intimidate any opposition. Such as *"Prepare a path for me that I may pass, O strong one, for I am Thoth"*[301] or, more directly, *"I am the Baboon, I am stronger than you"*.[302] Three of the spells in the *Book of the Dead* (95, 96 and 97) are for being beside Thoth and what better place could there be? *"I am the one who is beside Thoth."*[303]

A number of the funerary spells refer to ritual clothing, or objects, associated with the deities that will give the deceased additional protection. Most references are from the *Pyramid Texts* and refer to royal regalia which played a lesser role in the more democratic *Coffin Texts* and *Book of the Dead*. The king was *"girded as Horus and adorned as Thoth"*. There are a number of references to divine, and thus magical, garments. The deceased said they were *"clothed in the clothing of Thoth"*.[304] In one spell the deceased say that as they have left the constraints of earthly life they can now receive *"my fringed cloak for the heart of the Baboon"*.[305]

Magical and protective garments occur in many cultures, a reflection in part of the relative value of clothing when everything was laboriously spun and woven by hand. A fine piece of cloth, or garment, was a very valuable gift. If your deity gave you a garment it was a gratifying measure of your worth. Weaving and spinning also have an association with magic, we talk about spells being woven or spun. The texts refer to magic being woven around the deceased which will have acted as a protective cloak. Magic is created by joining together various energies in a specific way and so has a direct metaphor with activities such as spinning and weaving. Clothing metaphors may also have been used in regard to spiritual concepts, such being clothed in purity.

While associating yourself with a deity gave you power and protection becoming that deity was equally effective at other times. Sometimes the deceased associate parts of their body with that of the deity. At other times the deceased either enact part of a sacred myth or else describe the deity that they have become and their newly

---

301 *The Ancient Egyptian Coffin Texts Vol 3*, Faulkner. 2007:113. Spell 1013.
302 *The Ancient Egyptian Coffin Texts Vol 1*, Faulkner. 2007:190. Spell 243.
303 *The Ancient Egyptian Book of Two Ways*, Lesko. 1977:52. Spell 1047.
304 *An Early Egyptian Guide to the Hereafter*, Mueller. 1972:117.
305 *The Ancient Egyptian Book of the Dead*, Faulkner. 1989:73. Spell 75.

assumed powers. "*You will fly up as an ibis.*"[306] In a spell the deceased can be both themselves and the deity. "*I will not be judged in the lower year(?) which Thoth has fostered...I am the finger of Thoth.*"[307] In a spell for the Eye of Horus, the deceased states "*I am Thoth who protects you, I am not Seth who carried it off... there is no adversary who can oppose himself to my road, for I am Thoth, the mightiest of the gods*".[308]

In the afterworld the deceased must be careful to eat the right food and drink only water. It is essential that any food eaten is pure so the deceased will only accept food from a few trusted deities. The deceased state that they have pure food in the form of seven loaves of bread, four from the house of Horus and three from the house of Thoth.[309] Food from the house, or temple, of a deity would have been considered purified and so could provide the essential nourishment to the deceased. There are seven loaves as this was a significant and important sacred number. In another spell the deceased ask to be taken with Ra and Thoth so that they can eat and drink the same food and beverages as the gods. This concern over what the deceased will consume in the afterlife also reflects a fear of being dependent upon receiving funerary offerings, these cannot be guaranteed for any length of time.

A large number of the spells in the funerary texts, particularly the *Coffin Texts*, are against the strange (to us) fear of eating faeces and drinking urine. One explanation is that everything is inverted and reversed, or just plain confused, in the afterworld hence the fear of walking upside down and eating excrement. Maybe this is also a fear of spiritual contamination, or just that in a completely new existence you have no frame of reference and so your physical senses cannot be relied upon. Or, even worse, you have lost your mind and so don't know what you are doing. The deities live on *maat* and shun anything which is *isfet* or chaos. Just as eating inappropriately can defile a person so can acting inappropriately or associating with the wrong beings. Purity was an essential part of both spiritual life and the afterworld. These spells may also reflect the fear that someone might violate the tomb of the deceased by using it as a toilet. "*I reject urine*

[306] *The Liturgy of Opening the Mouth for Breathing,* Smith. 1993:34.
[307] *The Ancient Egyptian Coffin Texts Vol 2,* Faulkner. 2007:170. Spell 565.
[308] *The Ancient Egyptian Pyramid Texts,* Faulkner. 2007:196. Utterance 524.
[309] *The Ancient Egyptian Book of the Dead,* Faulkner. 1989:185. Spell 189.

just as Thoth protects the dead...I will be like Re, I will have acclaim like Thoth."[310]

In their travels through the afterworld the deceased will also re-enact the sacred myths, the most common being the conflict between Horus and Seth and the recovery of the Eye of Horus. The spell for going to Heliopolis refers to the sacred road which Thoth travelled on when he was going to pacify the two battling gods. During this re-enactment the deceased clearly state which side they are on. "*Cause that I be brought to you, O Thoth. I have not opposed you at night. I am the one who has brought the sound eye, who has rescued it from its [yellowness]. The mansion of the Moon is my witness. Hail to you, Thoth, in the suite of Re...I have not opposed you, O Thoth, at night.*"[311]

The deceased try to assist Thoth in gratitude and to further align themselves with him. They disassociate themselves from any rebellion and aid Thoth by bringing him his instruments of power, his writing materials. "*I am thy palette, (O) Thoth; I have brought thee thy water-bowl. I am not among those who betray their secrets. No betrayal shall come about through me.*"[312]

In the afterlife the deceased worship and serve various deities. "*I have opened the horizon for Re...that Thoth may be cheerful for me...I grasp the writing that I may receive the offerings, and that I may equip Thoth with what he has made.*"[313] In the illustration of a spell for "*not dying again*" the deceased and his wife are shown worshiping an ibis-headed Thoth who squats on a shrine holding an *ankh*.[314]

It was assumed that the deceased would have to work in the afterworld and what better way was there than assisting your patron deity? "*I am the scribe of Hathor, the writing materials of Thoth are opened for me, and I am his helper.*"[315]

In the *Liturgy of Opening the Mouth for Breathing* the deceased can become a messenger, a reflection of Thoth's emissary roles. "*Thoth will place a letter of dispatch in your hand. You will go forth to the sky*

---

[310] *The Ancient Egyptian Coffin Texts Vol 3*, Faulkner. 2007:111. Spell 1011.
[311] *The Ancient Egyptian Book of Two Ways*, Lesko. 1977:96. Spell 1094.
[312] *The Book of the Dead or Going Forth by Day*, Allen. 1974:183. Spell 175.
[313] *The Ancient Egyptian Book of Two Ways*, Lesko. 1977:103. Spell 1099.
[314] *The Ancient Egyptian Book of the Dead*, Faulkner. 1989:174. Spell 175.
[315] *The Ancient Egyptian Coffin Texts Vol 2*, Faulkner. 2007:158. Spell 540.

among the messengers of the great gods. Thoth will call you (by) your name among the great gods in Heliopolis."[316]

As no-one enters the afterworld free of sin the soul is probably in need of purification. This seems to have been the role of the Lake of Fire, in spell 126 in the *Book of the Dead*, and introduces the idea that salvation can be obtained by the purging of an individual's sins. The illustration of this spell in the *Papyrus of Ani* is of four baboons sitting on each side of a rectangular pool, which is coloured red. On each side of the pool is a brazier.[317] The blessed dead are refreshed by its burning waters but the wicked are tortured and destroyed by them. Thoth is not referenced directly but it is reasonable to assume that the baboons are portraying him, or are his agents, given their role and description. They are said to "*judge poor and rich...live on truth...whose hearts have no lies, who detest falsehood*".[318] The deceased ask the baboons to purge them of their misdeeds which the baboons do, in a way which was probably painful but effective.

At many times during this dangerous journey the most useful thing the deceased can do is say a prayer for assistance. "*Hail to you, Thoth, who was chosen as Lord in early morning. I am in possession of Maat. [Darkness] is (my) abomination. I see the light. I open the darkness.*"[319] In the presence of Thoth they are safe. "*Cause that I be brought to thee, O Thoth; May I not be held back from thee at night.*"[320]

But would Thoth know who they were? "*Be not unaware of me, O Thoth.*"[321] It is unlikely that Thoth is unaware of anyone. The deceased can take comfort with the fact that "*Thoth himself will come to you with the book of the sacred words, and he will set your hand on the horizon, at the place where your ka desires*".[322]

---

[316] *The Liturgy of Opening the Mouth for Breathing*, Smith. 1993:32.

[317] *Journey Through the Afterlife. Ancient Egyptian Book of the Dead*, Taylor. 2010:217.

[318] *Some Remarks on the Mysterious Language of the Baboons*, Velde. 1988:129.

[319] *The Ancient Egyptian Book of Two Ways*, Lesko. 1977:98. Spell 1092.

[320] *The Wandering of the Soul*, Piankoff. 1972:25. Spell 1094.

[321] *The Ancient Egyptian Pyramid Texts*, Faulkner. 2007:70. Utterance 262.

[322] *The Ancient Egyptian Book of the Dead*, Faulkner. 1989:170. Spell 170.

Judgement

"*You are examined before Thoth.*"[323] Thoth announces the deceased and brings them before the Divine Tribunal. "*Come to me when I go into the presence of the Lords of Ma'at*" the deceased request of him.[324] It is in his role as advocate and judge that Thoth is probably best known. The significance of the Weighing of the Heart becomes increasingly important in the New Kingdom. In the *Book of the Dead* there are two main spells referring to this scene.

Spell 30B is a spell to stop the hearts of the deceased speaking against them at the tribunal. As in life we can sabotage our best interests with inner conflict or suffer from a guilty conscience. The soul, being a spark of the divine, will also fight against untruths. After considerable pleading the deceased recite the words that they hope to hear from "*Thoth, judge of truth of the Great Ennead of the Gods*"[325] who is the Keeper of the Balance. Thoth, hopefully, will say that he has judged the deceased and found that their deeds overall weigh favourably against the feather of Maat and that they are without sin.

Spell 125, the Declaration of Innocence, covers the actual judgement and the Weighing of the Heart. The deceased enter the Hall of Justice, or the Hall of the Two Truths, and recite the Declaration of Innocence, which is often called the Negative Confession. They address each of the forty two assessors, and deny having committed specific sins, under the watchful eye of the baboon form of Thoth and two Maats carrying *was*-sceptres. The rubric says reciting this spell will purge the deceased of their sins, which is perhaps being a bit too optimistic.

The deceased are then interrogated before being brought before Osiris and the Ennead for the Weighing of the Heart. Having answered the questions they then say;

"*Announce me then to this god in his hour [of duty], tell this to the Interpreter of the Two Lands.*

And who is the Interpreter of the Two Lands?

---

[323] *The Ancient Egyptian Coffin Texts Vol 3*, Faulkner. 2007:57. Spell 902.
[324] *Thoth Or The Hermes Of Egypt*, Boylan. 1922:139.
[325] *The Wisdom of Ancient Egypt*, Kaster. 1993:135.

It is Thoth."326

Illustrations for the Weighing of the Heart show the deceased in the Hall of Justice escorted by Anubis who takes the role of psychopomp. The specific details do vary but all illustrate the moment of judgment. A vessel containing the heart of the deceased is weighed against the feather of Maat. The baboon form of Thoth often sits on the top of the balance although the squatting figure of Maat is sometimes present instead. Thoth, in his ibis-headed form, watches the balance and records the verdict. Staring intently at Thoth is the monstrous Ammut, '*Devourer of Hearts*'. If the heart is too heavy with sin it will be eaten and destroyed by Ammut.

This static scene gives the impression of an impersonal and automatic judgement, but it was considered a proper legal procedure and the deceased do have a chance to plead their case. Thoth acted as advocate for Osiris before the Divine Tribunal (see chapter 11) and so the deceased can ask Thoth to plead for them if they fear failure. "*O Thoth, who vindicated Osiris against his enemies, vindicate also N.N. against his enemies.*"327

It is worth noting that the deceased are judged on their behaviour and not on their religious beliefs. The Egyptians held that the existence of the deities was self-evident so such a thing was not required. There was no reward for believing and no punishment for disbelief or worshiping the '*wrong gods*'. Neither was entry to heaven automatic for those of wealth and status. This is an extract from the inscriptions in Petosiris' tomb.

"*No one reaches it unless his heart is upright in doing Maat.*

There is no distinction made between the humble and the great there.

Only that one who is found free from fault

When the balance and weight are before the Lord of eternity

No one is exempt from the assessment.

---

326 *The Wandering of the Soul*, Piankoff. 1972:9.
327 *Hathor and Thoth: Two Key Figures of the Ancient Egyptian Religion*, Bleeker. 1973:147.

Djehuti as baboon upon the balance will assess each person

By what he has done on earth. "[328]

Thoth is judge as well as advocate. "*Thoth, who contents the gods, he will judge me! Khonsu, the Scribe in Truth, he will defend me!*"[329] Here, Khonsu is apparently equated with Thoth. (See chapter 4.) Even though the deceased is tried before Osiris and the Ennead it is Thoth who has the final say on the verdict. He reports his conclusion to the Ennead and they endorse it. In many of the illustrations Ammut watches Thoth, not the balance, as the reading is not automatic. In the *Papyrus of Ani* Thoth is called the "*one who decides about justice*".[330] Thoth does more than record and announce the verdict, he calculates it taking into account all the facts and influences in the deceased's life. A person is judged "*according to the measure (?) of his term of life that Thoth wrote for him*".[331] In other words, the advantages and disadvantages of the life the person was born into is taken into account when assessing their actions.

Heaven

Ideas about heaven were rather vague and often contradictory. Whatever it is like, Thoth is the Opener of the Ways. He makes the good things of paradise available to those who follow the laws of Maat during their life. For the Egyptians there was no single goal and no single path in their spiritual and religious life. They accepted that we just don't know and that one person's path may be as valid as the next. There is no one single goal and path in a person's earthly life so why should the afterlife be any different?

One goal of the deceased was to become at one with a deity, or to join in their retinue, and re-enact the sacred myths. The Egyptian deities were not dictatorial. The vindicated deceased appeared to have had a say in their final destination in the afterlife, just as they could decide which deities they worshipped on earth. This choice is

---

[328] *Maat, the Moral Ideal in Ancient Egypt*, Karenga. 2004:121.
[329] *The Wisdom of Ancient Egypt*, Kaster. 1993:201.
[330] *Hathor and Thoth: Two Key Figures of the Ancient Egyptian Religion*, Bleeker. 1973:149.
[331] *Magical Bricks and the Bricks of Birth*, Roth & Roehrig. 2002:137.

emphasised in the *Book of Two Ways* with options of joining Thoth in his abode of the sky, going to the mansion of Osiris or joining with Ra. In what looks like competition between the cults the person who knows the most spells can join with Ra and the least with Thoth, which seems a surprising selection for the god of wisdom and magic. Section VI of the *Book of Two Ways* seems to be a local tradition of Hermopolis which puts more emphasis on Thoth. "*This is the way of Thoth toward the house of Maat. I shall be in the suite of Thoth at night towing them. Your way, O Thoth, is toward the house of Maat. I shall be in the suite of Thoth at night towing it.*"[332] (The Lunar Barque is being towed.)

Another goal was to enter a paradise similar to Egypt, presumably without the negative aspects, such as the Field of Reeds. The wonderful paintings on the tomb of Nebamun, now in the British Museum (London), show him hunting with his family in the marshes and at sumptuous banquets. The Egyptians expected to work in the afterlife either helping or serving the deities in some way or working as they did in life. In the *Book of Two Ways* the deceased state that they are "*the scribe of the plots of land beside Thoth*".[333] In the *Book of the Dead* for Horemheb, he prepares to resume his earthly profession "*bring me a water-pot and palette from the writing-kit of Thoth...See, I am a scribe*".[334] Now he can assume the role of Thoth as Scribe to the Gods. In the illustrations Horemheb receives a palette and water-pot from an ibis-headed Thoth who holds an *ankh*. Horemheb is then shown seated at a low table on which rest the palette and water-pot.

For a "*truly equipped spirit who will never die*" the ultimate destination has to be beyond our understanding of time.[335] A major desire for the Egyptians, indeed for any religion which seeks some form of rebirth in the afterlife, was not so much to conquer death as to conquer time, or at least the unpleasant aspects of it; those of decay and death. The soul wants to join with something eternal and outside of time, hence the frequent references to the "*boat of a million years*" and the "*imperishable stars*". The sun and moon were also seen as eternal in their cycles and so the solar and lunar barques offered a safe, eternal home.

---

[332] *The Ancient Egyptian Book of Two Ways*, Lesko. 1977:93-4. Spell 1093.
[333] *The Ancient Egyptian Book of Two Ways*, Lesko. 1977:53. Spell 1159.
[334] *The Ancient Egyptian Book of the Dead*, Faulkner. 1989:88. Spell 94.
[335] *The Ancient Egyptian Coffin Texts Vol 3*, Faulkner. 2007:163. Spell 1116.

Thoth's abodes were his lunar barque, the Western Mound of the Ibis, the House of Maat, the Mansion of Thoth or the Mansion of the Moon. For a lunar god the Mansion of the Moon is an obvious location for heaven. The moon, in its eternal role, is beyond time as is Thoth. In the lunar barque Thoth, as the Moon God, is accompanied through the night sky by the deceased in the form of stars. As a text from a sarcophagus states *"Plan to find yourself in the land of plenty amongst the followers of Osiris and among the servants of Thoth"*.[336]

Wherever they end up the vindicated deceased *"is with Thoth"*.[337] The *Coffin Texts* say that *"as for any person who is in his suite, he lives forever among the followers of Thoth"*. Variations on the above spell describe the entourage of Thoth as *"celebrated ones"* or as *"common folk"*, there is room for all.[338] Being able to see their deities was important to the deceased. *"As for anyone whose plots are in the Field of Offerings, he shall see Osiris and Thoth every day."*[339] Often on Middle Kingdom stele the deceased hope that they will be able to *"gaze on the beauty of Thoth"*.[340]

On the sarcophagus of Suti, a Chief Treasurer, Thoth says *"To you (belongs) the North; may you be satisfied [with it]...To you (belongs) the South; may you be pleased [with it]"*.[341] In a reflection of the unity of Upper and Lower Egypt the entire extent of the afterlife is made available to the vindicated Suti.

Deities in the Afterlife

The majority of Egyptian deities have roles in the afterlife and these vary over time, as does their relative importance. Many have only a brief mention in a funerary text or else have a very specific role such as Tayet, the weaving goddess, who is responsible for the funerary linen and afterlife garments. Prayers for assistance and protection, or just of worship, are addressed to many different deities. With the *Coffin Texts* there are a number of spells which occur only on

---

[336] *The Living Wisdom of Ancient Egypt*, Jacq. 1999:158. *Texts of the Sarcophagi.*
[337] *The Ancient Egyptian Coffin Texts Vol 3*, Faulkner. 2007:137. Spell 1051.
[338] *The Ancient Egyptian Book of Two Ways*, Lesko. 1977:100. Spell 1098.
[339] *The Ancient Egyptian Coffin Texts Vol 3*, Faulkner. 2007:184. Spell 1164.
[340] *Thoth Or The Hermes Of Egypt*, Boylan. 1922:139.
[341] *Ramesside Inscriptions Translated & Annotated. Vol III*. Kitchen. 2000:98.

one particular coffin which suggests that a person could chose, or had chosen for them, prayers to their personal deities.

There are deities who are present throughout the entire journey. Osiris, Horus and Ra dominate the funerary texts and the deceased frequently identify with them, either to act out sacred myths or to assume some useful attribute. Osiris and Ra also act as final destinations for the vindicated dead who aim to reach the Field of Reeds or the Solar Barque.

As mentioned previously, Anubis is an important afterlife god. He has a major funerary role, responsible for embalming and then protecting the mummy. He acts as a psychopomp and accompanies the deceased into the judgement hall. In some of the Weighing of the Heart illustrations he is shown adjusting the balance. In a number of areas Anubis has a similar role to Thoth but Anubis is primarily an afterlife god.

The goddess Hathor is present in the afterlife and in some ways her position is comparable to that of Thoth. She is a universal goddess who plays an important role in both the life and death of all Egyptians. She welcomes the deceased into the West just as she welcomes her father Ra at sunset. In a mirror of her mother-midwife role she helps everyone through the dangerous transition from life to death and rebirth. In the afterlife Hathor, as a tree goddess, provides the deceased with shade and food. During the Greco-Roman period many deceased women identified themselves with Hathor rather than with Osiris and the vindicated dead can become one of the followers of Hathor.

As well as writing the essential funerary texts Thoth is present throughout the afterlife journey, from mummification and burial through to the deceased's safe arrival at their destination. He is also, especially in the *Coffin Texts*, the desired destination of his followers who will join him in the Mansion of the Moon or in his Lunar Barque.

CHAPTER 7

JUDGE

"Be aware of eternity approaching. The vital thing is to practise justice."[342]

Lord of the Laws

One of Thoth's major roles was the creation and enforcement of laws in the cosmic, divine and human spheres. He is lawgiver, advocate and judge to the deities and this is reflected in his role and influence on earth. Central to Thoth's role in legal matters is his absolute devotion to Maat, the goddess of truth, justice and harmony, who is often portrayed as his partner. (See also chapter 11.)

Maat

The goddess Maat personifies a concept that the Egyptians held as crucial not only to the well being of Egypt but also to the whole of creation. From the earliest times Maat was central to their concept of ethics and cosmology. Kaster calls it an *'inner sense of right and justice'*.[343] Amongst other things Maat is truth and justice. She is also the very basis of order in society, both human and divine, and in creation; the latter being what we would term the laws of nature or

---

[342] *The Living Wisdom of Ancient Egypt,* Jacq. 1999:27. *Stories of the Oases.*
[343] *The Wisdom of Ancient Egypt,* Kaster. 1993:12.

science. Creation arose from the chaotic waters of the *Nun* and this chaos forever threatens it. Maat acts to preserve creation and unify all the aspects. There is a modern sentiment that change is not only inevitable within creation but it is also essential and beneficial. The Egyptians would not have shared this viewpoint. The Creator made the universe as it should be and the forces of change and chaos have to be kept at bay. Even though life was not static it should be circular and harmonious. Major changes and disruption were a consequence of the failure of *maat* and the encroachment of chaos. Assmann distinguishes three types of Maat. The *'raising of Maat'* to Ra was an offering performed by Thoth or the king on his behalf. *'Realising Maat'* was a political act again performed by the king which enabled the divine order to continue. Finally the *'saying'* or *'doing of Maat'* were the social actions which all people ought to follow.[344]

His wisdom and love of Maat make Thoth the great counsellor, judge and peacemaker, reconciling and overseeing justice for both people and deities. At the divine level Thoth safeguards the order in creation. He judges, punishes and controls the enemies of Horus and Osiris and gives protection to Ra during his nightly passage through the underworld. *"He who opens Maat for (or to) the Ennead."*[345] (See chapter 11 for further details.)

The Egyptians believed that *maat* applied to the deities as well as to the people. She is the standard against which all are judged. Deities were subject to their own laws and were expected to obey them. In many pantheons the deities do not feel constrained by morality, it is a case of *'do as I say and not as I do'*. The Egyptian deities were usually more law abiding and were subject to *maat*. Thoth is the *"Prophet of Maat"*.[346] He never abuses his power or breaks his own rules and so sets the perfect example for all people, from the king to the peasant, and to all deities.

From the tomb of Vizier Paser are the *"Words of Thoth, Lord of the hieroglyphs, Lord of Truth: 'Swallowed up is wrongdoing - he lives by truth"*.[347]

---

[344] *Review: Translating Ma'at*, Quirke. 1994:221.
[345] *The Legal Aspects of the Instructions of Amenemhet*, Anthes. 1957:178.
[346] *Ramesside Inscriptions Translated & Annotated. Vol I.* Kitchen. 1993:164.
[347] *Ramesside Inscriptions Translated & Annotated. Vol I.* Kitchen. 1993:286.

Maat in Everyday Life

The Egyptians were forever being exhorted to do and speak *maat*. Thoth is often shown creating *maat* and the Egyptians, particularly the king and officials, had to create *maat* every day, ensuring that earth was in harmony with heaven and so with creation. The king was an absolute monarch but he was still expected to obey the rules of *maat*, indeed it was his primary duty to rule the country according to *maat*. Whether he did or not is open to interpretation. There is nothing to be gained by idealizing Egypt. It was a tightly controlled, centralised bureaucracy and the king held the ultimate power assisted, or sometimes opposed, by a strong ruling elite. There will have been nepotism and corruption at the highest levels and fraud and abuse of power will have occurred alongside the everyday criminal activities. Some rulers and some periods will have been more unjust than others. The fact that the Egyptians had a legal system which was, in theory, available to anyone showed that they knew what was right and what ought to be and tried their best, with varying results, to achieve this. The poor will have found it harder to obtain justice and many crimes and injustices will have gone unpunished. In the periods of social disorder there are complaints about the breakdown of society and of law and order. At the end of the Old Kingdom they bemoaned that fact that Maat had been *"cast out and iniquity to sit in the council chamber. The plans of the gods are destroyed and their ordinances transgressed. The land is in misery, mourning is in every place, towns and villages lament"*.[348]

As Thoth is said to lift Maat to her father Ra so the kings are frequently shown offering Maat in the temples, signified by holding up small statues of Maat to the temple's chief deity. An inscription from the Temple of Edfu refers to the king as *"the lord of Maat who realises Maat, who strengthens the laws like Thoth"*.[349] On tombs and in inscriptions the kings and officials proclaim their integrity and compare themselves to the supreme example, Thoth. *"More accurate than the pointer of the scales, the very image of the balance."*[350] Whether they achieved this or not we don't know. Certainly no-one would admit in writing that they had failed to do *maat*. The ordinary

---

[348] *Myth and Ritual in the Ancient Near East,* James. 1958:184.
[349] *The Temple of Edfu,* Kurth. 2004:54.
[350] *Hathor and Thoth: Two Key Figures of the Ancient Egyptian Religion,* Bleeker. 1973:139.

people knew that anyone who escaped justice in this life would not be so lucky before the Judge of All.

Each person should strive for *maat* in their life as they would be judged on this in the afterworld. At the end of the Negative Confession, in the *Book of the Dead*, the deceased summarise their case by saying that they have followed *maat*. Thoth helps people to embrace *maat* and gives mankind the ability to understand and distinguish right from wrong. All actions on earth are eventually judged against the ultimate standard after death, namely the feather of Maat. *"The great god Thoth has set a balance in order to make right measure on earth by it. He placed the heart hidden in the flesh for the right measure of its owner."*[351] So all must *"appease the noble God who is content with the truth, Thoth"*.[352]

From the Middle Kingdom we have a lovely short story called the *Tale of the Eloquent Peasant*. A peasant who has been robbed appeals for justice to the High Steward in what is really a meditation on the need for justice. The entire story is well worth reading, here are a few of the complainant's words. *"You are equal of Thoth, one who judges without discrimination...Perform Ma'at for the sake of the Lord of Ma'at, for the constancy of his Ma'at is absolute..."(You are) the pen, papyrus and palette of Thoth, so keep far from the doing of wrong...Such is the integrity of the decree of God: It is a balance and it does not tilt; It is a scale, and it does not lean to the side...Speak Ma'at! Perform Ma'at! For it is great, it is exalted, it is enduring...Ma'at is the final end of falsehood."*[353]   True to the laws of Maat the peasant is finally recompensed.

Legislator

Thoth is said to have put the laws of Maat into writing and is regarded as the source of laws and the founder of social order, particularly in the New Kingdom and later. He was the *"lord of laws, (who makes) writing speak, whose words have brought order to the two*

---

[351] *Ancient Egyptian Literature Volume III*, Lichtheim. 2006:188. *The Instruction of Papyrus Insinger*.
[352] *Two Ramesside Stelas Pertaining to the Cult of Amenophis I*, Wente. 1963:32.
[353] *The Literature of Ancient Egypt*, Simpson et al. 2003:25-43. *The Tale of the Eloquent Peasant*. Trans. Tobin.

banks (of the Nile)".[354] It was said that Menes, the first king, received his laws direct from Thoth. The Stele of Tutankhamun refers to Thoth as "*the most ancient Legislator*". He is also known as him "*whose words have established the Two Lands*".[355] The kings were expected to model themselves on Thoth. They were described in terms such as "*he lays down laws like Thoth*" (namely just ones) and "*Who speaks justice like Thoth*".[356] Ramesses II said he "*governs the land by his plans like Thoth, and who enacts good laws in all his lands*".[357] Ptolemy V on the Memphis decree says of himself "*likewise causing justice to be done for the people in accordance with what Thoth the Twice-great did*".[358]

Thoth also verifies and protects legal documents. "*Thoth has said to me; 'The decree which is given to you is sealed.'*"[359]

Upholder of Law

Ultimately *maat* is upheld by "*Thoth the Chief Justice and Vizier*".[360] It is he "*who determines truth and reckons up right, who loves truth and gives justice to the doer of right*".[361] In a *Hymn to Osiris, Wepwawet and Thoth* on the tomb of Vizier Paser, it says "*Praise to Thoth, a million times (over), contented because of Truth (maat), successful in (his) deeds, who vindicates the Weary-hearted One over his foes*".[362]

One of the most well known images of Thoth is that in the Weighing of the Heart illustrations. Here he is the Keeper of the Balance. He also acts as judge to the gods. "*Thoth who judged the rivals.*"[363] On his stele the Chief Priest Rudjahau says that he is "*a Thoth in judging [matters]*".[364] In a hymn Thoth is praised as "*the one*

---

[354] *The Book of the Dead or Going Forth by Day*, Allen. 1974:196. Spell 182a.
[355] *Thoth Or The Hermes Of Egypt*, Boylan. 1922:89.
[356] *Hathor and Thoth: Two Key Figures of the Ancient Egyptian Religion*, Bleeker. 1973:145.
[357] *Ramesside Inscriptions Translated & Annotated. Vol II.* Kitchen. 1996:144.
[358] *Cracking Codes: The Rosetta Stone and Decipherment*, Parkinson. 1999:199.
[359] *The Ancient Egyptian Coffin Texts Vol 1*, Faulkner. 2007:116. Spell 134.
[360] *An Ancient Egyptian Book of Hours*, Faulkner. 1958:15.
[361] *Ramesside Inscriptions Translated & Annotated. Vol I.* Kitchen. 1993:317.
[362] *Ramesside Inscriptions Translated & Annotated. Vol I.* Kitchen. 1993:295.
[363] *An Ancient Egyptian Book of Hours*, Faulkner. 1958:15.
[364] *Ancient Egyptian Autobiographies Chiefly of the Middle Kingdom*, Lichtheim. 1988:71.

who loves justice (ma-a-t), who has justice done to him who practices justice".[365] He is *"That august god who is in charge of judgements"*.[366]

Thoth sets a divine example as a just judge and incorruptible official and judges used to wear an emblem of Maat to show that they followed, as well as enforced, her laws. In the New Kingdom there was an emphasis on Thoth as a just and forgiving judge. From Deir el-Medina, the village of the artists who decorated the Theban royal tombs, come a number of prayers to Thoth and Amun asking for their help to survive in an unjust society. Clearly the legal system at the time was not as devoted to *maat* as it should have been. It is to Thoth, the Lord of Justice, they turn; he who *"vindicates the loser, saviour of the wretched needy one and his possessions. (I) have driven away the darkness; I have scattered the clouds"*.[367]

A prayer from the statue of Horemheb refers to Thoth as: *"The measure which embodies correctness in the scales of justice...He rejects evil and welcomes the man who turns aside from unjust actions...the judge who weighs the words of men"*.[368] Petosiris says Thoth *"rewards every act according to its own merit"*.[369] Thoth describes himself as *"the Lord of Justice, one truly precise to the gods, who judges a matter so that it may continue in being"*.[370]

The deceased assure Thoth that they have upheld *maat* all their life. *"Hail to you, Thoth, who was chosen as lord of the morning. I possess righteousness, and what I detest [is wrong(?)]. My (?) light is my opening up of the darkness."*[371]

Thoth might be kind and forgiving but he punishes and corrects offenders. He is fair and assigns an appropriate punishment. *"O Moon-god, raise up his crime against him."*[372]

From the *Instructions of Amenope* come many admonitions to refrain from falsifying records, accounts or weights.

---

[365] *Hathor and Thoth: Two Key Figures of the Ancient Egyptian Religion*, Bleeker. 1973:138.

[366] *The Ancient Egyptian Coffin Texts Vol 1*, Faulkner. 2007:228. Spell 310.

[367] *The Book of the Dead or Going Forth by Day*, Allen. 1974:202. Spell 183b.

[368] *The Living Wisdom of Ancient Egypt*, Jacq. 1999:68. *Statue of Horemheb.*

[369] *The Living Wisdom of Ancient Egypt*, Jacq. 1999:88. *Petosiris.*

[370] *The Ancient Egyptian Book of the Dead*, Faulkner. 1989:181. Spell 182.

[371] *The Ancient Egyptian Coffin Texts Vol 3*, Faulkner. 2007:151. Spell 1092.

[372] *The Wisdom of Ancient Egypt*, Kaster. 1993:181.

"Tamper not with the scales, nor falsify the kite-weights,

nor diminish the fractions of the corn-measure...

The Ape sitteth by the balance,

his heart being the plummet.

Where is a god so great as Thoth,

he that discovered these things, to make them?"[373]

Peacemaker

From the literature and art of the Egyptians we get the impression that they were a peace loving people. They enjoyed the good life and abhorred strife and disorder. Despite being a military power there was no obvious warrior cult. Skill in magic and wisdom were more important, in most cases, for heroes than physical prowess. The aim was always that the north and south of the country were united and that a powerful government should maintain law and order and keep the country's borders secure.

As an upholder and lover of Maat the essential role of peacemaker inevitably belongs to Thoth who applies his wisdom to restore balance and harmony. His role as peacemaker seems to be mostly found amongst the other deities, this is covered in chapter 11.

In Summary

Thoth was considered a god of great truth and integrity, but also a compassionate one. *"Let us praise Thoth, the exact plummet in the midst of the balance, who passeth by(?) sin, who accepteth him that inclineth (?) not to do evil."*[374] It was common for people to claim that they had lived their life like Thoth. The *Stele of Intef* states *"I am accurate like the scales, straight and true like Thoth"*.[375]

---

[373] *The Teaching of Amenophis the Son of Kanakht. Papyrus B.M. 10474*, Griffith. 1926:214.
[374] *A Statue of Horemhab Before His Accession*, Winlock. 1924:3.
[375] *Ancient Egyptian Autobiographies Chiefly of the Middle Kingdom*, Lichtheim. 1988:111.

CHAPTER 8

THE MAGICIAN

"I have bedimmed the noontide sun, called forth the mutinous winds, and 'twixt the green sea and the azured vault set roaring war."[376]

Magic in Egypt

The Egyptian word for magic was *heka,* which is also personified by the god Heka. Magic was one of the forces that the Creator used to make the universe. Its power was then needed to protect the universe from the surrounding chaos of the *Nun.* When people use magic they are continuing this original process and so to perform magic the magician has to connect to the sacred myths and access their *heka.* All deities have *heka* as do supernatural beings, kings and special or unusual people. Thoth has the most *heka* amongst the gods, Isis amongst the goddesses.

Magic had a symbiotic relationship with religion in Egypt and it is impossible to separate ritual from magic. Being a magician was part of being a priest. Magic was also an integral part of healing and spells were an essential part of medicine. (See chapter 9.) Magic was considered a normal, if specialised, part of everyday life. The teachings of Merikare explain that the Creator *"has made for them magic, as a*

---

[376] *The Tempest,* Shakespeare. 1994:87. *Prospero.*

weapon to resist the events that happen".[377] *Heka* was a neutral force which, like most things, could be used for good or ill depending upon the intent of the person who wielded it. While there were occult aspects magic never had the sinister connotations to the Egyptians that it had to other cultures. Magic was certainly used for malicious purposes as some curse figurines from the Middle Kingdom illustrate. These were pierced and intended to inflict injury or death on enemies. This would not have been taken to prove that magic was bad of itself, only that someone had misused it. Using magic against enemies of the state was considered a normal part of military and political life.

The Egyptians were famous throughout the ancient world for their magical skills and they were well practiced. Magical texts have been found dating back to the 3rd millennium BCE. Before the Ptolemaic Period examples of anti-social magic are rare but it becomes noticeably popular throughout this period. A degraded form of magic seems to develop which is increasingly naive and which moves away from its divine source. This will have had a number of causes such as the decline of the old religion, increasing superstition and a shallow understanding of the old ways. Society had changed and the influence of the conquerors will have had an impact. The Greeks and Romans viewed magic as something occult and sinister so Egyptian magic, and the deities associated with it, began to receive a different sort of attention.

In the Greco-Roman Period there was an important development of alchemical and mystical writings, which were attributed to a composite Greek-Egyptian Thoth-Hermes. (This development is reviewed briefly in chapter 14.)

The Great in Magic

"*Great in magic in the boat of the millions of years.*"[378] Thoth has a number of attributes that make it inevitable that he is "*Great in hike*"[379] and "*Mighty of Magic*".[380] Magic requires a special knowledge

---

[377] *The Tale of Sinhue and Other Ancient Egyptian Poems,* Parkinson. 1998:226. *The Teaching for King Merikare.*
[378] *Hathor and Thoth: Two Key Figures of the Ancient Egyptian Religion,* Bleeker. 1973:119.
[379] *Thoth Or The Hermes Of Egypt,* Boylan. 1922:127.
[380] *An Ancient Egyptian Book of Hours,* Faulkner. 1958:14.

and power most of which is secret and sacred. The magician has to know the true nature and names of both beings and objects and the true relationship between them. As God of Wisdom, Thoth has all this knowledge. The moon also has a strong association with magic.

The creative power of words, both written and spoken, was the essence of magic. One term for magic was *"the art of the mouth"*.[381] Spells weren't just commands that some disembodied entity obeyed, they worked because the magician knew how to use the power inherent in words. Using puns and word associations allowed them to unlock the hidden meanings and make connections that weren't apparent at first hearing. By connecting together magical words the magician enabled the power to flow between them. It was this energy that activated the spell and brought about the desired effect. Because of this the correct words were an essential part of a spell and it was crucial that they were spoken precisely, again reflecting the first words spoken by Thoth when he created the world. A *'true'* voice was needed to enable the magician to control the energies of *heka* and to allow them to manifest in the material world. Any mistakes, false intonation or stumbling would render the incantation ineffective. Magical speech had to be distinguished from everyday speech. This was done by using archaic words or pronunciations and by chanting or singing. It was critical that the audience knew when they were listening to the important magical words. Puns and word play were also very important, something which is usually lost in translation.

The rubrics accompanying the spells often say when they are to be recited. Many were to be said at a particular time of day, or phase of the moon. One spell from the *Book of the Dead* has to be recited at the new moon. The rubrics also say how the spells are to be recited and how many times, this varied from four to seven. Four was a favoured number in rituals and magic. This may have sent the spell's power to the four cardinal directions as well as being the number representing balance and stability, and the earth. As in virtually all cultures seven was seen by the Egyptians as a mystical and sacred number and so repeating the spell seven times would have been considered particularly effective. It is likely that seven represented totality and perfection as it combined the earthly four with the heavenly three.

---

[381] *Magic in Ancient Egypt*, Pinch. 2006:68.

The power from written words could also be accessed via touch. Many inscriptions show signs of erosion where people have rubbed the words to transfer their power. This power could also be ingested by consuming the papyrus directly or by soaking the papyrus in water, or washing the inscription down with water, then drinking the magically charged water. In one story the magician copied everything from a particular book onto a sheet of papyrus. He then soaked the papyrus in beer and water until the ink dissolved. He drank the resulting draught and immediately knew everything that was in the book.[382]

As the inventor of writing and the *"Master of speech"* Thoth is inherently a magician.[383] He is considered the source of all magical texts and Scribe of the Divine Book. In the Edfu texts he is described as *"he who wrote magic-books"*.[384] He is *"mighty in his formulae"*[385] and so *"Thoth speaks with his great incantations which are in his body and which issue from his mouth"*.[386]

Several manuscripts, from the 1st century BCE to the 2nd century CE, claim to incorporate parts of the actual *Book of Thoth*. They begin with a dialogue between the person seeking knowledge and Thoth. These eventually evolved into the Hermetic Tradition (see chapter 14). It is no surprise that many have searched for the *Book of Thoth* and there are plenty of myths and stories about it. The book is described as follows in one Ptolemaic text. *"Thoth wrote the book with his own hand and in it was all the magic in the world. If you read the first page, you will enchant the sky, the earth, the abyss, the mountain, and the sea: you will understand the language of birds in the air...you will see the sun shining in the sky with the full moon and stars, and you will behold the great shapes of the gods."*[387]

Thoth is the ultimate Magician. He is *"Learned in Magic"*.[388] A lot of the descriptions about the strength of Thoth, such as *"Lord of strength"* are probably referring to the strength of his magical

---

[382] *Ancient Egyptian Literature Vol 3*, Lichtheim. 2006:131. *Setne Khamwas and Naneferkaptah.*
[383] *Ramesside Inscriptions Translated & Annotated. Vol I.* Kitchen. 1993:164.
[384] *Thoth Or The Hermes Of Egypt*, Boylan. 1922:125.
[385] *Thoth Or The Hermes Of Egypt*, Boylan. 1922:127.
[386] *The Ancient Egyptian Book of the Dead*, Faulkner. 1989:116. Spell 128.
[387] *Osiris*, Mosjov. 2005:43.
[388] *Thoth Or The Hermes Of Egypt*, Boylan. 1922:125.

power.[389] No evil thing can withstand the force of his words. *"My protection is Thoth's protection among you."*[390] The deceased state that they are the *"possessor of good protection from upon the hands of Thoth"*.[391]

Through his skills at magic Thoth protects and helps both deities and humans. At times even the deities need magical assistance and it is Thoth who provides it, even to those who have considerable *heka* of their own such as Isis. Thoth was said to know secrets unavailable to the other deities. He uses his magic many times in the sacred myths to assist other deities, such as Horus and Osiris, and to ensure that the equilibrium of creation is maintained. (See chapter 11.)

Thoth uses his *heka* to protect Ra against the serpent Apophis. Below are extracts from some of these ultimate protection spells, taken from the *Bremner-Rhind papyrus*. *"May ye not be, may Thoth make conjuration against (?) you with his magic. The great god is mighty against you, he has crushed you, he has caused men to hate you, the fire which is on his mouth comes forth against you, so burn, ye rebels! May ye not be; may Thoth make conjuration against (?) you with his magic; may he fell you, cut you up, destroy you, condemn you to the fiery glance of Horus which comes forth from the Eye of Horus...The spells of Thoth shall destroy thee, thy soul shall not be among the souls."*[392]

Despite his magical powers, even Thoth cannot completely annihilate Apophis. He merely withdraws to the *Nun* where he regenerates and emerges to challenge Ra again the following night. Apophis is outside of creation and so cannot be destroyed by any part of the created universe. *"The fingers of Thoth are in thine eyes, his magic lays hold on thee, and thy form is annihilated, thy shape destroyed, thy body is annihilated, thy shade and thy magic crushed, for he takes away thy life...Thoth cuts thee to pieces with his magic and thou canst not come against the barque of Re...Thoth, the efficacious of magic, lord of letters, is triumphant over his foe - four times."*[393] They

---

[389] *The Ancient Egyptian Book of the Dead*, Faulkner. 1989:181. Spell 182.

[390] *The Ancient Egyptian Coffin Texts Vol 1*, Faulkner. 2007:208. Spell 277.

[391] *The Ancient Egyptian Coffin Texts Vol 2*, Faulkner. 2007:160. Spell 544.

[392] *The Bremner-Rhind Papyrus: III: D. The Book of Overthrowing Apep*, Faulkner. 1937:170-172.

[393] *The Bremner-Rhind Papyrus: IV*, Faulkner. 1938:43,53.

might not have liked the concept but the Egyptians knew that the battle against chaos is eternal, even for the mightiest of the deities.

In the Horus myth from Edfu, Thoth uses his magic to calm the sea. *"Thereupon Thoth recited the spells for protecting the barque and the boats of the harpooners, in order to calm the sea when it is stormy"*.[394] In many of the myths Thoth's magical incantations are a powerful weapon on the side of order.

Magic is closely related to myth which the magician refers to paralleling events from *'first time'*, those of heaven and creation, with those on earth. Events of the present were considered echoes of the actions of the deities and so the magician could connect to these actions and use their power. The Egyptians didn't consider the time of the deities to be an event that had occurred in the distant past, it was something which was always happening. As he helped the deities with his magic Thoth will also help people. His assistance is particularly noticeable in his afterworld aspects. The funerary texts are in effect a series of magic spells to assist the deceased in reaching their goal.

As Thoth tutored Isis in magic so he will advance the initiate along the path of knowledge. He is the magicians' Magician. The pupils, however, must show that they are worthy to be taught and will not abuse this knowledge and power. Thoth may be willing to assist a magician but, as many of the stories indicate, he will not hesitate to intervene if the magic power is abused and *maat* is jeopardised. The perpetrator will either be punished or taught a lesson. In one story he appears as a baboon seven cubits high (3.7m) and prevents an inundation becoming too great.[395]

Magicians

Thoth is *"All-knowing"*[396] as well as being skilled in speech and so is inevitably the greatest of the magicians, the *"Chief Over the Mysteries"*.[397] His followers were also believed to have special magical knowledge. The magician equates himself with Thoth, his role model and source of *heka*. *"I am he who is in the nest, like the venerable ibis,*

---

[394] *The Myth of Horus at Edfu: I,* Fairman. 1935:35.
[395] *Magic and Mystery in Ancient Egypt,* Jacq. 1998:85.
[396] *Thoth Or The Hermes Of Egypt,* Boylan. 1922:103.
[397] *The Leyden Papyrus,* Griffith & Thompson. 1974:29.

Thoth is my name."398 A spell from the *Greek Magical Papyri* begins: "*I am Thoth, the inventor and founder of medicines and letters; come to me, thou that are under the earth, rise up to me, thou great spirit*".399

The temple at Hermopolis was famous for its collection of ancient and magical books and records. In stories priests and magicians often go to Hermopolis to obtain the necessary information or spell. There are allusions to special books containing the spells of Thoth. On one of his statues in Karnak, Amenhotep states "*I was introduced to the book of the god, I saw the transfigurations of Thoth and was equipped with their mysteries*".400

Spells found under mysterious circumstances were considered very effective. Here the light of the moon, being Thoth's wisdom, shines through the darkness. "*It was in the night that this protective spell was found, having descended into the broad hall of the temple in Coptos, as a mystery of this goddess, by the hand of a lector priest of this temple. Meanwhile this land was in darkness. It was the moon that shone on this scroll, on all its sides.*"401

Preparation and the correct state of mind were an essential part of magic. For one spell the magician is instructed to have an image of Maat painted on their tongue with scribe's ink.402 This no doubt will ensure that their words are true and that the spell is not malicious. They also needed to purify themselves for nine days, as Thoth himself did before reciting the spell for Ra.

It was important that spells were kept secret and never treated as mundane knowledge. "*Do not reveal it to the common man - (it is) a mystery of the House of Life.*"403

There is little information about female magicians, it is likely that their status and numbers paralleled those of priestesses. Reliefs from the reign of Hatshepsut show a royal priestess taking part in magical rites against the enemies of Egypt. Women would have been more likely to practice magic informally. Letters from the 2nd millennium

---

398 *Magic and Mystery in Ancient Egypt*, Jacq. 1998:84.
399 *Egyptian Magic*, Budge. 1971:43.
400 *The Secret Lore of Egypt. Its Impact on the West*, Hornung. 2001:5.
401 *Ancient Egyptian Magical Texts*, Borghouts. 1978:35-36.
402 *The Literature of Ancient Egypt*, Simpson et al. 2003:295. *The Book of the Heavenly Cow*. Trans. Wente.
403 *Ancient Egyptian Magical Texts*, Borghouts. 1978:87.

BCE have been found which refer to women called *rekhet*, knowing ones. A magical text from the 1st millennium BCE refers to a *rekhet* with the ability to diagnose what was wrong with a child.[404] Female magicians are frequently mentioned in the Roman Period.

State Magic

State magic was used against foreign enemies and for the benefit of society and the country as a whole. Magic was an integral part of religious ritual. The examples quoted below are from the Temple of Sety I, at Abydos.

The king, or the high priest on his behalf, assumes the role of Thoth. This may be because the power of the deity in their inner sanctuary is so great that only another deity can approach it. The priest also re-enacts the part of Thoth in the sacred myths. The daily temple ritual was performed throughout Egypt. In the spell for unfastening the seal the priest states *"Oh, Horus, I am Thoth who assesses the sound eye"*. In the spell for laying hands upon the deity, a particularly dangerous action, he states *"Thoth is come to see you....my arms are upon you as Thoth"*. In the ceremony of withdrawal he states *"Thoth comes, he has rescued the Eye of Horus from his enemies, and no enemy, male or female, enters into this sanctuary. Closing the door by Ptah, fastening the door by Thoth, closing the door and fastening the door with a bolt"*.[405] During the exit ritual the priest wiped out his footsteps using the *heden* plant. The *heden* plant is unidentified but had long, flexible stems. It was said to have been born before the sky and earth and was associated with Thoth. He had the epithet of *"He of the hdn"*.[406] The *heden* plant had the attributes of removing uncleanliness and hostile influences and was probably used in the form of a broom. It seems to have had an offensive smell, one spell in the *Pyramid Texts* is to stop the smell of the *heden* plant being used against the king. The temple of Ramesses III, at Medinet Habu, has a relief which shows the king leaving the shrine dragging a bundle of *heden* plant behind him. The inscription quotes from the withdrawal ceremony. The king takes the role of Thoth, the great magician, and banishes all demons from the sanctuary. This was done

---

[404] *Magic in Ancient Egypt,* Pinch. 2006:56.
[405] *Religion and Magic in Ancient Egypt,* David. 2002:350-355.
[406] *Thoth Or The Hermes Of Egypt,* Boylan. 1922:135.

through the medium of the *heden* plant. As Thoth was lord of the *heden* plant his magical powers were able to work through it. Demons would recoil at the smell of the plant just as vampires are believed to be repulsed by garlic.

Another daily ritual was the presentation of food to the royal ancestors. The correct magical ceremony purified the offering and transferred its essence to the deceased. Here the priest says *"[I am Thoth] and I have come to perform the ritual"*. Having completed the offering the priest states that *"Thoth is pleased"*.[407]

Personal Magic

A simple form of magic is practiced by the wearing of amulets which either attract what is good or repel what is harmful. Amulets have been found dating to as early as the 4th millennium BCE. Due to his association with the *wedjat* Eye Thoth is considered to be the provider of amulets, and the *heka* behind them. *"I have made an amulet against her who is warlike."*[408]

Potent images are needed to allow the magic to work. The *wedjat*, or Sacred Eye, is a common motif as it provides a powerful protection for both the living and the dead. Sacred Eye amulets are sometimes decorated with tiny troops of baboons to give the Eye, and the wearer, extra protection. The British Museum (London) has an impressive gold and silver circle amulet dating from 2000-1800 BCE. It is covered with protective symbols such as the *wedjat* eye, djed pillar and the *ankh*. Amongst the protective animals are a baboon, turtle, hare, snake and falcon.

Thoth is portrayed on wands in his baboon form. Egyptian wands are flat and slightly curved, they may have evolved from the shape of a throwing stick. The ibis form has less association with Thoth's magical aspects, though an Edfu text does refer to him as *"the Ibis splendid in hike [heka]"*.[409]

The magicians will invoke various deities. On the *Stele of Metternich* the magician appeals to Ra *"may you make Thoth come at*

---

[407] *Religion and Magic in Ancient Egypt,* David. 2002:357.
[408] *The Ancient Egyptian Coffin Texts Vol 2,* Faulkner. 2007:166. Spell 555.
[409] *Thoth Or The Hermes Of Egypt,* Boylan. 1922:132.

my call.[410] Regardless of the deities involved, the magician will always associate themselves with Thoth, or another deity with strong *heka*. By acting as Thoth they align themselves with Thoth's *heka* and acknowledge Thoth as the source of all magic incantations. One spell of the *Coffin Texts* is to "*become the secretary of Thoth and to open what his box contains*". Only a trusted secretary would have had authorisation to access these important documents. "*The seal is broken, [the cord(?)] is cut...I open the chest of the Great One...I open what the boxes of the god contain, I lift out the documents.*"[411]

Our knowledge of spells comes from a variety of sources; inscribed on amulets, ostraca, stelae and from magic books including the funerary texts. No spell can be treated in isolation from the actions and rituals which the magician performed alongside the words. Sometimes the actions are included in the text but for most spells we have only the words themselves. One spell from the Middle Kingdom *Book of the Heavenly Cow* is recited to a female figurine and starts "*O you to whom Thoth gives praise*".[412] A Ptolemaic spell to summon Thoth involves making a wax baboon over which a long spell for "*giving favour*" is recited. "*Come unto me...O Thoth, hasten; come to me. Let me see thy beautiful face here to-day... [Come unto me] that thou mayest hearken to my voice to-day, and mayest save me from all things evil and all slander(?)*".[413]

Funerary literature is basically magic as it gives the deceased the spells they will need in the afterworld. Most of the spells we have are in this category. Magic allowed the deceased to traverse the afterworld and arrive safely. "*O Thoth, N will not be forgotten yonder at the Gate by reason of her magic.*"[414] (See chapters 6 for funerary magic and 9 for healing magic.)

Some of the funerary spells were also used by the living, such as spell 135 of the *Book of the Dead*. When recited successfully this spell will ensure that the magician will be like Thoth, will be protected from the anger of the king and fevers and will live to a happy old age.

---

[410] *Magic and Mystery in Ancient Egypt*, Jacq. 1998:85.
[411] *The Ancient Egyptian Coffin Texts Vol 3*, Faulkner. 2007:100. Spell 992.
[412] *The Literature of Ancient Egypt*, Simpson et al. 2003:297. *The Book of the Heavenly Cow*. Trans. Wente.
[413] *The Leyden Papyrus*, Griffith & Thompson. 1974:81.
[414] *The Ancient Egyptian Coffin Texts Vol 2*, Faulkner. 2007:82. Spell 446.

The *Leyden Papyrus* is thought to be the book of a practicing sorcerer and dates to the 3rd century CE. It is an interesting amalgamation combining beliefs and rituals from all ages with a dash of magical gibberish thrown in. Even the script is a jumble of hieratic and demotic. This was probably done so that it looked impressive but, of more importance, was indecipherable to the uninitiated. It refers to Thoth as the Chief Physician and at times merges him with Anubis as Hermanubis. This is part of a spell to invoke Thoth. *"Come to the earth, show thyself to me here to-day. Thou art Thoth, thou art he that came from the heart of the great Agathodaemon."* Another one starts *"Thoth, let creation (?) fill the earth with light; O (thou who art) ibis in his noble countenance, thou noble one that enters the heart, let the truth be brought forth, thou great god whose name is great"*.[415] It is always wise to verify the entity who answers a magical summons. The magician then asks *"Art thou the unique great wick of the linen of Thoth?"*[416]

Protection spells were widely used against physical threats, demons and the evil eye. It is *"Thoth who exorcises demons"*.[417] The following are all extracts from magical texts which refer to Thoth. *"A spell against people with the evil eye: Sakhmet's arrow is in you, the magic of Thoth is in your body."*[418]

Garlic was believed to protect against snakes and scorpions. This spell had the added benefit of repulsing the dead as well. *"Garlic will protect Wennofer's dwelling: ...it is the arms of Thoth."* The garlic was pulverised, mixed with beer and sprinkled on the ground.[419]

Crocodiles were a major hazard for those in or on the water, or merely by the river banks. *"Oh egg of water and earth-spittle - the egg-shells of the Ogdoad gods - great one in heaven....This spell is to be said [over] a clay egg...If something on the water surfaces, [it] should be thrown upon the water."*[420] The egg alludes to the Hermopolitan creation myth (see chapter 12).

Being in the water was dangerous. *"Hail to you, baboon of seven cubits whose eyes are electrum, whose lips are fire, and each of whose*

415 *The Leyden Papyrus*, Griffith & Thompson. 1974:29-31.
416 *The Leyden Papyrus*, Griffith & Thompson. 1974:53.
417 *An Ancient Egyptian Book of Hours*, Faulkner. 1958:15.
418 *Ancient Egyptian Magical Texts*, Borghouts. 1978:2.
419 *Ancient Egyptian Magical Texts*, Borghouts. 1978:82-83.
420 *Ancient Egyptian Magical Texts*, Borghouts. 1978:87.

words is a glowing flame. Keep steady the swimmer, so that [I] may go forth in safety!"[421] Another spell was *"an invocation of the sun-god against a crocodile...May you cause Thoth to come for me at my voice, that he may drive away Grim-Face for me...Oh you water dwellers...your tongues are cut out by Thoth...Retire now, retreat now for me - I am Thoth".*[422]

There are numerous spells against snakes, which were a constant threat in Egypt. *"Spells for conjuring a viper: Oh Thoth who has come from Hermopolis, assembling the gods....See, I have slain a viper of one cubit."*[423] And again *"An incantation of a snake: Oh you who are in the hole, who are at the opening of the hole, who are on the road...You will not bite him! He is Re - you will not sting him! He is Thoth - you will not shoot your poison at him!"*[424]

This would have been a very useful spell; *"To call magic to mind. I am one to whom (things) were given, a son of Re and a son of Thoth...the letter goes out from the house of Re, having been sealed in the house of Thoth, and I have called to mind all the magic which is in this my belly".*[425] An even better one was for *"Knowing what Thoth knows of protective spells".*[426] Protective spells threatened to turn the anger of the deities against any aggressor and then slip easily into curses. Despite having no association with violence Thoth is still invoked. Akhmim, in 4th century BCE, carved a spell against anyone who would harm him on a spell board. The transgressor will, amongst other things, *"be penetrated by the heka of Thoth".*[427] Thoth is asked to punish the offenders. *"[But as for him] who will destroy this image and efface this inscription...he will not see success, he will not achieve that on account of which he has come. It is [Thoth, lord of] Hmnw and it is Anty, Lord of [Tjerty] who will punish (?) him."*[428]

A more severe threat comes from a New Kingdom text. *"As for anybody who will not recite this....he shall be burned together with the damned, since Thoth has condemned him...As for anybody who will*

---

[421] *Ancient Egyptian Magical Texts*, Borghouts. 1978:89.
[422] *Ancient Egyptian Magical Texts*, Borghouts. 1978:85-86.
[423] *Ancient Egyptian Magical Texts*, Borghouts. 1978:92.
[424] *Ancient Egyptian Magical Texts*, Borghouts. 1978:93-94.
[425] *The Ancient Egyptian Coffin Texts Vol 2*, Faulkner. 2007:228. Spell 657.
[426] *The Ancient Egyptian Coffin Texts Vol 1*, Faulkner. 2007:132. Spell 154.
[427] *Magic in Ancient Egypt*, Pinch. 2006:73.
[428] *An Additional Fragment of a 'Hatnub' stela*, Simpson. 1961:25.

displace this stele from the tomb which I have built, he will not stand before Thoth and Maat shall not judge him."[429]

Thoth was invoked in the Ptolemaic Period for malicious magic which shows a total lack of awareness of his character. As Lord of Justice such misuse of his *heka* would not have met with his approval. Anubis, with his strong association with the dead and the afterlife, also suffered a similar fate becoming a god favoured by necromancers.

In the Roman Period, according to Cicero, the Egyptians were reluctant to speak Thoth's name for fear of his magic. *"The Egyptians deem it sinful to pronounce his name."*[430] This is a sad reflection of how an obsession with dark magic has obliterated the just and kind god of earlier times when a worshipper could proclaim *"O Thoth, for me you are more than a champion; I shall never fear what you do"*.[431]

Magicians in Stories

Magicians were often the hero, or at least the protagonist, in many Egyptian stories. This is a noticeable contrast to early Western literature, such as Norse or Celtic, where the hero is usually a warrior. The following are extracts from stories relating specifically to Thoth.

King Khufu and the Magicians

The papyrus bearing this tale dates from the Hyksos Period. King Khufu is introduced to the magician Dedi. At court Dedi shows his skills by reattaching the severed heads of birds and animals, after refusing to do this to a prisoner saying that it was not permitted. Having watched the entertainment what the king really wants to know is *"the number of the (shrines) of the enclosure of Thot"*.[432] The king is seeking this information so he can replicate them for himself. Dedi tells the king that he doesn't have the information but knows where it can be obtained. It is kept in a chest with the flint knives, in a chamber of a temple in Heliopolis. Why the number or arrangement of

---

[429] *When Justice Fails: Jurisdiction and Imprecation in Ancient Egypt and the Near East*, Assmann. 1992:155.
[430] *De Natura Deorum*, Cicero. 1951:341. Trans. Rackham.
[431] *Hymns, Prayers and Songs*, Foster. 1995:146. *Hymn to Thoth*.
[432] *The Literature of Ancient Egypt*, Simpson et al. 2003:18. *King Cheops and the Magicians*. Trans. Simpson.

these secret chambers is important is unclear and the story soon moves on to other things. Simpson suggests that it might be an architectural plan for part of Khufu's pyramid complex. Gardiner translates the phrase as "*secret sanctuary*" and suggests that it is the secret archive where Thoth stores his records.[433] It is possible that the king is seeking more esoteric knowledge. The House of Thoth is the Mansion of the Moon and the king may be trying to uncover secrets of the afterlife. Ensuring that your tomb or mortuary temple was a reflection of heaven would have been considered very advantageous for the deceased.

Setna I

This cautionary tale is an example of demotic literature, from the Ptolemaic Period. A magician, Naneferkaptah, enters the treasury of Thoth and kills its guardian. He steals a scroll belonging to Thoth, who had written it with "*his own hand when he was going down following the gods*". One of the spells allows him to enchant heaven, earth and the seas and to understand the speech of birds and reptiles. The other enables him to behold Ra and the Ennead and the "*moon in its manner of rising*".[434] Unsurprisingly, Thoth is angry when he discovers what Naneferkaptah has done and he complains to Ra who sends down a slaughtering demon. Naneferkaptah and his family perish and are interred along with the scroll. Many years later Prince Setna, a royal magician, learns about the scroll and goes to Naneferkaptah's tomb and steals the scroll. He suffers a distressing vision in which he is enchanted by a beautiful woman. In his lust for the woman he allows her to kill his children. Relieved to find he has not actually committed this terrible crime Setna hurriedly returns the scroll.

Setna II

This story is from the Roman Period. The hero, Si-Osire, is involved in a dual with a Nubian magician who is attacking the king. A magician, Horus-son-of-the-Wolf, prepares an amulet to protect the king. Going to Hermopolis he makes offerings and libations to Thoth

---

[433] *Comparative Studies in Egyptian and Ugaritic*, Ward. 1961:32.
[434] *The Literature of Ancient Egypt*, Simpson et al. 2003:456. *Setna Khaemuas and the Mummies*. Trans. Ritner.

and then prays before him asking for his help in protecting both the king and Egypt from the Nubians. "*You are the one who [created] magical writings. You are the one who suspended the heaven as he established the earth and underworld ... Let me learn the way to save Pharaoh.*"[435] Thoth appears to him in a dream and directs the magician to the library in the temple at Hermopolis. In a chest in a sealed chamber is a papyrus. It is the *Book of Magic* written in Thoth's own hand. Armed with such powers the hero is able to defeat the Nubian magician.

The Wax Baboons

There is a Greco-Roman story of a magician, Petese, who learnt that he had forty days to live. Amongst other preparatory work for his death he made "*two baboons of wax. He [cast] a spell upon them. He let them live. He commanded for them to let [...] daily 35 bad and 35 good stories[...] handed over books and palette to them to write down the stories*".[436] These were moral tales which he kindly gave to his wife for her continued instruction. Let us hope he also bothered to leave her something to live on.

---

[435] *The Literature of Ancient Egypt*, Simpson et al. 2003:483. *The Adventures of Setna and Si-Osire.* Trans. Ritner.
[436] *The Carlsberg Papyri 4: The Story of Petese Son of Petetun*, Ryholt. 1999:56.

CHAPTER 9

THE HEALER

"I have come to see you that I may drive out your vexations, that I may annihilate all ailments."[437]

Healing in Egypt

Magic and religion were inseparable from healing and only minor health problems would have been treated without magic. Spells and amulets were used as preventative medicine, probably viewed the same way as we do vitamins and inoculations.

Thoth as Healer

It was his wisdom and skill in magic which made Thoth the patron of physicians, reflecting his role in healing the Eye and the assistance he gave to Isis and Horus. What is said about Thoth as magician applies equally to his role as a healer for the two were inextricably linked. The Egyptian word *sunu* is translated as physician or doctor. Thoth, Isis and Horus are also referred to as *sunu*.[438] The *Turin Papyrus* states *"No sickness alighteth on him: he is Thoth the Great"*.[439] Thoth has the knowledge and ability to heal himself. This is

---

[437] *Ancient Egyptian Magical Texts,* Borghouts. 1978:3.
[438] *Magic in Ancient Egypt,* Pinch. 2006:53-54.
[439] *Thoth Or The Hermes Of Egypt,* Boylan. 1922:130.

reflected in the constant waxing and waning of the moon which is seen to restore itself to full each month. *"O Thoth, [make] me hale even as [you] make [yourself] hale."*[440] This quote also appears to allude to an arm wound that Thoth sustained when he intervened in the battle between Horus and Seth.

One of Thoth's great healing acts was to restore the wounded Eye of Horus. He is the Physician of the Eye of Horus. *"I restored the Eye after it had been injured on that day when the Rivals fought."*[441] Alternatively, the Eye was sick because it wept with sorrow or rage. Some of the myths have Thoth heal the Eye by spitting in it. Unhygienic as it sounds this was a method of healing in the ancient world. Perhaps the saliva was considered magical as it was impregnated with the healing incantation which the physician had uttered.

Thoth states, *"I am Thoth, that physician of the Eye of Horus"*[442] and so he is called upon for many healing spells for eye diseases. *"A spell of applying a medicine to the two eyes: That Eye of Horus has come which the souls of Heliopolis created, which Thoth brought from Cusae...protection behind protection, protection has arrived! This spell is to be said 4 times [while] applying a medicine to the two eyes."*[443]

Thoth performs many healing acts during the Contendings of Horus and Seth. Even Isis, herself Great in Magic, calls upon Thoth when her child, Horus, is poisoned. When Isis discovered Horus dying of a scorpion sting her shrieks of anguish stopped the solar barque and plunged the world into darkness until she obtained divine assistance. *"Thoth comes, furnished with magic power, to charm the poison so that it may not gain power over any of the limbs of the sick one."* Thoth then says *"at Re's command I have come from the sky to protect you day and night on your sickbed"*.[444] Thoth uses his incantations to save the Horus child from the scorpion's poison. He then states that as he has restored Horus to life he will do the same for any person, or animal, suffering from poison. By saving Horus, Thoth has saved the divine order because, with the exception of

---

[440] *The Ancient Egyptian Coffin Texts Vol 2*, Faulkner. 2007:256. Spell 691.
[441] *The Ancient Egyptian Coffin Texts Vol 1*, Faulkner. 2007:263. Spell 335.
[442] *Ancient Egyptian Magical Texts*, Borghouts. 1978:49.
[443] *Ancient Egyptian Magical Texts*, Borghouts. 1978:47-48.
[444] *Hathor and Thoth: Two Key Figures of the Ancient Egyptian Religion*, Bleeker. 1973:142.

Osiris, deities are not meant to die. Maat is thus restored. *"It means that Horus lives for his mother - and that the sufferer lives for his mother likewise. The poison is powerless. Then the skilled one will be praised on account of his task when delivering his report to the one who sent him. Let your heart rejoice, Rehorachte: your son Horus has been assigned to life - and all men and all animals that are suffering from poison live likewise."*[445]

The *Metternich Stele* is devoted to Thoth's role as a healer. It tells of the healing of the Horus child and is illustrated by the ibis-headed Thoth standing on a snake, another well known healing symbol, making a protective gesture towards the Horus child. The stele is covered with every deity and symbol of significance. Thoth also appears in smaller scale at the top of the stele with eight solar worshiping baboons. The stele is inscribed with Thoth's spells against poisonous creatures.

Even though Thoth protects and defends Horus in his battles with Seth he is also willing to heal Seth. He restores Seth's damaged testicles which were torn off in one of these fights. *"Pick up the testicles of Seth, that you may remove his mutilation."*[446] By healing both combatants Thoth demonstrates the approach of a true physician; namely that it is healing which is a healer's task not determining if the injured party deserves healing.

Healing spells reflected events which occurred in *'first time'*, the time of creation and when the actions told of in the sacred myths occurred. They refer to the part of a myth in which one of the deities is injured and then healed by another. This enabled the physician to connect to the cosmic energy and to direct a small part of it to the patient. Such spells usually invoke Thoth, or another healing deity, and during the spell the physicians associated themselves with the healing deity and their patients with the inflicted deity. By identifying with the characters in the myths the patient is encouraged to believe that their healing is possible. They become an active participant in the healing process rather than a passive recipient. Such an attitude will encourage the body to fight illness and to recover regardless of the effectiveness of any medicine or treatment. Reference to these myths will also have helped people to accept illness as an inevitable, if

---

[445] *Ancient Egyptian Magical Texts*, Borghouts. 1978:69.
[446] *The Ancient Egyptian Pyramid Texts*, Faulkner. 2007:42. Utterance 215.

unpleasant, part of life. The deities suffered from illness and injury so it was foolish to believe that people could escape such things.

Eye diseases and scorpion bites, in a reflection of the myths, appear to have been Thoth's speciality. *"Break out, you who have come from heaven, scorpion who has come forth from the fundament! ... Thoth arrests you."*[447] When a person had been bitten there was *"A tooth [against] a tooth, while Re guards the poison...The barque of Re was moored and Thoth stood on it"*[448] and also *"Another conjuration against scorpions...The voice of the conjurer is loud while calling for the poison, like the voice of Thoth for his writings"*.[449] The physician was *"a messenger of Thoth, having come to bring protection"*.[450]

Some other spells which invoke Thoth are: *"A spell for warding off an haemorrhage...Backwards, you who are on the hand of Seth! ... Have you ignored the dam? Backwards you, from Thoth! This spell is to be said over a bead of carnelian"*.[451] (As an aside, in Medieval Europe carnelian was also believed to staunch blood.)

For an unexplained swelling, which might signal an unpleasant disease or injury, there was, *"[A book of Conjura]tions for any evil swelling...Thoth, the great one, sojourning in heaven, the scribe [of righteousness] of Re (and) of the Ennead, the first-born child of Re, who ensures an infinite period for all the gods, who pacifies the lords of shrines, who offers the Sound Eye through me to its lord. He has made the spell applying to you, you evil swelling! He has taken away (the effects of) [your] utterance!"*[452]

The *Ebers Papyrus*, dating to about 1515 BCE, relates how Thoth cured Horus of a bad cold and also of a headache.[453] *"[My] head! said Horus. The side of [my] head! said Thoth."*[454] References to such minor forms of mythical healing may well have been used in domestic medicine. Thoth's compassion even extends to animals. *"A spell for*

---

[447] *Ancient Egyptian Magical Texts*, Borghouts. 1978:77.
[448] *Ancient Egyptian Magical Texts*, Borghouts. 1978:78-79.
[449] *Ancient Egyptian Magical Texts*, Borghouts. 1978:82.
[450] *Ancient Egyptian Magical Texts*, Borghouts. 1978:80.
[451] *Ancient Egyptian Magical Texts*, Borghouts. 1978:23.
[452] *Ancient Egyptian Magical Texts*, Borghouts. 1978:33.
[453] *Thoth Or The Hermes Of Egypt*, Boylan. 1922:131.
[454] *Ancient Egyptian Magical Texts*, Borghouts. 1978:31.

conjuring a cat...You cat here - your breast is the breast of Thoth, the lord of righteousness. He has given you air to let your throat inhale."[455]

The physician declares that he has been given the ability to heal by Thoth himself. *"The followers of Re who give praise to Thoth. See, I have brought your (appropriate) medicine against you, your protective drink against you."*[456] The physician was skilled because, *"His guide is Thoth; he turns the script into words. He makes compilations; he gives useful (knowledge) to scholars, to the physicians who are in his following, to liberate someone whose god desires that he should keep him alive".*[457] The actual medical procedure was often omitted from the medical texts, probably on the assumption that the physician knew what to do. Easily treatable conditions, such as bone setting, rarely had incantations. The more difficult the condition was to diagnose and heal the greater the amount of magic that had to be applied. For severe conditions the physician had to access the healing skills and knowledge possessed by the deities.

Thoth is credited with inventing healing formulae due to his association with the *wedjat* Eye. As mentioned in chapter 4, the fractions of the eye were used to work out the relative proportions of the ingredients for medicines.

Strange and exotic ingredients for medicines shouldn't be taken literally. Crucial ingredients were given obscure or secret names for professional secrecy. Sometimes they were merely the descriptive names for herbs. A rubric for one spell states that, *"heart of baboon"* is oil of lily.[458] A study of the uses given for *"ibis wing"* or *"Thoth's feather"* in both Greek and Demotic medical texts concluded that it is a variety of the plant species *potentilla*.[459]

Thoth's role and popularity in healing seems to have grown considerably during the Ptolemaic Period when he was associated with Asklepios the Greek god of healing and medicine. In a number of illustrations from this period Thoth is shown holding a staff entwined with serpents, still a healing symbol today, which was associated with Asklepios. One is in a temple at Philae, where he is called *"Thoth of*

---

[455] *Ancient Egyptian Magical Texts,* Borghouts. 1978:56-57.
[456] *Ancient Egyptian Magical Texts,* Borghouts. 1978:34.
[457] *Ancient Egyptian Magical Texts,* Borghouts. 1978:45.
[458] *Magic in Ancient Egypt,* Pinch. 2006:80.
[459] *Studies in the Egyptian Medical Texts: IV (Continued),* Dawson. 1934:186.

Pnubs", another is in the Nubian temple of Dendur. Thoth responded quickly to the petitioner's plea. In Philae he is referred to as "*He who comes to him that calls him*" so the petitioner can confidently invoke Thoth. "*Thou grantest that Thoth comes to me when I call.*"[460] He will remain with the patient for as long as needed. "*Thoth will not depart.*"[461]

---

[460] *Thoth Or The Hermes Of Egypt,* Boylan. 1922:131-132.
[461] *Ancient Egyptian Magical Texts,* Borghouts. 1978:59

CHAPTER 10

DEFINING THE EDGES

"God is older than the sun and moon and the eye cannot behold him nor the voice describe him: and still, this is the god Hermes, sitting by my hearth."[462]

Negative Aspects

The preceding chapters have focused on the key attributes of Thoth. One area as yet untouched is the more negative aspects of his character. Is there anything corrupt, destructive or evil in the Maat loving Thoth?

There are a few sections in earlier texts that assign a malevolent character to Thoth and align him with Seth. *"Thoth aids Set against Osiris."*[463] In an early version of the *Pyramid Texts* Seth and Thoth are referred to as the brothers of Osiris who *"do not know how to mourn"*.[464] Utterance 219 warns both Seth and Thoth that Osiris has been restored to life and will punish them. This may be an echo of an ancient alliance between the nomes of Thoth and Seth against that of Horus. Involvement in the murder of Osiris is the opposite of any action expected from the upholder of *maat*. Later on in the *Pyramid Texts* Thoth is back on the side of Osiris, as he is in the other funerary

---

[462] *The Complete Poems of D H Lawrence,* Lawrence. 1994:579. *Maximus.*
[463] *The Wisdom of Ancient Egypt,* Kaster. 1993:82.
[464] *The Ancient Egyptian Pyramid Texts,* Faulkner. 2007:46. Utterance 218.

texts. It seems strange that the accomplice of Seth should be helping bring Seth and his followers to justice. There are many references to Thoth rounding up Seth and his followers and bringing them to trial. *"I am the baboon with the strong name... who has felled the gang of Seth. I have come here speaking and reciting the Book of Divine Words."*[465] Plutarch says *"Typhon when pursuing pig towards full-moon found the wooden coffin in which the body of Osiris lay dead".*[466] Maybe Thoth was implicated in the crime because, as god of the moon, he provided the light so that Seth could see the body of Osiris.

Seth was originally a benevolent god (see chapter 11) who was later demonized. My interpretation of this part of the texts is that we are seeing a time when Thoth has taken over the positive aspects of Seth, but in a few instances the text has allotted Thoth some of Seth's evil traits as well. There are some sections in the funerary texts where Seth is comparable to Thoth and where his older, positive attributes still survive. Spell 17 in the *Book of the Dead* refers to Seth and Isdes as the Lords of Justice.[467] Another example of Seth in his helpful aspect is *"the Eye of Horus is placed on the wing of his brother Seth".*[468] This seems unlikely given that Seth was the one who injured it in the first place; also Seth has no bird symbolism that I am aware of.

Another reference to an apparently dangerous aspect of Thoth appears in spell 534 of the *Pyramid Texts*. *"If Thoth comes with this his evil coming, do not open your arms to him, but let there be said to him his name of 'Motherless!'"*[469] The rest of the spell also includes the repulsion of Osiris, Horus, Isis and Nephthys as well as Seth. Its purpose is not clear. It might be to drive away demons masquerading as good deities. Bleeker uses the phrase *'evil gait'* rather than *'coming'.*[470] If the spell does refer to demons perhaps their disguise is not perfect and their walk provides a way of distinguishing between the real deity and the demon. Another suggestion is that it is a much older spell which has been misunderstood or copied incorrectly, or

---

[465] *An Early Egyptian Guide to the Hereafter,* Mueller. 1972:110.
[466] *Plutarch: Concerning The Mysteries Of Isis And Osiris,* Mead. 2002:189.
[467] *The Ancient Egyptian Book of the Dead,* Faulkner. 1989:47. Spell 17.
[468] *The Ancient Egyptian Pyramid Texts,* Faulkner. 2007:256. Utterance 615.
[469] *The Ancient Egyptian Pyramid Texts,* Faulkner. 2007:201. Utterance 534.
[470] *Hathor and Thoth: Two Key Figures of the Ancient Egyptian Religion,* Bleeker. 1973:117.

even one from a previous theology which was trying to displace these new, usurping deities.

The only other negative trait I can find is Thoth catching souls in his net. Some illustrations of spell 153B from the *Book of the Dead* show three baboons catching souls, represented by fish, in a net.[471] Other illustrations of the spell show three gods in human form. "*Do you know that I know the name of its fishermen? They are baboons. Do you know that I know the name of the plateau on which it is pulled tight? It is the Mansion of the Moon.*"[472] The deceased fears this net, for some reason, but given his role as psychopomp it is not clear why Thoth should be catching souls unless they were what we might term 'lost souls' in need of rescuing. Could these be the souls who were unable to transfigure and develop and have instead reverted back to a basic fishlike form? If this is the case then the deceased may fear the net in case they are unable to develop into a transfigured spirit. An alternative explanation may be that these are souls who know they will not be vindicated at the Weighing of the Heart and are trying to escape justice.

"*Great in slaughter and mighty in dread*" is more of an appellation for Seth than the benevolent Thoth.[473] Some earlier authors cite these as violent and demonic traits of Thoth. The quotes have to be read in context though. Thoth is fighting the enemies of *maat*, the forces of darkness and chaos. Law enforcers must be backed up by force or else they become as inadequate as chained guard-dogs. To scare away demons you must be stronger and scarier than they are. Horus continually fights Seth, to avenge his father and to claim his rightful inheritance, yet his actions are not viewed as inherently evil.

Thoth is credited in an Old Kingdom text from Wadi Kharig, in Sinai, with assisting the king to defeat his enemies. "*Thoth, the lord of terror, the subduer of Asia.*" He also "*treads on the rebels*".[474] This is not surprising; the victors have always thanked their favoured deities for intervening in their battles. We need only recall how many times the pacifist Christ has been credited with both supporting wars and winning battles.

[471] *Men and Gods on the Roman Nile,* Lindsay. 1968:270.
[472] *The Ancient Egyptian Book of the Dead,* Faulkner. 1989:152. Spell 153B.
[473] *Thoth Or The Hermes Of Egypt,* Boylan. 1922:134.
[474] *Texts From the Pyramid Age,* Strudwick. 2005:136,85.

Being biased, I do not feel that this is sufficient evidence to allocate any negative or morally wrong aspects to Thoth. One hymn, on a stele from the 20th Dynasty, calls Thoth *"great in dread power, kind and merciful"*.[475] All deities, by their very essence, will appear frightening to mortals, even one renowned for being approachable and helpful. The awe we feel is a mixture of wonder and fear.

If Thoth was anything less than the embodiment of *maat* he could not carry out his cosmic duty of the preservation of *maat* at all levels. *"I am Thoth, the excellent scribe, whose hands are pure...the scribe of right and truth, who abominates wrongdoing."*[476]

Excluded Aspects

What a god is not defines him as much as what he is. In a polytheist religion some deities will have more aspects than others, reflecting a deeper and broader personality and age, but by its very nature polytheism has no need for a god who encompasses everything. Little is to be gained from listing all the things that Thoth is not, but some absent aspects are worth commenting upon.

We would not expect Thoth to have the same character as a god such as Osiris who has a different role and function. A fertility or sacrificial vegetation god would not fit easily with Thoth's personality as we understand it. Neither is he a chthonic or nature deity, he is a god of the moon and stars rather than of the earth.

Thoth has no sexual or fertility aspects, unlike Geb and Osiris whose relationships with lovers and wives were sexual and fertile. Thoth has consorts but no obvious sexual relationships with them. There is no indication that Thoth is hostile towards women, sex or bodies in general, which is the same as the other Egyptian deities. Apart from ritual purity demanded at certain times the Egyptians had a love of life, attested to by their literature and art, which they hoped to continue with in the afterlife. The Egyptians were considerably less sexist and misogynist than the other cultures of their time and this is reflected in their religion. Women are not blamed for the evils of the world or rated as second best by their Creator. Thoth shows no bias towards women. Following the Egyptian reasoning; as Thoth helps Nut

475 *Ramesside Inscriptions Translated & Annotated. Vol III.* Kitchen. 2000:492.
476 *The Wisdom of Ancient Egypt*, Kaster. 1993:72.

and Isis so he will help all women, as he works with Seshat so he will work with all women. Thoth is more of an intellectual god so it is not surprising that he has cerebral rather than physical relationships. As a god who *"knows what is in the heart"* he will see beyond gender seeking a soul mate rather than a lover.[477]

Thoth has no war aspects, although he is a protector and will punish the enemies of *maat*. Despite being a military power the Egyptians did not have a strong warrior culture, they valued order and harmony. Compared to other cultures of the period they were relatively peaceful, but it must be remembered that the Egyptians had a large and effective military infrastructure. Egypt retained its autonomy for nearly 3,000 years, strong evidence of its military capabilities. As mentioned previously, their heroes were magicians and scholars and this is reflected in their deities. Although Horus was a warrior there was no need for the other gods to be. There were specific war deities such as Montu the falcon headed god of Thebes and the goddess Sekhmet in her savage aspect.

Another noticeable absence in Thoth's character is the lack of trickery and chaos. Trickery can be an aspect of wisdom deities in other pantheons; some use it for their own ends, others use it to teach. While tricksters often view rules as plastic objects Thoth views them as an essential component of creation. He abides by his own rules because *maat* applies to him as much as it does to everyone else. Some deities will introduce chaos into a situation to force it to change. Even if the intent was honourable and the outcome ultimately beneficial this is the antithesis of any action that would come from the *isfet* disliking Thoth.

"I am Thoth, the trusty one."[478]

Balance and Completeness

As well as representing order and harmony Thoth personifies everything which is exact and complete. He is the full moon, the restored Eye of Horus. Budge suggests that the baboon form of Thoth who sits on the balance is the *"God of Equilibrium"* who keeps the

---

[477] *Thoth Or The Hermes Of Egypt*, Boylan. 1922:101.
[478] *The Ancient Egyptian Coffin Texts Vol 1*, Faulkner. 2007:96. Spell 97.

opposing forces of creation in balance.[479] Bomhard notes that Thoth is the divinity for the sixth hour of the day, noon, when the sun is at its height.[480] He is also connected with the sixth hour of the night in the *Amduat*. At this hour the sun is in the utmost depths of the *Duat* where it connects to the *Nun*, the primeval chaos which surrounds the created world. Thoth is thus the point of balance between sunrise and sunset when the day and night are at their fullest. Thoth could also be considered the God of the Equinoxes; the two times of the year when day and night are in perfect balance throughout the Earth.[481] In all aspects he is a prime illustration of the path of the *'middle way'* avoiding extremes of anything.

Conclusion

A classification of Thoth, indeed any deity, using titles such as Moon God and Wisdom God is a quick and practical approach. At its best it can give us a rough approximation of the god without getting entangled in multidimensional and abstract theology. While appreciating that it is no good trying to understand a deity as you would a person, it has to be said that contemplating various aspects of their character does help to give an area of reference and make it easier for their worshippers to connect to them.

Sadly, but not surprisingly, we have lost huge amounts of the Egyptians' writings. Throughout the surviving literature there are often references which we can't understand because they allude to unknown myths and symbols such as in the following statement. "*My soul has been godly in the presence of Sokar like the goose in the presence of Thoth.*"[482] These lost myths might have identified aspects of Thoth which we are unaware of and the sampling by fate and time lent a bias towards certain attributes. That said we have enough evidence to know that the Egyptians loved and respected him highly. "*He enters praised and comes forth loved.*"[483]

---

479 *The Gods of the Egyptians Vol 1*, Budge. 1969:403.
480 *The Egyptian Calendar A Work For Eternity*, Bomhard. 1999:79.
481 *The Gods of the Egyptians Vol 1*, Budge. 1969:403.
482 *Some Egyptian Sun Hymns*, Allen. 1949:354.
483 *The Book of the Dead or Going Forth by Day*, Allen. 1974:10. Spell 9.

CHAPTER 11

RELATIONSHIPS

"Set your deeds throughout the world that everyone may greet you."[484]

The characters of the deities are often best illuminated through their relationships with each other and Thoth is no exception. How they interact shows the various aspects of their personalities and over the 5,000 years of the Egyptian religion these relationships change and develop.

His Consorts

Three goddesses are linked with Thoth and are referred to as his wife or consort: Maat, Seshat and Nehmataway. We are told virtually nothing about the relationship between Thoth and his partners. He works with Seshat at times and worships Maat but that is all. There is no hint of a sexual, or marital, relationship as there is between other divine couples such as Isis and Osiris. All of his consorts have their own distinct character, though in the case of Nehmataway we know very little about her, and none of them can be considered merely the female counterpart of Thoth.

---

[484] *The Literature of Ancient Egypt,* Simpson et al. 2003:230. *The Instruction of Amenemope.* Trans. Simpson.

Maat

As discussed in chapter 7, Maat is truth and justice, not because it is an aspect of her character but because she personifies the cosmic harmony established by the Creator. She has always been closely associated with Ra and was often shown standing behind him in the solar barque. By the 18th Dynasty Maat was known as the Daughter of Ra. She protects Ra and eases his path. Maat is the air he breathes and is his vital power, his *ka*. The gods are said to live off *maat*. "*Thy nourishment consists of Ma-a-t, thy beverage is Ma-a-t, thy bread is Ma-a-t...the garment of thy body is Ma-a-t.*"[485]

Maat is depicted as a goddess wearing an ostrich feather in her hair. An ostrich feather on its own could represent her as could the hieroglyph used to write her name - the plinth which statues stood on. From the 14th century BCE Maat is often shown as a winged goddess. Like Isis, it was said that she could revive the dead by fanning air with her wings.

The main duty of a king was to uphold *maat* and they are often depicted as offering a small figurine of Maat to the temple deity. There is a silver gilded image of a king offering Maat from the 18th Dynasty (now in the British Museum, London). A hymn to Maat during the Persian occupation urges her to reside in the Persian king's head so that he will understand this fundamental concept, so precious to the Egyptians, and consequently will do *maat*.[486]

There is one myth about the golden age of Egypt, when Maat was a ruler on earth.[487] Maat grew upset with the wickedness of humans and so retreated to heaven. She was still prepared to help individuals though and 'joining Maat' became a euphemism for death. Maat lost her central place in the Ptolemaic Period and Isis took over some of her functions. Her decline probably parallels the decline in the old religion and changing society at that time.

Thoth is clearly devoted to Maat and it was said he carried her in his heart. In an illustration in the *Papyrus of Ani* he is shown painting her ostrich feather emblem. They both sail in Ra's barque as part of

---

[485] *Hathor and Thoth: Two Key Figures of the Ancient Egyptian Religion*, Bleeker. 1973:122.
[486] *Hymns, Prayers and Songs*, Foster. 1995:123. *Hymn to Maat*.
[487] *Egyptian Mythology*, Pinch. 2002:160.

his retinue ensuring the continuation of cosmic order. "*Daily Thoth writes Ma-a-t for thee.*"[488] An illustration from Vizier Paser's tomb shows him offering libation to "*Maat at the prow of the Barque of Thoth*" and saying "*I have adored Re...(with) Thoth and Maat upon his hands*".[489]

Thoth strives to ensure the stability of creation and cosmic order at all levels; from the workings of the universe, the lives of the deities, the state of Egypt and down to each individual on earth. Who else but Maat could be his consort in this effort?

Seshat

Seshat is often shown as the consort of Thoth but there are references to her as his daughter and his assistant. An inscription for Sety I describes her as "*sister of Thoth*" which is assumed to mean wife.[490] A literal translation of her name is "*female scribe*" and she is "*the lady of writing*".[491] Like Thoth, Seshat was equated with the art of writing. The scribe Hori, writing in the 19th Dynasty, described himself as "*a champion in valour and in the art of Seshyt*".[492] Seshat is the goddess of all forms of notation and writing, including the maintenance of the royal annals, record-keeping, accounting and census. Seshat was the patron of all libraries, the "*chief of the library*",[493] where she was referred to as "*she who is foremost in the house of books*".[494] Seshat "*dwells in the house of god's documents; she who dwells in the "school of the nobility*".[495] With her counting and calculating ability she was also the patron of astronomy and mathematics.

Seshat is an early goddess; she is sometimes referred to as "*the primeval one*".[496] Another epithet is "*she who wrote for the first*

---

[488] *Hathor and Thoth: Two Key Figures of the Ancient Egyptian Religion*, Bleeker. 1973:119.
[489] *Ramesside Inscriptions Translated & Annotated. Vol III.* Kitchen. 2000:3,5.
[490] *Ramesside Inscriptions Translated & Annotated. Vol I.* Kitchen. 1993:162.
[491] *Temple Festival Calendars of Ancient Egypt,* El-Sabban. 2000:48.
[492] *Ancient Egyptian Science - A Source Book Vol I,* Clagett. 1989:35.
[493] *Temple Festival Calendars of Ancient Egypt,* El-Sabban. 2000:48.
[494] *The Complete Gods and Goddesses of Ancient Egypt,* Wilkinson. 2003:166.
[495] *Texts From the Pyramid Age,* Strudwick. 2005:84.
[496] *The Ancient Egyptian Book of Thoth,* Jasnow & Zauzich. 2005:20.

time".[497] Her worship was most widespread in the Old Kingdom, after that she was seen mostly attending to the king. In later periods she tended to become merged with the other major goddesses, such as Isis, though her important role in temples continued into the Late Period. Seshat is depicted as a goddess wearing a seven pointed star, which is topped by a bow or inverted horns, and usually wears a leopard skin. This is a very ancient form of dress and was only worn by *sem*-priests after the Old Kingdom. These priests officiated at the funeral rites which illustrates Seshat's very old afterlife aspect. At times she is portrayed carrying a palm frond which is notched to mark the passing years. In a 19th century BCE relief from Luxor she is shown inscribing the rib of a palm leaf, the hieroglyph used to denote the word *renpet* or year.[498] This also shows her antiquity as notching a stick formed the earliest method of counting before writing had been invented.

In an Old Kingdom 4th Dynasty text she records the herds of livestock seized as booty by King Sahura from his Libyan enemies. In the 12th Dynasty temple of Senusret I, at el-Lisht, Seshat records the names and tribute from foreign captives. In the New Kingdom temples of Karnak and Luxor she is shown recording the royal jubilee. Here she holds a notched palm branch topped by a tadpole, signifying an eternity of years.[499]

In a painting from the early 2nd Dynasty she is shown helping King Khasekhemwy in the ritual of the *"stretching of the cord"* ceremony, which was always carried out before starting construction work on temples.[500] In her speech to Sety I, Seshat says: *"I stretched out the measuring-cord within its walls, my mouth was (devoted) to it with great incantations, while Thoth was there with his books."*[501] As *"Mistress of the rope"* she was the patron of architects.[502] Seshat established the ground plan on the founding and extension of every sacred building. This Lady of Builders presumably oversaw the actual construction as well. In the temple at Edfu she is described as *"Seshat*

[497] *The Rainbow. A Collection of Studies in the Science of Religion*, Bleeker. 1975:97.
[498] *Hieroglyphs and the Afterlife in Ancient Egypt*, Foreman & Quirke. 1996:10-11.
[499] *The Routledge Dictionary of Egyptian Gods and Goddesses*, Hart. 2005:143.
[500] *The Complete Gods and Goddesses of Ancient Egypt*, Wilkinson. 2003:166.
[501] *Ramesside Inscriptions Translated & Annotated. Vol I.* Kitchen. 1993:161.
[502] *The Ancient Egyptian Book of Thoth*, Jasnow & Zauzich. 2005:36.

of Lower Egypt, the lady of plans, the lady of writings in the House of Life.[503]

In life Seshat is largely a goddess for the king rather than for the ordinary people. She does play a role in the afterlife where her roles reflect her earthly duties, she records events and is responsible for the construction of the mansions of the gods and the *"mansions in the West"* for the vindicated dead.[504] In the *Coffin Texts* both Thoth and Seshat aid the deceased. She gives access to the afterlife, *"the portal is opened for you by Seshat"*.[505] With Thoth, she provides the deceased with the essential magical texts. *"He shall bring Thoth to me in his shape, he shall bring [Seshat] to me [in] her [shape], he shall bring [this writing to me]."*[506]

Seshat plays a significant role in the *Book of Thoth* (described in chapter 5) where she is the major goddess. This is not surprising given the book's emphasis on the scribe's profession and the House of Life. She is *"Mistress of the Sustenance of the Foremost of the Chamber of Darkness"* and *"She-who-is-wise, this one who first established (the) chamber, she being...a lamp of prophecy"*.[507] It is Seshat who helps bring the light of understanding, of gnosis, into the darkness of ignorance.

Nehmataway

The goddess Nehmataway is mentioned as a consort of Thoth from the New Kingdom. We know little else about her. She was venerated alongside Thoth in his major cult centres and is often depicted as a goddess nursing a child on her lap. Her *sistrum* headdress differentiates her from other nursing goddesses such as Isis.

One myth tells us that Thoth was given Nehmataway as a consort as a reward for retrieving the Eye of Ra. She might be one of a pair of goddesses worshipped as the aggressive and pacified Eye of Ra, such as Ayet and Nehmataway who are worshipped at Herakleopolis.[508] As the pacified Eye Nehmataway is an obvious consort. There is a

---

[503] *The House of Life,* Gardiner. 1938:174.
[504] *Egyptian Mythology,* Pinch. 2002:190.
[505] *The Ancient Egyptian Coffin Texts Vol 1,* Faulkner. 2007:7. Spell 10.
[506] *The Ancient Egyptian Coffin Texts Vol 3,* Faulkner. 2007:122. Spell 1022.
[507] *The Ancient Egyptian Book of Thoth,* Jasnow & Zauzich. 2005:20,22.
[508] *Egyptian Mythology,* Pinch. 2002:130.

reference to *"Nehmataway, the Eye of Re"* on a Late Period stele.[509] At Hermopolis she was also linked to a local version of Hathor.[510]

A Late Period stele from Hermopolis links Nehmataway with oracles for Nectanebo I. As a general he came to the city to put down an uprising. Whilst there *"His mother, the Mighty, Nehmataway...announced to him that he would be king"*. Sure enough *"his father, Thoth, [the twice great] Lord of Hermopolis, and his mother [Neh]me[t]awa...caused him to appear in glory"*.[511] And so started the 19th Dynasty.

Nehmataway appears to have been a goddess of justice; her name means *"the rescuer of him who is robbed"*.[512] Petosiris, the High Priest of Thoth in Hermopolis, restored her temple at Hermopolis. He refers to her as *"the one who-made-what-is"* and *"mother of god"*.[513] Nehmataway was also considered the consort of the serpent deity Nehebu-Kau. He is a snake god, often shown as a snake-headed man, and was seen as a powerful and benevolent god. His name means *"he who harnesses the spirits"*.[514]

Children

Unlike some of the other Egyptian deities Thoth does not appear to have had children. Child gods were usually associated with triads. These family groups of god, goddess and child were used to order and associate the deities and to give the significant number of three. The duality of two, the god and goddess, bringing forth a third. Despite having consorts Thoth is not part of any triad. His priests and priestesses never felt the need for such an alignment. Maybe he was too independent, or busy, to be forced into such an arrangement. He does not come across as a *'family'* deity as he works beyond family ties and obligations.

---

[509] *Two Overlooked Oracles*, Klotz. 2010:250.
[510] *Hathor and Thoth: Two Key Figures of the Ancient Egyptian Religion*, Bleeker. 1973:67.
[511] *Two Overlooked Oracles*, Klotz. 2010:250.
[512] *Hathor and Thoth: Two Key Figures of the Ancient Egyptian Religion*, Bleeker. 1973:122.
[513] *Ancient Egyptian Literature Vol 3*, Lichtheim. 2006:47. *The Long Biographical Inscription of Petosiris.*
[514] *The Routledge Dictionary of Egyptian Gods and Goddesses*, Hart. 2005:99.

In some of the writings there are references to Thoth's daughter and Thoth's son but it isn't clear whether they refer to actual divine offspring. It is more likely to be a term indicating a close and honoured relationship. Both his followers and his priests and priestesses may well have used the term 'son of Thoth' and 'daughter of Thoth'. There is no mention of any children of Thoth in the surviving myths. Spell 201 of the *Coffin Texts* refers to Wnpy the son of Thoth, who is a minor deity, but there doesn't appear to be any other references to him.

Relationships with Other Deities

There are two major themes in Egyptian religion; the solar tradition of the Sun God Ra and the earth-rebirth tradition of Osiris. Thoth moves easily between the two of them. As he is a major deity in his own right it is not surprising that he was incorporated into both traditions as they gained in popularity and strength. It is worth noting that there was no battle for supremacy between the deities except that of Horus and Seth, representing the ever-present battle between order and chaos. It is highly likely though that the major cults would have competed for power and influence. There is no evidence of a tradition that was specific to Thoth, although he is associated with the Hermopolitan creation theology (see chapter 12). The city of Hermopolis never became a dominant political power which is probably why a tradition specific to Thoth never developed, as far as the evidence shows.

Ra

Thoth is sometimes considered *"the son of Re"* and says *"I am Thoth, the eldest son of Re"*.[515] Thoth also acts as Ra's deputy. *"Thou shalt be writer in the nether-world...Thou shalt take my place as deputy, thou shalt be called Thoth substitute of Re."*[516]

The *Book of the Heavenly Cow* describes how Thoth came into being. *"Thou shalt be in my place, my representative. Men shall address thee as 'Thoth the Representative of Re'...So came into being*

---

[515] *Hathor and Thoth: Two Key Figures of the Ancient Egyptian Religion,* Bleeker. 1973:112.
[516] *Hathor and Thoth: Two Key Figures of the Ancient Egyptian Religion,* Bleeker. 1973:119.

the ibis of Thoth... 'I shall cause thee to encompass both skies with thy beauty and with thy light'. So came into being the moon of Thoth. 'I shall cause thee to turn back the Haunebu.' So came into being the baboon of Thoth."[517] (The Haunebu were one of the enemies of Egypt.)

In another text Thoth is appointed as successor to Ra. He discharged his duties so well that he had the epithet "*the one with whose word Atum is content*".[518] A limestone plaque from the Ptolemaic Period shows Thoth, in his baboon form, offering the *wedjat* eye to Ra who is portrayed as a winged sun disc. Thoth performs three essential services for Ra; he is messenger and secretary, protector of the solar barque and peacemaker.

As the Messenger of Ra, Thoth does a lot of summoning of the deities particularly during the struggles between Horus and Seth. On a papyrus from Thebes, dating to around 950 BCE, a falcon-headed Ra-Horakhty sits on a throne while the ibis-headed Thoth stands in front of him.[519] He holds a reed and palette and is poised ready to write. Thoth could be described as the perfect secretary. He certainly comes across as longsuffering with the number of letters he has to read and write during the Contendings of Horus and Seth. Letters are written to Osiris and Neith and their replies read out. Thoth is also said to report everything that has happened during the day to Ra.

Along with a number of other deities, Thoth is a protector of Ra and the solar barque. The *Book of the Heavenly Cow* also explains how Ra sends Thoth into the afterworld to record and to destroy any who rise up against him. Thoth is usually shown accompanying Ra in the solar barque. Each day he determines the course of the sun. "*I am Thoth, who issues the decree at dawn, and whose sight follows on after the overthrow of his season, the guide of heaven and earth.*"[520] He ensures the safe passage of the solar barque and removes any opposition to the boat's transit. "*I have knotted the cord and have put the ferry-boat in good order, I have fetched East and West.*"[521] Along with Seth, Thoth protects Ra from the chaos serpent Apophis who attacks the solar barque as it descends into the afterworld each night.

---

[517] *Ancient Egyptian Science - A Source Book Vol 1*, Clagett. 1989:541.
[518] *Hathor and Thoth: Two Key Figures of the Ancient Egyptian Religion*, Bleeker. 1973:119.
[519] *Egyptian Drawings*, Peck. 1978:125.
[520] *The Wisdom of Ancient Egypt*, Kaster. 1993:73. Spell 182.
[521] *The Ancient Egyptian Book of the Dead*, Faulkner. 1989:181. Spell 182.

"(Thoth) whose spells protect the one who bore him (Re), who dispels rebelliousness and ends strife."[522] It is only with the assistance of Thoth and the other deities that the sun can rise again each morning. *"Thoth is established in the bow of your Sacred Barque, destroying all your foes."*[523]

The following extracts from a hymn to Thoth, from the statue of Horemheb, summarises Thoth's relationship with Ra. *"Praise to Thoth, son of Re...contenting Re, reporting to the Sole Lord (?) reading and causing him to know all that happens...contenting the Morning Ship...rejoicing with the joy of the Evening Ship at the Feast of Traversing Heaven, overthrowing the fiend, seizing the Western Horizon. The ennead of the gods that is in the Evening Ship give praise to Thoth, they say to him, 'Praise [to...]praised of Re."*[524]

Death, a necessity for rebirth, was considered an essential part of the cycles of existence, so the perilous descent into the underworld was as important for Ra as it was for the deceased. Thoth accompanies the weary, setting Sun God on his journey to meet with Osiris, the lord of the underworld and of resurrection. Only when the soul of Ra joins with Osiris can the sun begin its ascension towards sunrise. Thoth protects and guides Ra and ensures that the two gods are reconciled and reunited, in doing so he also allows the two traditions (solar and earth-rebirth) to be united. *"I cause Re to set as Osiris, Osiris having set as Re. I cause him to enter the secret pit to revive the breast of the Weary-hearted one, the sacred soul within the west."*[525] Osiris and Ra are seen here as the polarities of a single deity. Ra, representing the *ba*, was visible during the day and Osiris, representing the body, was hidden in the underworld. The union of the two, protected and guided by Thoth, brought new life not only to the sun but also to everyone.[526]

In the New Kingdom another funerary text occurs known as the *Amduat*, or *What is in the Netherworld*. Thutmose III and Amenhotep II have this text in their tombs. It gives a very detailed, concise account

---

[522] *Hathor and Thoth: Two Key Figures of the Ancient Egyptian Religion*, Bleeker. 1973:119.
[523] *The Ancient Egyptian Book of the Dead*, Faulkner. 1989:41. Spell 15.
[524] *A Statue of Horemhab Before His Accession*, Winlock. 1924:3.
[525] *The Book of the Dead or Going Forth by Day*, Allen. 1974:196. Spell 182a.
[526] *Journey Through the Afterlife. Ancient Egyptian Book of the Dead*, Taylor (ed). 2010:20.

of the solar barque as it journeys through the twelve hours of darkness.[527] In the fourth hour the sun has lost its light and the Solar Eye has been injured by evil forces. An ibis-headed Thoth and a falcon-headed Sokar hold the Solar Eye. (Sokar is an underworld god, an aspect of Osiris.) They will protect and restore the Eye. The sixth hour is midnight and the uttermost depths for the barque. Thoth is portrayed as a baboon-headed man. He offers a small ibis to a goddess, who holds the solar eyes behind her, and thus offers himself. He is offering his service, wisdom and skills for the resurrection of the sun and for the continuance of creation. The text says that Thoth will be *"guided by these eyes to his fields"*.[528] By the tenth hour the Solar Eye has been restored. A baboon-headed Thoth sits holding the Eye, facing him are eight forms of Sekhmet in her healing aspect. This lion-headed daughter of Ra is no longer angry and destructive but has reverted back to her more helpful, healing aspect. At the twelfth hour the sun is reborn with the dawn. Thoth is not present in this hour but the eight gods of the Ogdoad are. They were present at the first creation and so are present at this re-creation.[529] (See chapter 12.)

Peace-making is one of Thoth's important functions and he is in great demand as a diplomat and peacemaker. He uses his wisdom and power with words to pacify the angry, to reconcile enemies and to ensure that *maat* is upheld. A number of the texts give the impression that Ra is weary of the strife around him but he is unable to resolve it and so relies on Thoth to restore *maat* and *"bring him peace through godly power"*.[530]

Thoth retrieves and pacifies the Angry Eye of Ra, a role complementary to his retrieving and healing the injured Eye of Horus (see below). The myths about the Solar Eye are inconsistent probably because they are so old and have been adapted to various local traditions. Either the Eye was sent on a mission by Ra or she argued with Ra and left him. The Eye became lost and Thoth searched for her. *"I am Thoth who wanders abroad to seek the eye for its owner (Re), I come and I have found it."*[531]

---

527 *Knowledge for the Afterlife*, Abt & Hornung. 2003:59.
528 *Knowledge for the Afterlife*, Abt & Hornung. 2003:82.
529 *Knowledge for the Afterlife*, Abt & Hornung. 2003:118-120.
530 *Hymns, Prayers and Songs*, Foster. 1995:64. *The Cairo Hymns to Amun-Re*.
531 *Hathor and Thoth: Two Key Figures of the Ancient Egyptian Religion*, Bleeker. 1973:120.

In another variation of the myth the returning Eye is angry because Ra has replaced her with another. Thoth pacifies the Angry Eye. He gives her a position on Ra's forehead and she becomes the cobra headed *uraeus* who wards off his enemies. *"Thoth brought the Sound Eye, he pacified the Sound Eye, after Re sent it forth (when) it was greatly enraged."*[532]

From the Demotic literature of the Ptolemaic Period we have another tale of the Angry Eye this time in the form of Ra's daughter. Again the tales vary, the Eye goddess can be Bastet, Hathor, Sekhmet or Tefnut. She quarrels with her father and leaves Egypt. The Angry Eye takes the form of a lioness, or wild-cat, and lives in either Nubia or Libya. Not only is she dangerous and destructive in the land of her self-imposed exile she has left Ra vulnerable for he has lost his protective *uraeus*. Her extreme power is lethal even for the other deities. Ra sends his peacemaker, Thoth, to pacify the Eye and to persuade her to return. Thoth, in his baboon form, seeks out the Eye and eventually manages to placate her. In one version he finds her in Nubia in the Eastern Mountains of the sunrise at *Bwgm*, the Place of Finding. Using a mixture of persuasion and haranguing Thoth finally persuades her to return to Egypt. One version of the myth states that he had to ask her 1,077 times. This myth has been used as a vehicle for a collection of fables. One of them, the *Lion in Search of Man*, is given in a condensed form in the *Fables of Aesop*.[533]

It is probable that there was another myth, that of the Distant Goddess, incorporated into the myth of the Angry Eye. In this myth a wild goddess, native to Nubia, is persuaded by Thoth to come to Egypt.[534] A 19th Dynasty ostraca shows the baboon Thoth persuading the Distant Goddess, portrayed as a seated lioness, to return to Egypt.[535] Once in the civilised land of Egypt the more amiable aspects of the goddess emerge. She does not forsake her wild nature entirely and Thoth constantly has to pacify her; she is appeased by music, dance and wine which symbolise the benefits of civilisation over the untamed wilderness.

---

[532] *The Book of the Dead or Going Forth by Day*, Allen. 1974:162. Spell 167.
[533] *Egyptian Mythology*, Pinch. 2002:71-74.
[534] *Hathor and Thoth: Two Key Figures of the Ancient Egyptian Religion*, Bleeker. 1973:128-130.
[535] *The Animal World of the Pharaohs*, Houlihan. 1996:215.

The Earth-Rebirth Tradition

The tale of Isis and Osiris and the Contendings of Horus and Seth incorporate Thoth into the second major tradition. The cult of Osiris becomes prominent during the 5th Dynasty and the myths evolve until the Christianisation of Egypt, consequently the myths are complicated and contradictory and have many variations. Only the parts of the story relevant to Thoth are included here.

Osiris

Isis and Osiris ruled the earth until Osiris was murdered by his brother Seth. After a long story the corpse is retrieved and mummified by Anubis. Seth and his followers try to destroy the body but it is protected by Anubis, the guardian of the tomb, and Thoth's magic. *"Thoth recites your liturgy, and calls you with his spells."*[536] Thoth supports the grieving Isis and Nephthys and helps them in their efforts to revive Osiris. He *"catches the suffering of Isis...as though in a net"*.[537] The two mourning goddesses are often shown as kites and in the *Pyramid Texts* are referred to as kites on the wings of Thoth; that is, under his protection.

Having reassembled the various parts of the body of Osiris Thoth raises the north wind, viewed as health giving by the Egyptians, which enables Osiris to breathe again. He then recites the ritual for the opening of the mouth and gives the power of speech back to Osiris. Thoth and Horus then raise Osiris and enable him to stand up. Through his mastery of magic Thoth makes Osiris a being of light and ensures his eternal life. *"Thoth has protected you...Thoth has made you a spirit."*[538]

Thoth then restrains the followers of Seth and brings them to justice. *"O Thoth, set your hand against them and your knife into them, turn them back upon the roads."*[539]

Thoth acts as an advocate for the dead Osiris before the Ennead. *"I am Thoth who vindicated Osiris against his foes on that day of*

[536] *Ancient Egyptian Literature Vol 3*, Lichtheim. 2006:120. *The Lamentations of Isis and Nephthys.*
[537] *Hathor and Thoth: Two Key Figures of the Ancient Egyptian Religion*, Bleeker. 1973:118.
[538] *The Ancient Egyptian Coffin Texts Vol 1*, Faulkner. 2007:69-70. Spell 74.
[539] *The Ancient Egyptian Coffin Texts Vol 1*, Faulkner. 2007:43. Spell 47.

judgement in the great Mansion of the Prince which is in Heliopolis."[540]
The *Pyramid Texts* tell how at the tribunal Thoth issued a decree making Osiris god of the afterlife rather than of the earth as he had previously been. The assembled deities were said to be content with this *"great and mighty word which issued from the mouth of Thoth"*.[541] Thoth protects Osiris during his journey through the afterworld and then establishes him as ruler of the Westerners. *"Tehuti protecteth thee; he causeth thy soul to be established within the Maadet boat, by the power of thy name of 'Iah'...Tehuti proclaimeth thy Heb-festival, and invoketh thee with his protecting formulae.*"[542]

Spell 313 of the *Coffin Texts* gives a summary of what Thoth has done for Osiris. *"O Thoth - so says Atum - travel for us upon the Island of Fire, see Osiris for us, for you will find him in Ninsu...regrant his crown for me, for you are the god for the protection (?) of Osiris...Behold, I have come - so says Thoth (to Osiris) - and I have brought to you truth and joy, I have brought to you authority and vindication...I have placed your foes in bonds and the Scorpion in fetters: so says Thoth to Osiris. I have come that I may do again what is good for you, I will raise up Truth for you, I will gladden you with what you desire, for I have smitten, subdued and felled your foes.*"[543]

Isis

Isis, through her magic, revitalises Osiris and conceives a son by him. Seth then imprisons Isis in a spinning house. It is Thoth who urges her to escape with his help. *"I am Isis. I had come from the spinning-house where my brother Seth had put me. Now Thoth, the great god, the chief of justice in heaven and on earth said to me: 'do come, Isis divine! For it is well to listen - the one lives while the other one leads him. Conceal yourself with the young boy Horus.*"[544] As Isis is herself Great in Magic it appears surprising that she should allow herself to be imprisoned in the first place and then to be reluctant to escape without the prompting of Thoth.

---

[540] *The Ancient Egyptian Book of the Dead*, Falkner. 1989:34-5. Spell 1.
[541] *Thoth or the Hermes of Egypt*, Boylan. 1922:22.
[542] *The Burden of Isis*, Dennis. 1910:23,26.
[543] *The Ancient Egyptian Coffin Texts Vol 1*, Faulkner. 2007:233-4. Spell 313.
[544] *Ancient Egyptian Magical Texts*, Borghouts. 1978:59.

This myth appears to align Isis with those women who would have been at the mercy of men throughout their lives. Weaving and spinning were the time-consuming, and not always welcome, chores of many women. It may have consoled them to know that even Isis had to spin. At another level the symbolism of spinning, or weaving, suggests fate and destiny. Was Isis constrained by her fate until *"the orderer of fate"* enabled her to break free of its bindings?[545] Cloth was an essential component of the funerary rites and so Isis imprisoned and spinning may show her trapped by her intense mourning of Osiris unable to concentrate on their son Horus. It is assistance from the *"lord of kind-heartedness"*[546] that helps her overcome this stasis. Horus, son of the late Osiris, is born in the papyrus swamps of the Delta where Isis is comforted and protected by Thoth and Amun-Ra.

As discussed in chapter 9, Thoth saves Horus when he is stung by a scorpion which was sent by Seth. Despite being Great in Magic herself Isis is unable to save her child and insists that Ra save him. Thoth is despatched to save Horus and restore *maat*. *"And Isis sent her voice to heaven, her cries to the barque of millions. The sun-disc halted in front of her and did not move from its place. Thoth came, provided with his magic power and with the high command of justification."* Once he has cured Horus he states *"I am Thoth, the eldest one, the son of Re, whom Atum, the father of the gods has ordered to heal Horus for his mother Isis - and to heal the sufferer likewise"*. Thoth then tells the local gods and people to watch over the Horus child. *"And Thoth said to these gods and spoke to the inhabitants of Khemmis: 'oh nurses who are in Pe...be watchful over this child, look for his path among men, confuse the ways of those who rebel against him until he has taken for himself the throne of the Two Lands."*[547]

Horus

When Horus is older he takes revenge on Seth, and his colleagues, for his father's murder. He calls on Thoth, as the avenger of injustice, to help him. *"Sharpen your knife, O Thoth, which is keen and cutting,*

---

[545] *Thoth or the Hermes of Egypt*, Boylan. 1922:185.
[546] *Cracking Codes: The Rosetta Stone and Decipherment*, Parkinson. 1999:148.
[547] *Ancient Egyptian Magical Texts*, Borghouts. 1978:65, 68.

which removes heads and cuts out hearts!"[548] The crescent moon can be seen to represent a particularly sharp, curved knife or sword. Thoth, acting as criminal judge, pronounces the punishment of Seth which is to carry Osiris on his back. This was usually portrayed as Osiris riding on a donkey, one of the animal forms of Seth. "*He has set you on his back that he may not thwart you.*"[549]

The subsequent hostility between Horus and Seth leads to endless battles. A text from the Horus Temple, at Edfu, tells of Horus' on-going struggle with Seth. Thoth praises the day of eventual victory. "*A happy day, O Horus, lord of this land.*"[550] There are many versions of this myth in which Thoth uses his magic in various ways to defend Horus. The myths do get confusing as they were actively evolving and being adapted to local circumstances.

The Contendings of Horus and Seth

In this myth Thoth acts as advocate to Horus and also as scribe to the deities. The story comes from the New Kingdom, from a papyrus from the reign of Ramesses V. There is a strong element of coarse humour mixed in with the serious parts, which seems to be a characteristic of this age. The story starts with Horus claiming the throne of his father, Osiris, in front of Ra and the Ennead. Shu and Thoth both support the claim against Seth, arguing that as the son Horus should inherit his father's throne. Ra, however, wants to grant Seth the throne because he is more powerful than Horus. Thoth overrules this because it is not following the inheritance laws, it is not *maat*. The Ennead tell Thoth, the Clerk of the Court, to write a letter to the creator Goddess Neith. He later reads out the reply which confirms Horus as the rightful heir.

Seth challenges Horus to a fight and both transform into a pair of battling hippopotamuses. In one version of the myth, from the New Kingdom *Papyrus Sallier*, Horus is furious when Isis intervenes and allows Seth to survive so he cuts off her head. Thoth heals Isis by replacing her missing head with a cow's head. It is tempting to tie this in with our expression of '*losing your head*'. Has Thoth calmed Isis down, using his diplomatic skills, allowing her to regain her dignity?

---

[548] *The Ancient Egyptian Pyramid Texts*, Faulkner. 2007:165. Utterance 477.
[549] *The Ancient Egyptian Pyramid Texts*, Faulkner. 2007:123. Utterance 372.
[550] *The Myth of Horus at Edfu: II.C. (Continued)*, Blackman & Fairman. 1943:5.

Plutarch says that Horus *"drew off the crown from her head. Whereupon Hermes crowned her with a head-dress of cow-horns"*.[551] This more dignified rendering allows Thoth to align Isis with Hathor who also wears a cow-horn crown.

The story gets more bizarre at this point. Seth attempts to rape Horus who catches Seth's semen in his hand. Isis cuts off the corrupted hand and throws it into the river. She then takes semen from Horus and spreads it on some lettuce which Seth eats. Seth tells the Ennead what he has done. When Horus denies this Thoth determines who is speaking the truth. He orders the semen of both gods to come out. The semen of Seth answers him from the river, the semen of Horus answers from inside Seth. Thoth orders it to come out of Seth's head where it emerges as a golden sun disc. Thoth takes this and places it on his own head.

One myth says Thoth was born from the union of Horus and Seth, which might refer obliquely to the disc from Seth's head.[552] It perhaps means that equilibrium and wisdom, personified by Thoth, are born out of the resolution of conflict and are not attainable through the obliteration of one of the opposing sides.

The dispute continues for eighty years and you can't help feeling sympathy for Ra who has to go and lie down at one stage in the proceedings. Thoth continues patiently and suggests writing a letter to Osiris and letting him decide between the two contenders. Thoth then reads out the reply. When Horus is finally given the throne Ra takes Seth with him in the solar barque because his chaotic power is a powerful weapon against Ra's enemies. Thoth becomes *"Thoth who judged the rivals"*.[553] Might does not win automatically, the victor has to be vindicated to be morally and legally in the right. *"I am Thoth who vindicated Horus against his foes."*[554]

The Reconciliation of Horus and Seth

One of Thoth's important missions was the reconciliation of these two battling gods. *"N has gone out of the House of Thoth, he has broken*

[551] *Plutarch: Concerning The Mysteries Of Isis And Osiris,* Mead. 2002:202.
[552] *Hathor and Thoth: Two Key Figures of the Ancient Egyptian Religion,* Bleeker. 1973:112.
[553] *An Ancient Egyptian Book of Hours,* Faulkner. 1958:15.
[554] *The Ancient Egyptian Coffin Texts Vol 1,* Faulkner. 2007:236. Spell 314.

up the fight and has quelled the uproar."[555] The deities looked on in dismay at this endless, unholy battle. "*The earth was hacked up when the Rivals fought, their feet scooped out the sacred pool in On. Now comes Thoth adorned with his dignity, for Atum has ennobled him with strength, and the Two Great Ladies are pleased with him.*"[556]

The myths tell of one specific major conflict between Horus and Seth. In their fury Seth tore out one of Horus' eyes and Horus removed Seth's testicles. Both gods have inflicted serious injury on each other. Seth has lost his virility and thus his power. This might have pleased Horus but it has endangered creation as Ra needs Seth in the daily battle with Apophis. The Eye of Horus has many meanings such as soundness and perfection, the strength of the monarchy and the celestial bodies of the sun and moon. Damage to the Eye, and thus these associations, is damage to *maat*. Thoth intervenes at this point and heals both the injured parties. The powers of both gods are essential and in trying to disable each other they have imperilled creation.

In some versions of the myth Thoth retrieves the Eye. The inference is that Seth escapes with the Eye, or throws it away, or the Eye itself escapes from the violence. "*I have returned from searching for the Horus-eye, I have brought it back*" or "*Thoth comes after having taken the eye of Horus away from his opponent*".[557] Where the Eye has been damaged Thoth makes it whole again. This produces the *wedjat* Eye, the full, healed Eye. The *wedjat* Eye symbolises divine life and the overcoming of death. This scene is illustrated with Thoth handing the *wedjat* Eye to Horus. "*I am Thoth who brings justice, who healed the Sacred Eye.*"[558]

Thoth eventually separates and reconciles the warring parties. "*So the fighting is ended, the tumult is stopped, the fire which went forth is quenched, the anger in the presence of the Tribunal of the God is calmed.*"[559] Separating two combatants is easy if you are more powerful than they are but it can be inflammatory as it pours violence upon violence. At best it only produces a temporary solution as the

---

[555] *The Ancient Egyptian Coffin Texts Vol 2*, Faulkner. 2007:245. Spell 678.
[556] *The Ancient Egyptian Coffin Texts Vol 1*, Faulkner. 2007:3. Spell 7.
[557] *Hathor and Thoth: Two Key Figures of the Ancient Egyptian Religion*, Bleeker. 1973:125.
[558] *The Ancient Egyptian Coffin Texts Vol 1*, Faulkner. 2007:190. Spell 242.
[559] *The Ancient Egyptian Coffin Texts Vol 1*, Faulkner. 2007:3. Spell 7.

root cause of the conflict remains. Skill and application are needed to reconcile them, which is the outcome that Maat demands. *"I have satisfied Horus, I have calmed down the two companions in the moment of their rage, I have washed off the blood, I have ended the quarrel."*[560] The other deities could truly say, *"Hail to you, O Thoth, in whom is the peace of the gods".*[561]

The Legend of the Winged Disc

Another version of the Horus and Seth conflict comes from a Late Period text from Edfu. Horus of Behdet is battling against his foes, while Ra and Thoth appear in the text as narrators. A large proportion of Thoth's words are to do with the naming of places and people. *"And Thoth said to Re: Therefore shall the name of this town shall be called...Thoth said to Re 'therefore shall Horus be called the Winged Disc'....and Thoth said to Re 'therefore the priest of this god shall be called 'Lord of Combat' from this day"* and so on. Thoth also sets up the winged disc in every temple, thus sanctifying the image. *"And Thoth set up this image everywhere and in every place in which they are (now) and in which any gods or goddesses are to this day."*[562]

Reading the story you get the impression that Ra and Thoth have been drafted in to enhance the reputation of Horus of Behdet. As Horus is described as Lord of Lower Egypt and Seth as Lord of Upper Egypt it reads very much as a war between the two countries where the victor claims that the gods were on his side.

In conclusion, Thoth is an essential friend, protector and advocate for Isis, Osiris and Horus. In spell 110 from the *Book of the Dead* the deceased identifies with Thoth and gives a good summary of his role in the whole affair. *"I pacify the Combatants...I drive away mourning from their elders, I remove turmoil from their young; I wipe away harm of all kinds from Isis, I wipe away harm of all kinds from the gods."*[563]

---

[560] *Hathor and Thoth: Two Key Figures of the Ancient Egyptian Religion,* Bleeker. 1973:126.
[561] *The Ancient Egyptian Coffin Texts Vol 1,* Faulkner. 2007:5. Spell 9.
[562] *The Myth of Horus at Edfu: I,* Fairman. 1935:30-35.
[563] *The Ancient Egyptian Book of the Dead,* Faulkner. 1989:104. Spell 110.

Seth

Although Thoth opposes Seth, and fights on the side of Osiris and Horus, he does not have a direct, hostile relationship with Seth.

In his original form Seth was the god of Ombus and was seen as a benevolent deity. In some parts of the *Pyramid Texts* he is referred to as the brother of Thoth and he appears as an ally of Horus. In some reliefs and illustrations Seth holds the ladder with Horus for the deceased to ascend into the afterworld. He also appears with Horus tying together the heraldic plants of Upper and Lower Egypt. These scenes illustrate the importance of reconciliation and of duality; there is harmony through the balance of equal but opposite forces. The tension between the two opposing gods provides the force that holds the ladder firm and gives stability to the intertwined plants. Seth also played an important part in the early coronation ceremonies. With time, and changing politics and religion, Seth becomes increasingly demonised and his functions are taken over by Thoth. This seems to have started in the 18th Dynasty. One suggestion is that it was connected with the occupation of Northern Egypt by the Hyksos who worshipped Seth due to his similarity to their storm god, Ba'al.

In the stories of their battles Horus and Seth are opposites and inevitably always in conflict, but they are both essential components of creation just as order (*maat*) and chaos (*isfet*) are. They are equals, neither one can destroy the other and their power needs to be brought back into balance. Seth represents chaos, aggression and energy. Without these aspects, albeit in a regulated form, creation will stagnate and there will be no power strong enough to fight off the chaos of the *Nun* which constantly threatens the created order. With time the myths change and Seth becomes increasingly demonised. He is transformed into the evil which has to be defeated, the darkness which must be overcome by the light, rather than being part of the natural duality of the created order. Thoth is seen as fighting against the chaos of Seth which threatens order and *maat*.

Thoth, by of his very nature, must be in opposition to Seth. He abhors the disorder and disruption which threaten *maat*. He strives to keep balance and order in creation, he is eternally vigilant against the powers of chaos. Thoth constantly acts to restore equilibrium and harmony by opposing the forces of chaos. His opposition is in keeping with his character; wise, compassionate and level headed. Even though he fights the perpetrators of injustice he is not hot-tempered like Horus who fights from passion. Thoth fights and punishes because that is what is needed to safeguard creation and *maat*. Wherever possible he uses his wisdom and skill to reconcile, but when this fails he will become the *"dread avenger of injustice"*.[564]

Seth represents disorder in individuals, societies and nature but he is not the enemy of creation. He journeys in the night barque with Ra and uses his powers against the real enemy of creation, the chaos serpent Apophis. No matter how destructive Seth is he will fight on the side of Ra in the end, as the annihilation of creation would be his own annihilation. This is echoed by Thoth healing Seth when he was injured during his fight with Horus. Thoth does not destroy Seth even though he may well have the power to do so. His task is *"to reconcile contradictory forces and to bundle them together in order to create harmony, peace and order"*.[565]

Hathor

Bleeker considers Hathor and Thoth to be two key deities in Egyptian religion.[566] In heaven Ra is the creator and Osiris the giver of eternal life. On earth Hathor and Thoth act as counterbalances to each other even though they are not particularly linked through myths. He suggests that Hathor is the dynamic deity bringing creativity and fertility while Thoth is the harmonic deity bringing peace and maintaining order. Part of Thoth's duty is to calm Hathor down, to control the dynamic element to ensure that it does not bring chaos. Hathor acts to inject energy into order to ensure that it does not stagnate. Sekhmet can be perceived as an aspect of Hathor at her most destructive, as seen in the Angry Eye myths.

An inscription from a temple at Dakhla, for the *"House of the nbs-tree"*, shows the baboon form of Thoth resting beneath a tree. This associates him with Hathor in either her Wandering Goddess or Angry Eye aspect.[567] The Egyptian artists did observe the natural world in

---

[564] *Hathor and Thoth: Two Key Figures of the Ancient Egyptian Religion,* Bleeker. 1973:134.
[565] *Hathor and Thoth: Two Key Figures of the Ancient Egyptian Religion,* Bleeker. 1973:127.
[566] *Hathor and Thoth: Two Key Figures of the Ancient Egyptian Religion,* Bleeker. 1973:159-60.
[567] *The Goddesses of the Egyptian Tree Cult,* Buhl. 1947:87.

detail and Thoth may also be enjoying the shade at noon as no doubt many baboons would have done.

In the temple of Dendera, Seshat and Hathor are associated and it is Hathor who is described as the *"queen of writing, mistress of the book"*.[568] Rather than linking Hathor to Thoth, through his relationship with Seshat, this is probably just another illustration of the fluidity of the Egyptian deities and a reflection of Hathor's literacy.

Shu

Shu and his sister Tefnut were the first children of Ra. He is the god of sunlight and dry air, she the goddess of moist air. In some variations of the Distant Goddess and Angry Eye myths Shu appears interchangeable with Thoth, in others he accompanies Thoth. As Tefnut can sometimes be the goddess concerned it would make sense for her brother, Shu, to be the one who searches for her. To the Egyptians Shu would have been viewed as the sky, or the air, that separated heaven and earth. As the moon traversed the sky they would perceive a relationship between the two gods that we might not, with our more scientific approach, immediately recognise. There are a few instances where Shu is equated with Thoth. At the Sokaris Chapel at Dendera, Shu is depicted with Thoth in the illustration of the full moon (see chapter 4). In a *Hymn to Maat*, from the Temple of Amun at el-Hibis, it refers to *"Shu commingling with Thoth"*. [569]

Spell 161 of the *Book of the Dead* illustrates another connection between the two gods. This spell is to break open the sky which will allow the deceased to breathe, to give them the breath of life. Early illustrations show four ibis-headed figures of Thoth holding the hieroglyph sign for the sky on a pole. In later illustrations the sky signs have disappeared and the four figures of Thoth grasp the edges of doors. Once opened these doors will allow the winds of the four directions to revive the deceased and allow them to breathe. In a reference to this the 19th Dynasty coffin of Henutmehyt has an ibis-

---

[568] *Hathor and Thoth: Two Key Figures of the Ancient Egyptian Religion*, Bleeker. 1973:69.
[569] *Hymns, Prayers and Songs*, Foster. 1995:123. *Hymn to Maat*.

headed Thoth at each corner of the coffin, each holding the hieroglyph sign for the sky.[570]

In one of the Horus myths, Thoth is able to calm the stormy sea which indicates a sky god's power over the weather. (See chapter 8.) There is also a Roman reference to Hermes Aerios, Hermes of the Air, which reflects the perceived connection between these two gods. The magician Harnuphis served with the army under Marcus Aurelius. He is credited with not only summoning rain for the army but also with conjuring a thunderstorm which helped defeat the enemy. Harnuphis invoked Hermes Aerios, who appears to be a weather god through a fusion of Thoth and Shu.[571]

In Western beliefs the element of air is equated to the power of the mind, wisdom and communication providing another link between Shu and Thoth.

Anubis

Anubis is concerned exclusively with the dead and the afterlife. He works with Thoth in the embalming of the dead, the protection of the tomb and as a psychopomp. He is often shown escorting the deceased into the Judgement Hall and is the *"overseer of adjustments"* of the balance used to weigh the deceased's heart.[572]

Hapi

"Thoth is upon the arms of Hapy."[573] Hapi was the god of the Nile inundation and from the New Kingdom onwards there seems to have been a relationship between Hapi and Thoth, though it is not immediately obvious why this should have developed.

In one spell from the *Book of the Dead* Thoth is referred to as *"Thoth the Great who came forth from the Inundation"*.[574] Flocks of ibises no doubt took advantage of the bounty of food the overflowing Nile brought, which will have helped reinforce this relationship. The

---

[570] *Journey Through the Afterlife. Ancient Egyptian Book of the Dead,* Taylor. 2010:108, 116-117
[571] *Men and Gods on the Roman Nile,* Lindsay. 1968:215-217.
[572] *An Ancient Egyptian Book of Hours,* Faulkner. 1958:9.
[573] *Wine and Wine Offering in the Religion of Ancient Egypt,* Poo. 1995:83.
[574] *The Book of the Dead or Going Forth by Day,* Allen. 1974:187. Spell 178f.

Winding Waterway of the afterlife was also under the control of Thoth and Hapi. *"Opened for me are the double doors of the sky, parted for me are the double doors of the celestial waters, by Thoth and Hapi."*[575]

The first month of the inundation is called *Dhwty* (after Thoth) and the festival of drunkenness is held during this month. The myth of the Distant Goddess whom Thoth brought back from the south may, at one level, refer to the inundation which came from the south and was initially violent and dangerous before transforming into a benevolent blessing. During the inundation the Nile turned red due to the colour of the sediments it carried. As wine was red and couldn't have been made without the annual inundation it made an obvious offering at this time. Thoth is responsible for the wine offering to Hathor, in her angry aspect, hence his appellation of *"Lord of Wine"*. Thoth and Hapi are seen as providers of wine and of purification. *"May Osiris-N be purified upon the arms of Hapy, may Thoth cause that Osiris-N drink his water, his beer, his wine."*[576]

---

[575] *The Book of the Dead or Going Forth by Day,* Allen. 1974:55. Spell 60.
[576] *Wine and Wine Offering in the Religion of Ancient Egypt,* Poo. 1995:157.

CHAPTER 12

CREATION

"Before the High and Far-Off Times, O my Best Beloved, came the Time of the Very Beginnings; and that was in the days when the Eldest Magician was getting Things ready."[577]

Creation

The origin of creation and the birth of deities are impossible to ascertain, but that has never stopped anyone from speculating about them and trying to explain the unexplainable. The Egyptians, like most cultures, considered the created universe to consist of heaven, earth (which was focused on Egypt) and the afterworld or *duat*. Three main cosmogonies emerged from the three main cult centres.

The Three Theologies

The Heliopolitan theology emphasises the power of the sun god with Ra-Atum as creator. Atum, who is self-generated, creates the god Shu and the goddess Tefnut who in turn create the god Geb and the goddess Nut.

The Memphite theology focuses on the power of thought and expression with Ptah, the craftsman god, as the creator. Ptah is said to have created everything through his heart and tongue, personified

[577] *Just So Stories, The Crab That Played With the Sea*, Kipling. 1976:171.

as Horus and Thoth. He *"transmitted [life] to all the gods and to their kas by means of the heart in which Horus has taken shape and by means of the tongue in which Thoth has taken shape"*.[578]

The Hermopolitan theology focuses on the latent power of the *Nun*, or pre-creation chaos. It is believed to date back to the 3rd millennium BCE. The *Nun*, which is the primordial ocean, has a female aspect - the *Nanuet*, which is sometimes described as the celestial expanse above the abyss. This gives rise to the attributes of the *Nun*: *Heh* and *Hauhet* who represent the boundless and imperceptible expanses of the chaotic and formlessness, *Kek* and *Kauket* who represent its darkness and obscurity and *Amun* and *Amaunet* who represent the intangible secrets of the chaos and are likened to the wind. These four pairs of deities form the Ogdoad. They are usually shown as four frog-headed gods and four snake-headed goddesses. Another explanation for the Ogdoad is that Thoth was an ancient god of the Delta region and these eight deities were his souls.[579] The Ogdoad is seen as subordinate to Thoth. A Ptolemaic inscription at Karnak says the Eight created *"light in the Height [of Hermopolis] and took their place in Hermopolis with their father, the Venerable One"*.[580]

This theology appears quite scientific with its description of the initial creation of the universe out of nothing. Current theories of cosmology with its unknown, undetectable dark energy and dark matter appear similar to the concept of the *Nun*, where the nothing isn't a complete vacuum but seething with creative energy. A dense cloud of matter in the very early stages of the universe is thought to have collapsed into itself, compacted and ignited to form the first sun and the first light. In the Hermopolitan theory the wind churned part of the *Nun* which congealed and formed solid land, a hill called the Isle of Flames. On this hill an ibis laid the egg from which the sun god emerged. He caused the first sunrise, illuminating creation for the first time, and began the creation of life. Hermopolis was considered to be this place of high ground where Ra rested when he rose for the first time. The cult centre of Thoth was believed to be on this primal mound and the eggshell was said to be held in the sanctuary. The sacred district of Hermopolis was a rectangle surrounded by high

---

[578] *Ancient Egyptian Science - A Source Book Vol 1*, Clagett. 1989:600.
[579] *Creation and Cosmology*, James. 1969:17.
[580] *Ancient Egyptian Science - A Source Book Vol 1*, Clagett. 1989:304.

walls inside which was a representation of this instant of creation; an Island of Flame in the Lake of Two Knives.[581] The Egyptian name for the town was *Hmnw* - the Town of the Eight. Although the Greeks called it Hermopolis, after Hermes who they associated with Thoth, the current Egyptian name is el-Ashmunein - the Two Eights.[582] Thoth is *"lord of the Eight"*.[583]

Some scholars have suggested that there were only four deities and that the male-female split is only grammatical. Certainly the high priest of Hermopolis had the title *"Chief of Five"*[584] and *"great one of the five"* rather than *'of the Nine'*.[585] Four deities, or pairs of deities, were significant as four represents the balance and stability which was needed for an enduring creation. Four also represents the cardinal points. The following hymn to the Ogdoad supports the theory of four deities. *"Salutations to you, you Five Great Gods, Who came out of the City of Eight."*[586]

The idea that divine order was created out of the swamps of chaos associated the ibis, as a wetland bird, with the first stages of creation. The remains of this first egg were said to be preserved in the temple of Thoth in Hermopolis. *"It is there that the two halves of the egg lie, together with all the [beings] which emerged from it."* The concept of the primordial egg may have come from the marshes of the Delta where it would have been an obvious method of creation for an ibis god. This theory may have then been appended onto the existing Hermopolitan theory of the Ogdoad. *"Go, go to the two [halves of the] egg, go to Pe, to the Abode of Thoth."*[587] (Pe was a city in the Delta region.)

These are not the only creation myths, the Egyptians were quite happy to have multiple creators. *"The Great Throne which the gods made, which Horus made and which Thoth brought into being."*[588] They knew that they were attempting to describe the indescribable and that a number of different points of view might better achieve what they

---

581 *Ancient Egyptian Religion*, Cerny. 1952:44.
582 *Egyptian Myths*, Hart. 1990:20.
583 *Stelae of the Middle and New Kingdoms in the Museum of Archaeology and Anthropology, University of Cambridge*, Dodson. 1992:278.
584 *The Gods of the Egyptians Vol 1*, Budge. 1969:404.
585 *Hathor and Thoth: Two Key Figures of the Ancient Egyptian Religion*, Bleeker. 1973:152.
586 *Gods and Myths of Ancient Egypt*, Armour. 2001:125-26.
587 *Egyptian Religion*, Morenz. 1992:178.
588 *The Ancient Egyptian Pyramid Texts*, Falkner. 2007:187. Utterance 511.

were trying to do. The sacred myths were not meant to be taken literally anyway, many ideas would have come about through word play and puns.

Thoth as Creator

Thoth may have originally been considered a creator god. When the other theologies became dominant Thoth was absorbed into them. He lost his role as a creator and was subsequently viewed as a creative logos sprung from another god. Thoth was the first god, self-begotten. He is the personification of divine intelligence and is omniscient and omnipotent. "*Lord of Khemennu, self-created, to whom none hath given birth.*"[589] The *Edfu Texts* treat Thoth as a creator in his own right. "*The maker of all that is*" and "*the Great one who hath created all things.*"[590] He was "*the one who suspended the sky, establishing the earth and the underworld*".[591] Thoth creates by utterance. He speaks what is in his heart, or mind, and his words of power produce a physical manifestation of his heart. The idea of speaking the world into existence is similar to the later concept of Logos, which introduces the *Gospel of St. John*; "*In the beginning was the Word, and the Word was with God, and the Word was God*".

The Maintenance of Creation

Regardless of the differing details of the various creation theories they all portray creation as a precious ordered bubble of light, air and substance existing in the chaotic waters of the *Nun*. The *Nun*, like anti-matter, permanently threatens to break through and annihilate creation. It needs constant work to maintain creation against the hostile, chaotic powers of the *Nun*. Thoth is intimately involved with the protection of creation by ensuring that *maat* is maintained at all levels. Indeed, it is the responsibility of everyone to strive to maintain *maat* and ultimately creation.

---

[589] *The Gods of the Egyptians Vol 1*, Budge. 1969:400.
[590] *Thoth Or The Hermes Of Egypt*, Boylan. 1922:120.
[591] *The Liturgy of Opening the Mouth for Breathing*, Smith. 1993:69.

Thoth's Becoming

There are various myths about Thoth's origins. In one spell of the *Pyramid Texts* Thoth is referred to as *"Motherless"*. This passage is hostile towards Thoth so it is probably the equivalent of calling someone illegitimate.

So who is Thoth and where does he come from? *"Thou art the god sprung from the god (i.e. the sun-god) himself, for whom the gates of the horizon opened on the day of his birth: every god came forth at his command: his word passes into being: thou art Chons-Thoth."*[592]

From Ra

Thoth is often considered the son of Ra, having issued *"from the lips of Ra"*.[593] He is *"Thoth, thrice great, Lord of Hermopolis, the glorious ibis, presiding over Egypt, sprung from Re, born at the beginning"*.[594] Thoth was referred to as the heart of Ra, with the epithet *"veritable heart"* and considered the source of all creative thought.[595] *"What comes from his heart, at once takes place."*[596] (Thoth's relationship with Ra is covered in chapter 11.)

We know from a Ptolemaic Period text that the Greeks were speculating about the origin of the epithet *"Heart of Re"*. It is likely that the priests of that time had lost much of the ancient knowledge of their religion and those that had some knowledge were not prepared to divulge their secrets. It should be remembered that nearly 3,000 years separated those priests from the origins of their religion, compared to the well documented 2,000 years that separate us from the birth of Christianity. Over the centuries the myths and religion will have constantly been reinterpreted and their focus changed, but nothing was ever discarded. *"An ibis was begotten of the thought of his (i.e. Shu's) heart - Thoth, the great one, who created all things, the tongue and heart that knows everything which is with him (i.e. Re)."*[597]

As in many religions the concept of a trinity of deities was widespread in Egypt. Three in one gives unity within plurality.

[592] *Thoth Or The Hermes Of Egypt*, Boylan. 1922:121.
[593] *Egyptian Mythology*, Pinch. 2002:209.
[594] *Thoth Or The Hermes Of Egypt*, Boylan. 1922:118.
[595] *The Liturgy of Opening the Mouth for Breathing*, Smith. 1993:52.
[596] *Thoth Or The Hermes Of Egypt*, Boylan. 1922:120.
[597] *Thoth Or The Hermes Of Egypt*, Boylan. 1922:117.

Although not a part of a formal triad, Thoth is called *"the heart of Re, the tongue of the Tatenen [= Ptah], the throat of the one with the hidden name [Amon]"*.[598]

From Horus and Seth

In some variations of the Contendings of Horus and Seth, Thoth is called the son of Horus having emerged from Seth's forehead. (See chapter 11.) Elsewhere he is referred to as *"the one who emerged from the skull"*. This story may have arisen from a play on words. *Wp.t* - skull, is very close to *wp.wpw* - judge, and similar to *wpw.tj* - messenger, both of which are Thoth's roles.[599]

Self Creating

As Lord of the Ogdoad, Thoth was considered a self-creating god who produced the cosmic egg on the Island of Flame. He also hatched out of this egg in his ibis form. *"Thoth, son of the stone, who came forth from the twin eggshells."*[600] The *Turin Papyrus* considers Thoth to be self-created. *"Hail to thee Lunar-Thoth, thou self-engendered, the unknown!"*[601]

The Rule of the Gods

The *Turin Papyrus*, dating from the period of Ramesses II, lists the earthly reigns of the gods, in the *"Time of Horus"*. Thoth reigned for 7,726 years.[602] The number may have had a significance we can only guess at.

The Creation of Humanity

There is little speculation about the origins of humanity in the literature, which is surprising. Possibly it hasn't survived. Ra was said to have made humans from his tears. He is quick, however, to distance himself from the evil which humans are capable of. *"I did not*

---

[598] *Egyptian Religion,* Morenz. 1992:144.
[599] *Hathor and Thoth: Two Key Figures of the Ancient Egyptian Religion,* Bleeker. 1973:112.
[600] *The Book of the Dead or Going Forth by Day,* Allen. 1974:109. Spell 134.
[601] *Thoth Or The Hermes Of Egypt,* Boylan. 1922:63.
[602] *Ancient Egypt: Anatomy of a Civilization,* Kemp. 1989:65.

ordain that they commit iniquity, it is their hearts which destroyed what I had ordered."[603]   Alternately the potter god, Khnum, fashioned humanity out of clay. There is no mention of Thoth creating humans. Maybe he didn't, otherwise we might have been better disposed towards *maat.*

---

[603] *The Wandering of the Soul,* Piankoff. 1972:35. Spell 1130.

CHAPTER 13

WORSHIP OF THOTH

"Celebrate the feast of your God, and begin it at the correct time. God is unhappy if He is neglected."[604]

The Extent of the Cult of Thoth

The cult of Thoth probably arose in Predynastic times, about 3200 – 2686 BCE, although it is impossible to determine how old it was and where it originated. He was referred to as the *"Great God of primeval times, the primeval one"*.[605] Ibis and baboon figurines and inscriptions have been found from earliest times and Thoth was an important god during the Old Kingdom. In the Old Kingdom there are references to the *"Feast of Thoth"* and a *"House of Thoth"*. From the 3rd Dynasty there is reference to a priest of the *"temple of Thoth"*.[606]

In a polytheistic society it was unlikely that Thoth would have been the sole god worshipped by an individual, even by his priests and priestesses, but to some he would have been the major focus of their devotions.

---

[604] *The Living Wisdom of Ancient Egypt,* Jacq. 1999:44. Ani.
[605] *Some Remarks on the Mysterious Language of the Baboons,* Velde. 1988:33.
[606] *Thoth Or The Hermes Of Egypt,* Boylan. 1922:148.

Royalty

A number of royal princes of the 4th Dynasty held the office of High Priest of Hermopolis but Thoth's popularity within the royal circles became increasing important in the later dynasties. Several New Kingdom monarchs had names incorporating Thoth, such as Thutmose - born of Thoth, indicating that his cult was popular amongst the nobility at this time. In the 18th Dynasty there was intense veneration of Thoth by the elite. The popularity of personal names containing Thoth is evidence of this.[607]

Queen Hatshepsut boasted of her devotion to Thoth, saying that she doubled the offerings in his temples and erected new sanctuaries. One of these is at Speos Artemidos, near Beni Hasan. In the temple of Deir el-Bahri she recorded her expedition to the distant land of Punt. Thoth is shown recording the treasures they brought back. Thutmose III and Amenhotep IV built shrines for Thoth in Hermopolis.

In the 19th Dynasty Sety I and Ramesses II erected several shrines to Thoth. Sety refers to Thoth as his father and paintings in his tomb show him being embraced by an ibis-headed Thoth. Ramesses II built temples in Memphis, at Tell-om-Harb in the Delta and in Derr in Nubia. Ramesses III was also a devotee of Thoth building two temples near Hermopolis.[608]

The Rest of Society

Royal patronage of a major god does not always reflect the beliefs of the rest of the population, but the worship of Thoth seems to have had a wide base amongst the Egyptians. There are many references to him in the tombs of non-royals and to offerings made on his feast days. The usual offerings were bread, beer, cattle and poultry.

Certainly for the scribes, and some other professionals, Thoth was their patron deity and so it was natural that his worship was an integral part of their lives. At first it might appear that Thoth was more of a god for the educated people and wouldn't have been very popular with the labourers, farmers and craftsmen but this is not the case. As a healing god he would have been needed by everyone. He was also considered an approachable and just god, so a wide class of

[607] *Thoth Or The Hermes Of Egypt*, Boylan. 1922:159.
[608] *Thoth Or The Hermes Of Egypt*, Boylan. 1922:162.

people probably appealed to him over issues of injustice given his role as a judge and mediator of the gods. A lot evidence of Thoth's worship amongst the poorer people of Egypt has been found. This is in the form of manuscripts and stelae from Deir el-Medina, in the Theban necropolis, dating to the 19th Dynasty. It is clear that these all come from a similar class of people as they were found in the small temples serving the artisans and attendants. All show a very personal relationship with the deities addressed, Thoth being prominent amongst them. A lot of the prayers and hymns which come from kings and priests reflect the high status confidence of their beliefs. Although polite, such people have a high opinion of themselves and view themselves as comparable with deities, on conversational terms with the ones they worship. The texts from the poorer people speak from their hearts and appeal for mercy and assistance, hoping to be saved through the grace of their deities.[609]

Temples are referred to in many districts in Middle Kingdom texts, both *"north and south"* indicating a widespread public cult. The cult of Thoth is prominent in temple inscriptions in the New Kingdom and seems to have expanded out of Egypt by this date. Horemheb built a shrine near Abu Simbel in Nubia.[610] The Late Period also saw a resurgence in the popularity of Thoth's cult. After a general religious decline there was a revival in the Ptolemaic Period when old temples were restored and new ones built.

Specifically Amongst Women

We do not know how many women worshipped Thoth, only that he had priestesses in his temples. The majority of women may have only celebrated his feast days and worshipped him because he was the god of their nome. Some may have adopted him as their household god because their husband or father worshipped him. A few women were literate, perhaps they held Thoth as their patron god as did their male counterparts (see chapter 5).

To the Egyptians both gods and goddesses were integral parts of the divine order and their religion and society did not have a hostile attitude towards women. There is no logical reason to suppose that more women worshipped and favoured the goddesses. The record that

---

[609] *The Religion of the Poor in Ancient Egypt,* Gunn. 1916:82.
[610] *Thoth Or The Hermes Of Egypt,* Boylan. 1922:159-160.

Egyptian women have left behind is sparse so we can only speculate. It is probable that the Egyptians appealed to the deity most likely to help them, just as we select a different professional for health problems compared to legal ones. Pregnancy, childbirth and the survival of their children were the major preoccupations of most Egyptian women and their choice of deities will have reflected this. Thoth does not have any direct connection with these concerns, although he was a protector of the child Horus and he is a healer. Bes (a protective dwarf deity) and Taweret (a hippopotamus goddess often associated with childbirth) were the more popular household deities and it is likely that they were called upon more often for such matters.

The myths do not show Thoth treating goddesses and women any differently to gods and men. He assists Isis on many occasions, persuades the Distant Goddess to return to Ra and uses his wisdom and skill to enable Nut to give birth to her children. In the Weighing of the Heart illustrations Thoth is shown judging men and women impartially. Surely such a wise and kind god loves and protects his female worshippers as effectively and generously as he does their male counterparts.

Temples in General

The huge and magnificent remains of Egypt's temples astound us and those who are fortunate enough to visit them can easily be transported back to the ancient ceremonies and be filled with feelings of religious awe. We need to remember though that these were not the cathedrals of their time. They were the houses of the deities and were reserved for them and a few select attendants. The temples were full of symbolism, from the largest scale down to the smallest detail, and were decorated with mythical scenes. At their heart lay the inner sanctuary where the deities dwelt whilst on earth. This was a piece of *'heaven on earth'* and was so sacred that virtually no one was permitted to enter. The temple was the interface between the divine and the mundane, representing *maat* balancing on the fulcrum between order and chaos. Temple complexes were also major centres of administration, learning and commerce. They employed large numbers of people and owned considerable land and resources. Temples were dedicated to one specific deity (or triad) but they frequently had minor temples and shrines for associated deities who were also depicted throughout the temple. There were no jealous gods in Egypt.

Temples were usually sited in, and orientated to, specific points in the landscape whether it was the Nile, other religious complexes or astronomical points. Surveying precision was vital especially when lining up with rising stars or significant lunar and solar phenomena. For this reason Seshat, the goddess of measurement and architecture, was involved in every temple founding or change. She presided over the king as he went through the highly important and symbolic *pedj-shes* ceremony (the stretching of the cord) and established the orientation using the *merkhet*. This was the first ritual carried out as the foundations of the temple were established. The *merkhet* was a wooden instrument used to determine the astronomical orientation of the temple layout. It is likely that the professionals would have already established the correct sightings making the king's role more symbolic.

Dedications on temples in the New Kingdom often contain building inscriptions affirming that they were constructed *"According to the word of the knower of the Two Lands"*.[611] The deities helped make their own temples. *"It was the god Ptah who issued instructions (for the building), while Thoth put them into writing. The tightening and loosening of the measuring rope (were performed) by the King himself and the goddess Seshat."*[612] The inscriptions at Dendera tell how the temple's structure and arrangement corresponded to the plans of Thoth. *"The correct position of the temple chambers was determined by the gods of the creator-word together with the Lord of the Heden Plant (Thoth)."*[613] The Ramesses Temple of Amun was built *"by the work of the knower of the Two Lands, by that which his heart created"*.

Statues were placed *"as Thoth has decreed thereon"* and the depictions are *"in their shape which Ptah has fashioned, according to that which Thoth has written concerning their bodies in the great register (?) which is in the Library"*.[614] Inscriptions from the Ramesside

---

[611] *Thoth Or The Hermes Of Egypt*, Boylan. 1922:89-90.
[612] *The Temple of Edfu*, Kurth. 2004:27.
[613] *The Temple of Edfu*, Kurth. 2004:49.
[614] *Thoth Or The Hermes Of Egypt*, Boylan. 1922:90-91.

Court at Luxor describe Ramesses II as *"wise in knowledge like Thoth, knowing how to instruct, skilled (?) in craftsmanship"*.[615]

Most temples had a *per ankh*, a House of Life, at which Thoth would be honoured daily. These acted as a library, archive and scriptorium as well as a centre of learning. An inscription from Abydos describes the ideal structure for the House of Life. It was to have depictions of Isis, Nephthys, Horus and Thoth on each of the four sides. *"It shall be very hidden and very large. It shall not be known, nor shall it be seen...The people who enter into it are the staff of Re and the scribes of the House of Life...the scribe of the sacred books is Thoth, and it is he who will recite the (ritual) glorifications in the course of every day, unseen, unheard...The books that are in it are the emanations (of) Re wherewith to keep alive this god and to overthrow his enemies."*[616] Another inscription from Abydos describes Ramesses IV as *"excellent of understanding like Thoth, and he hath penetrated into the annals like the maker thereof, having examined the writings of the House of Life"*.[617]

Not everyone treated these wonderful temples with the respect that they deserved. New Kingdom pilgrims and tourists visited these sites, which were already a thousand years old, and many left graffiti recording their opinions. On the temple precinct of Djoser, in Saqqara, one such vandal complained of his predecessors, *"Their work is awful. They are not scribes trained by Thoth"*.[618] Even graffiti must be worthy of the God of the Scribes.

Thoth's Cult Centre

The Egyptians divided their country into forty two administrative districts called nomes. Each nome had a principal deity. Thoth was principal deity of the 15th nome of Upper Egypt, the hare nome, which was centred around Hermopolis. He is *"Thoth, Chief over the Two Mounds of the Hare (XV th) Province"*.[619] Thoth also had strong associations with the 15th nome of Lower Egypt, the ibis nome, which

---

[615] *The Earliest Years of Ramesses II, and the Building of the Ramesside Court at Luxor,* Redford. 1971:113.
[616] *The House of Life,* Gardiner. 1938:168.
[617] *The House of Life,* Gardiner. 1938:162.
[618] *The Temple of Edfu,* Kurth. 2004:19.
[619] *Ramesside Inscriptions Translated & Annotated. Vol I.* Kitchen. 1993:169.

was in the North East Delta region. Greek city names reflect the two cult centres of Thoth; Hermopolis Parva in the Delta and Hermopolis Magna in the Nile Valley.

The main cult centre of Thoth was at Hermopolis Magna (referred to as Hermopolis throughout this book). It was called Khmun by the Egyptians and is known today as el-Ashmunein. There is no evidence that this was the original cult centre but it was certainly the chief centre of worship in Dynastic times and an important pilgrimage site. Khmun, or *'eight-town'*, was named for the eight primeval deities of the Hermopolitan cosmology (see chapter 12). The Greeks called it Hermopolis - City of Hermes, as they equated Thoth with Hermes (see chapter 14). Many of the prayers reference Hermopolis. "*O Thoth, take me to Hermopolis, your city where it is pleasant to live.*"[620] Thoth's epithets frequently refer to his cult centre, such as "*Bull in Hermopolis*".[621]

The Temple in Hermopolis was renowned as a centre of wisdom and learning and both in real life and in stories priests and magicians travelled there to seek information or to gain wisdom. The *Famine Stele* tells how King Djoser asked his priests for advice on how to end a seven year drought and famine. He needed to know where the source of the Nile was and which deities lived there so he would be able to persuade them to restore the annual Nile flood. His chief lector priest, Imhotep, did not know but he went to the Temple of Thoth at Hermopolis and found the answers in one of the sacred books kept in the House of Life.

Temples of Thoth

The *Festal Song of Thoth*, inscribed in a stele in Hermopolis, gives a poetic description of a temple constructed by Merenptah.

"*For you have built a noble Temple, on Thoth's forecourt,*

that he may dwell in his great shrine, to the west ('right') of his House.

It is wrought in fine white (lime)stone,

in all (manner of) excellent work.

---

[620] *Hymns, Prayers and Songs*, Foster. 1995:147. *Prayer to Thoth.*
[621] *A Statue of Horemhab Before His Accession*, Winlock. 1924:3.

Your Potentates are the gods (with)in the sacred (shrine),

hearing (people's) prayers.

Its pylon-towers reach up to the sky,

equipped with mighty doors of gold, (with) bolts of copper,

[......] are its mighty double portals.

It is planted with every (kind of) fruit-tree,

sparkling with flowers.

Its gardens have lotuses and (other) blooms,

reeds, lotus-buds and papyrus.

They are presented as the daily bouquet at the forecourt of Thoth,

they freshen up (again) the foliage of the House of Thoth."[622]

No doubt there were many magnificent temples dedicated to Thoth but none remain. Some of the ones found to date are listed below.

- **Abu Simbel**. At the Great Temple of Ramesses II, to the left of the main entrance, there is a separate chapel dedicated to Thoth.[623]

- **Dakhla Oasis** is in the Western Desert, 350km west of Luxor. The remains of a Ptolemaic or Roman temple of Thoth are now buried under houses.[624]

- **el-Ashmunein** (Hermopolis). Unfortunately very little remains of Thoth's cult centre. The most memorable are the quartzite baboon colossi of Amenhotep III. The central sacred area of the city was enclosed by massive brick walls in the 13th Dynasty. Several temples stood here, the largest one for Thoth. This was rebuilt by Nectanebo I in the 30th Dynasty and may well have replaced a very ancient temple. Further additions were made to Thoth's temple in the time of Alexander the Great and Philip

---

[622] *Ramesside Inscriptions Translated & Annotated Vol IV.* Kitchen. 2003:25-26. *Festal Song of Thoth.*
[623] *The Complete Temples of Ancient Egypt,* Wilkinson. 2000:225.
[624] *The Complete Temples of Ancient Egypt,* Wilkinson. 2000:235.

Arrhidaeus. Until the 1820s a magnificent portico was still standing, it was unfortunately demolished to provide building stone.[625] In the 4th century BCE the High Priest of Thoth, Petosiris, renovated his cult centre at Hermopolis. It had been left in a derelict condition in the wake of the Persian invasion. The tomb of Petosiris is decorated with images of Thoth, in his ibis and baboon forms, and is inscribed with texts alluding to his great local importance.[626]

- **The Temple of the Net.** There are references to the Temple of the Net in Hermopolis. Although this is a temple of Thoth it is not clear what the Net refers to. It may relate to a lost myth. A painting shows Ramesses II as Horus and Amun catching birds in a net while Thoth directs them.[627] There is also a myth in which Horus catches Seth in a net, or it could refer to the net used to catch souls in the afterworld. The *Book of Thoth* contains references to the *"House of the Fish-net"*. This appears to be a temple or sacred precinct within Hermopolis which represented the place where Thoth captured the enemies of Ra.[628] It was said that a net was preserved and venerated at this temple. Thoth will have used magic to capture the enemies of Ra and a net is a good way of illustrating a magical energy field. There is a lot of symbolism attached to nets, ropes and knots in all cultures. The net may also allude to the limitations of physical existence, to the soul's entanglement in sin or to the web of fate as Thoth was responsible for an individual's destiny. It is likely to have had several layers of meaning on which we can only speculate.

- **Island of Flame.** Late Period texts refer to a temple on the Island of Flame, which is in the necropolis at Hermopolis.[629] In Old Kingdom texts the Island of Flame is mentioned in association with hymns to Thoth. He is said

---

[625] *The Complete Temples of Ancient Egypt*, Wilkinson. 2000:139-140.
[626] *The Complete Gods and Goddesses of Ancient Egypt*, Wilkinson. 2003:217.
[627] *Thoth Or The Hermes Of Egypt*, Boylan. 1922:153.
[628] *The Ancient Egyptian Book of Thoth*, Jasnow & Zauzich. 2005:10.
[629] *Thoth Or The Hermes Of Egypt*, Boylan. 1922:154-155.

to have built shrines for the deities on this island. In the *Pyramid Texts* the dead have to cross the Island of Flame as part of their journey through the afterworld.

- To the west of Hermopolis is the necropolis of **Tuna el-Gebel**. Here the mummified bodies of ibises and baboons, sold to pilgrims as votive offerings, are held in the Ibeum. (See chapter 3.)

- **el-Baqliva** (Hermopolis Parva). There are the basic outlines of the temple enclosure walls. King Apries, 26th Dynasty, dedicated a shrine to Thoth there. A mound now marks its site.[630] (Some sources cite el-Baqliva as the site of Hermopolis Parva others Damanhur.)

- **el-Dakhla**. The Greco-Roman Temple of Thoth at Dakhla was originally sited 100km south of the Aswan High Dam. It was moved 40km upstream to its new site at el-Sebua.[631] A carved relief from the sanctuary shows Thoth in his baboon form sitting under a sycamore tree. In the Roman side chapel the baboon is shown worshipping the goddess Tefnut, who is portrayed as a lioness.[632] (Tefnut was the Distant Goddess in some of the myths.)

- **el-Kab**. This is an important area of Predynastic settlement and home to the vulture-goddess Nekhbet. In the 18th Dynasty Amenhotep II began construction of a temple to Thoth. The outer pylon area was completed by Ramesses II.[633]

- **Karnak.** North of the temple, outside the Nectanebo enclosure wall, recent excavations have revealed the gateway of a temple dedicated to Thoth dating to the reign of Ptolemy IV.[634]

- **Luxor**. A red granite colossus of Thoth in his baboon-headed form was recently discovered in the 18th Dynasty funeral complex of Amenhotep III. The statue is 3.5m high

---

630 *The Complete Temples of Ancient Egypt,* Wilkinson. 2003:106.
631 *The Complete Temples of Ancient Egypt,* Wilkinson. 2003:219.
632 *Ancient Egypt,* Oakes & Gahlin. 2004:218.
633 *The Complete Temples of Ancient Egypt,* Wilkinson. 2000:202-203.
634 *News From Egypt,* Taher. 2009:9.

and is thought to have been part of an avenue of statues leading to the temple of Thoth.[635]

- **Qasr el-Agueze.** There are the remains of a temple dedicated to Thoth by Ptolemy VIII. One relief shows an enthroned ibis-headed Thoth wearing a crown. Others show Ptolemy receiving the *heb sed* symbol from Thoth, and Ptolemy opening a shrine with the figure of Thoth inside.[636]

- **Saqqara.** A Late Period temple to Thoth was found in the Memphis necropolis. The area was also a major sacred animal necropolis (see also chapter 3). The site had a long standing connection with Imhotep, who was closely identified with Thoth at this period. A large number of ritual vessels called *situla* were found at this temple site. These are metal vessels with a wire handle used to hold water or milk for rituals. Some were inscribed with prayers to Thoth, asking for health and long life, and would have been left as offerings.[637]

- **Serabit el-Khadim** in Sinai was an important Egyptian settlement. The temple complex was dedicated primarily to Hathor but Thoth and Soped (the god of the eastern desert) were also worshipped there.[638]

Temples and shrines to Thoth have been found within other temple complexes. In the Temple of Isis at **Philae** a number of chambers and a library are dedicated to Thoth.[639] These date from Greco-Roman times. Thoth is an important deity in the temple of Hathor at **Dendera** with his own special shrine and cult. He was also a significant deity in the Horus temple at **Edfu**. Here he was revered as *Chons-Thoth* emphasising his lunar aspects.[640] This is not unexpected given Thoth's role in restoring and returning the lost Eye of Horus and the help he gives to Horus in his battles with Seth. Temples of Iah usually had a cult of Thoth. The guardian of the moon

---

[635] *News From Egypt,* Taher. 2011:12.
[636] *News From Egypt,* Taher. 2008:13-14.
[637] *The Life of Meresamun,* Teeter & Johnson. 2009:44.
[638] *The Routledge Dictionary of Egyptian Gods and Goddesses,* Hart. 2005:159.
[639] *The Complete Temples of Ancient Egypt,* Wilkinson. 2000:214.
[640] *Thoth Or The Hermes Of Egypt,* Boylan. 1922:165.

thus has a house on the moon. *"I have made provision for Thoth in the house of Iooh."*[641]

South Karnak. A child form of Thoth has been found at the temple precinct of the Goddess Mut. From the 21st Dynasty there was a *mammisi* here. This was a birth house dedicated to the birth of child-gods and the divine birth of kings. In this case the child-god was Khonsu, the moon god and son of Amun and Mut. There was a rise in child-god worship in the Greco-Roman period. A lintel relief from this period shows five child-gods. The first is Khonsu and the fifth is described as *"Khons-Thoth of Amenemope, who gives years (i.e. a long life) to the one who is loyal to him"*.[642] It is unusual to have a self-begotten god, or at least one that was not born in the normal way, to be shown as a child and there is no known child mythology relating to Thoth. As a moon god Thoth has an obvious link with Khonsu and if Thoth's worship was strong in the local area it would seem natural to the temple builders to incorporate one of the local gods into their pantheon. Arguably the constant renewal of the moon could be seen as rebirth and the new crescent moon as a child. On an inscription for Sety I, Seshat says *"Thou shalt renew thy youth; thou shalt flourish again like Iooh-Thoth when he is a child"*.[643]

Priests and Priestesses

A full time priesthood served in the temples augmented by a much larger number of part time staff who served in the temple on a rotating basis. The prestigious and powerful posts were either hereditary or by appointment of the king. The Famine Stele of King Djoser, 3rd Dynasty, refers to priests as the *"staff of the Ibis"*.[644] In the Ptolemaic Period, tomb inscriptions in Alexandria and Thebes refer to *"the lector of the monkey"* and the *"lector of the ape"*.[645]

Petosiris, the High Priest of Thoth at Hermopolis, has left a grand and well decorated tomb. It was built at the end of the 4th and the beginning of the 5th century BCE. For five generations the role of High

---

[641] *Thoth Or The Hermes Of Egypt*, Boylan. 1922:63.
[642] *Recent Work at the Mut Precinct at South Karnak*, Fazzini & van Dijk. 2007:10-11.
[643] *Thoth Or The Hermes Of Egypt*, Boylan. 1922:63.
[644] *The Literature of Ancient Egypt*, Simpson et al. 2003:387. *The Famine Stele*. Trans. Ritner.
[645] *Men and Gods on the Roman Nile*, Lindsay. 1968:281.

Priest was handed down from father to son. Petosiris was originally the Controller of the Temple which seems to have been a financial position. He inherited the role of High Priest on the death of his elder brother Djedthothefankh, because *"I was on the water of the lord of Khnum since my birth. All his counsel was in my heart"*. To be on the water of a deity was to be loyal and obedient to their wishes.[646]

In his biography recorded on his tomb Petosiris explains how he rebuilt the temple and its estates after its neglect and destruction in the Persian wars. *"[He] chose me to administer his temple, knowing I respected him in my heart...I put the temple of Thoth in its former condition. I caused every rite to be as before."* He describes the former dereliction of the site. *"For it is the birthplace of every god, who came into being at the beginning. This spot, wretches had damaged it, intruders had traversed it...Egypt was distressed by it, for the half of the egg is buried in it."*[647]

He also rebuilt the temple of Thoth's consort in Hermopolis, Nehmataway (see chapter 11). On a stele Petosiris describes how the site was selected. A procession of priests carried a statue of Nehmataway through the flooded ruins of Hermopolis until it *'stopped'* to show where the goddess wished her new temple to be.[648] Such processions were common and were used as oracles as well as allowing the deity, in theory at least, to make decisions and answer questions.

All this restoration work seems to have gone well for Petosiris. *"My lord Thoth distinguished [me] above all [my] peers, as a reward for enriching him."*[649]

Women appeared to have served more often in the temples of goddesses but not exclusively. Priestesses were more prevalent in the Old Kingdom where many women have the title *hmt-ntr* – *'Servant of God'*. There is a reference to a *"priestess of Thoth"*[650] and Queen Meresankh is described as a *"High Priestess of Thoth"*.[651] On the

---

[646] *Maat, the Moral Ideal in Ancient Egypt,* Karenga. 2004:121,293.
[647] *Ancient Egyptian Literature Vol 3,* Lichtheim. 2006:46-8. *Biographical Inscription of Petosiris.*
[648] *Two Overlooked Oracles,* Klotz. 2010:253.
[649] *Ancient Egyptian Literature Vol 3,* Lichtheim. 2006:48. *Biographical Inscription of Petosiris.*
[650] *Thoth Or The Hermes Of Egypt,* Boylan. 1922:148.
[651] *Women in Ancient Egypt,* Watterson. 1997:43.

Mastaba of Khamerernebty II, at Giza, both the mother of the king and his eldest daughter are described as *"priest(ess) of Thoth"*.[652] There is a gradual decline in records of priestesses in the Middle Kingdom. This seems to be a result of changing social attitudes plus a trend towards having a dedicated full time priesthood. Many priestesses were from royal and noble families or were the wives and daughters of the priests.

Priestesses would have been needed to take the role of the goddesses in any re-enactment of the sacred myths.[653] There is a 4th Dynasty reference to *mrt* - a musician-priestess, who is shown on reliefs receiving the king as he enters the temple. *Mrt* is the title of the High Priestess of Thoth at Hermopolis. It might be that the king, who takes the role of Thoth as the master of all temple ceremonies, is received by the High Priestess acting as the wife of Thoth.[654]

Women worked for the temples in other capacities. The archive of Hor refers to two women who interpreted an ibis oracle and there is a reference to women working in the ibis catacombs. *"May Thoth the ibis, the great god, give life to the children of the Maidservant of the Ibises."*[655]

Rituals, Feast Days and Festivals

The daily and seasonal rituals carried out to Thoth are unknown but they would have been similar to those documented for other deities; feeding and clothing the statue, making offerings and re-enacting significant myths. Feast days and festivals of some of the deities, such as Hathor, and Isis and Osiris, are well documented. In contrast we know very little about those of Thoth. In a temple at Tod there is an inscribed inventory of books held by the temple. One tantalisingly reads *"a book of the Festival of Thoth in the temple of Khons"*.[656] Sadly all we have is a list of festival dates. The festival of Thoth is known to be an ancient festival as it is mentioned in the *Pyramid Texts*. The *Cairo Calendar*, 19th Dynasty, describes the

---

[652] *Texts From the Pyramid Age*, Strudwick. 2005:381.
[653] *The Complete Temples of Ancient Egypt*, Wilkinson. 2000:93-94.
[654] *On the Position of Women in the Ancient Egyptian Hierarchy*, Blackman. 1921:8-9.
[655] *The Life of Meresamun*, Teeter & Johnson. 2009:49.
[656] *The Priests of Ancient Egypt*, Sauneron. 2000:136.

Festival of Thoth as the day when the Ennead celebrated a great feast and when the procession of Thoth took place in the necropolis.

The start of the Egyptian year was the First month of the Inundation (named *Dhwty*) and was a time of great celebration, coinciding with the rising of the Nile. "*You shall follow Thoth, on that beautiful day of the start of Inundation.*"[657] During this month there were three festivals for Thoth, held on the 4th, 19th and 21st. Entries from various calendars give the following descriptions of these feast days. 4th day - a "*Festival of Thoth*". 19th day - a "*Festival for Thoth, the very great, in the whole country*". The countrywide celebration would probably be a general holiday, but we don't know if it was celebrated by the people as a whole or was confined to the temples. 21st day - a festival to "*celebrate 'the triumph of Thoth' in the presence of Re*".[658] This might have been a procession or a re-enactment of the myth. All the major festivals for Thoth appear to be in the month of *Dhwty*. He is mentioned in festivals in the other months as one of the participating deities. On the 1st day of the Second month of Inundation the entry reads "*guarding(?) the eye of Horus...Making the procession of Heqa, Khonsu, Thoth; union with the disc; return*". On the 1st day of the First month of Summer was "*Feast of Khnum, of Nebtu and of Heqa and Thoth and of the gods and goddesses...Shu-Thoth bring the eye back to its owner*".[659]

Some of the papyri state which days were considered lucky or unlucky. According to the *Papyrus Sallier* the 19th *Dhwty* is "*wholly lucky. A day of festival in heaven and upon earth in the presence of Ra*". The 26th *Dhwty* was "*wholly unlucky*" as "*this was the day of the fight between Horus and Set*". Offerings were made to Thoth and Osiris on this day.[660]

Bomhard suggests that the first day of the new year, which coincided with the rising of Sirius, was the 19th July.[661] This would give the festivals in *Dhwty* the following modern dates; the 4th as the

---

[657] *Ancient Egyptian Literature Vol 3*, Lichtheim. 2006:53. *Speech of Thothreky Son of Petosiris.*
[658] *Hathor and Thoth: Two Key Figures of the Ancient Egyptian Religion*, Bleeker. 1973:152.
[659] *Temple Festival Calendars of Ancient Egypt*, El-Sabban. 2000:160,165.
[660] *Egyptian Magic*, Budge. 1971:226.
[661] *The Egyptian Calendar A Work For Eternity*, Bomhard. 1999:XII.

22nd of July, the 19th and 21st as the 6th and 8th of August and the 26th as the 13th of August.

There is a suggestion that the Feast of Thoth, mentioned from very early documents, has an association with the dead, rather like our Halloween or Day of the Dead, but there is little direct evidence for this.[662] The *wag*-festival on the previous day is a day of the dead where offerings were made in the tombs and candles lit for deceased ancestors. A statue of a Royal Scribe Amenmose does refer to articles *"offered(?) in the Wag-feast of Thoth"*.[663]

The festival to celebrate the return of the Wandering Eye goddess was held in many temples. Graffiti and inscriptions on rocks suggest that people went into the desert to help bring back the goddess just as Thoth had done. This may have been viewed purely as a pilgrimage or as a legitimate excuse for an excursion and a change of routine and scenery. The desert was seen as a dangerous place and it might not have been a comfortable trip.

The burning of incense and anointing the statues with fragrant oils and unguents played a major part in the temple's daily rituals as did music and offerings. An incantation is recorded which was used when priests re-enacted Thoth presenting Horus with the restored Eye.[664]

An inscription from the Late Period lists offerings made on various feasts, including the Thoth Feasts. These include bread, beer, cakes, oxen, fowl, alabaster, clothing, incense and unguents. Illustrations and inscriptions from the Royal Tombs at Hierakonpolis refer to the Feast of Thoth being celebrated in the *"great houses"* and oxen are shown being offered in sacrifice to Thoth in his ibis form.[665] The *Victory Stele of Piy*, Late Period, describes how he freed Hermopolis from the *'Asiatics'*. In thanks Piy sacrificed cattle and poultry in the Temple of Thoth to his *"father Thoth, lord of Khmun, and the Ogdoad in the Temple of the Ogdoad"*.[666]

---

[662] *Thoth or the Hermes of Egypt*, Boylan. 1922:136-137.
[663] *Ramesside Inscriptions Translated & Annotated. Vol III.* Kitchen. 2000:150-1.
[664] *Sacred Luxuries*, Manniche. 1999:34.
[665] *Thoth or the Hermes of Egypt*, Boylan. 1922:147.
[666] *Ancient Egyptian Literature Vol 3*, Lichtheim. 2006:72. *The Victory Stele of King Piye*.

The *Festal Song of Thoth* is a *"copy of the Song-of-Praise...which Thoth made, on the Festival of Thoth, when he reposed in the [Temple] of Amun-of-Merenptah"*. It describes some of the preparations and offerings made on the Feast of Thoth.

"I have come to see your beauty,

to accept the oblation which you have made,

on the days of the Feast of Thoth.

...Pure are you limbs, clean [is your body?],

your purification was made in the House of the Living (?)

See, the House of Life is [festoon]ed with foliage,

like the Delta [....]

All the royal (?) offerings are by millions,

in all goodly varieties:

oxen and calves without limit,

seprat-cattle and short-horns:

gazelles, ibex and oryx,

milch-cows(?), many goats, and geese."[667]

As guardian of the moon, and restorer of the Sacred Eye, Thoth would have been one of the major deities celebrated in the regular lunar festivals. From the Buto stele of Thutmose III we have details of some of these lunar festivals. On the New Moon festival offerings of bread, beer, vegetables and a jar of wine were made. Similar offerings, but without the wine, were made on the sixth day festival (the 1st quarter) and the monthly festival (the full moon).[668] The 3rd quarter was associated with the death of Osiris so wasn't celebrated.

Processions would have been a popular element of the sacred calendar. Known as the *'coming forth'* a statue of the deity was processed through the streets followed by the public. It is thought that

---

[667] *Ramesside Inscriptions Translated & Annotated Vol IV*. Kitchen. 2003:22-3. *Festal Song of Thoth*.
[668] *The Egyptian Calendar A Work For Eternity*, Bomhard. 1999:43.

every major feast day included a procession. This was the one time that the deity left the secret seclusion of the inner temple and went out to be seen by the people. On these days the boundary between sacred and profane and secret and public was suspended. The deities did not always live on earth but during festivals they were considered to return to their people.

The *Stele of Iykhernofret* gives his biography, part of which is a description of how he conducted the procession of Wepwawet. "*I caused the god's barque to sail on, with Thoth leading the voyage.*"[669]

It is difficult to know how ordinary people celebrated feast days. It will have varied depending upon their status, wealth and inclination. Plutarch says that "*on the nineteenth of the first month, when they keep a feast to Hermes, they eat honey and figs, saying when so doing, 'Truth is sweet'*".[670] Some idea of what was considered proper comes from the *Instructions of Merikare*. "*A man should do what is good for his soul. Performing the monthly service, putting on white sandals, joining the temple estate, keeping confidential the mysteries, entering into the sanctuary, eating bread from the temple! Making the offering tables flourish, make the provisions great, increase the daily offerings!*"[671]

From Deir el-Medina there is a letter from the 20th Dynasty scribe Qensety to his brother. He asks for reed brushes and ink "*with which he was going to fill his scribal palette on the day of Thoth*".[672] This may be for an offering to Thoth or Qensety may have presented the tools of his profession to be blessed for the coming year. There are prayers to Thoth which "*are spoken by a man after he had presented offerings to Thoth*".[673]

From the stele of Iykhernofret we have a description of some of the activities of the cult of Osiris. The priests re-enacted the story as part of the festival in the last month of the inundation. The public who

---

[669] *The Literature of Ancient Egypt*, Simpson et al. 2003:427. *The Stele of Iykhernofret.* Trans. Simpson.
[670] *Plutarch: Concerning The Mysteries Of Isis And Osiris*, Mead. 2002:242.
[671] *The Tale of Sinuhe and Other Ancient Egyptian Poems*, Parkinson. 1997:221. *The Teaching for King Merikare.*
[672] *Do Not Celebrate Your Feast Without Your Neighbours Academic Dissertation*, Jauhiainen. 2009:87.
[673] *Egyptian Religion*, Morenz. 1992:93.

travelled to see these plays were referred to as the *"followers of Thoth"*.[674]

Although not related to a feast day of Thoth, inscriptions from the Horus Temple at Edfu give details of the acting out of the conflict between Horus and Seth. This would probably have been similar to the Medieval Mystery or Passion plays. A Mystery play was performed by the 12th Dynasty king Senusret as part of his coronation rituals. He took the part of Horus at the death of Osiris and in the Contendings of Horus and Seth. The corpse of Osiris was *'found'* by priests called *"spirit seekers"* who took the role of Thoth.[675]

---

[674] *Myth and Symbol in Ancient Egypt,* Clark. 1978:173.
[675] *Myth and Ritual in the Ancient Near East,* James. 1958:87.

Personal Worship and Veneration

In General

What the general public saw of the temples was restricted to processional avenues, the external walls and doors and, on a few occasions, the outer courtyard where they could make offerings and pray. Their involvement was restricted to that of making offerings and participating in feast days and processions. Some temples had shrines for public worship, usually at the rear of the temple. State religion was considered to be for the benefit of society as a whole not for the individual. Despite this barrier to the divine the Egyptians were considered a very religious and pious people. Herodotus says they were *"religious to excess, beyond any other nation in the world"*[676] and this was at a time when the ancient religion was declining. The Egyptians had a close and personal relationship with their deities which was conducted in private at home and in the workplace. Numerous altars, shrines and figurines have been found in private houses and there are a large volume of personal votive offerings in temples.

Some deities were venerated as part of the official cult while others, such as Bes and Taweret, were considered *'domestic'* deities and had little, if any, place in the official pantheons. Certain deities crossed boundaries, Thoth being one of them. Other examples are Hathor, Amun, Ptah and some local deities. Religious life was not restricted to one cult, the majority of people didn't claim to be followers of a particular deity. They would have called upon the deity most relevant to their request, the deity of their home town or the local deities of the area they were in. A letter from the 20th Dynasty scribe Thutmose to his employee starts *"I am calling upon Arsaphes, lord of Herakleopolis, Thoth, lord of Hermopolis, and every god and goddess by whom I pass, to give you life, prosperity, and health"*.[677]

Along with gods such as Ra, Osiris and Ptah, Thoth is called the *"Greatest God"*.[678] If there was rivalry between cult centres it was only

---

[676] *Herodotus: The Histories.* 2003:110. Trans. Selincourt.
[677] *The Egyptian Book of the Dead,* Faulkner & Goelet. 2008:144.
[678] *Conceptions of God in Ancient Egypt,* Hornung. 1996:187.

for human reasons, such as power and wealth, the Egyptians never felt that their deities were battling for supremacy. The only divine battles were those of light against darkness, order against chaos. The hymns often address the deity as if they were the only one. This is not for monotheist reasons. The deity being addressed was the only one that mattered to the worshipper or was, at least, the main focus of their devotion. One prayer address Thoth as the *'only'* god then in the same paragraph goes on to mention the other gods.[679] A 13th Dynasty royal stele, from Hermopolis, refers to Thoth as *'Son of Ra'* making him subordinate to Ra then to Thoth as *'Chief of the Gods'* and thus superior to Ra.[680] The contradiction only worries us, the Egyptians probably didn't even notice it. Petosiris, High Priest of Thoth, calls him *"the Only One, who has no equal".*[681] Maybe it was considered polite when addressing an important deity to refer to them as the creator. *"Praised be thee, Thoth, Lord of Hermopolis, who hath created himself, he was not born, the sole god."*[682] Flattery is an important part of praise. *"He is the most supreme of the gods and of all of the goddess for he commands the great ennead."*[683]

We are fortunate to have a lot more evidence of the worship of Thoth by individuals than we do of his official worship. He may have been particularly popular or this may just be a consequence of random survival rates. Hymns and praise poems to Thoth are particularly common. One reason is that they were considered illuminating, as well as educational, for pupils to copy. What we have found is only a pitiful fragment of what must have existed throughout the thousands of years of Egyptian history. It is ungrateful, though, to complain given the treasures we have when the religious literature of other ancient cultures is inaccessible to us for various reasons.

All scribes were expected to start the day with a prayer to Thoth and to make a libation from their water bowls. We don't know if this was a standard prayer learnt at school, the mention of his name or something personal, probably it depended upon the inclination of the

---

[679] *Hymns, Prayers and Songs*, Foster. 1995:113. *Hymn to Thoth and Maat.*
[680] *Conceptions of God in Ancient Egypt*, Hornung. 1996:236.
[681] *The Living Wisdom of Ancient Egypt*, Jacq. 1999:42. *Petosiris.*
[682] *Hathor and Thoth: Two Key Figures of the Ancient Egyptian Religion*, Bleeker. 1973:153.
[683] *Hathor and Thoth: Two Key Figures of the Ancient Egyptian Religion*, Bleeker. 1973:20.

individual. Thoth, like many of the other major deities, wasn't a remote presence but was an integral part of human life. The divine formed the background to human experience and divine energies were believed to be manifest in the natural world and human behaviour. The Egyptians believed that the deities could and did work through humans. Many religious documents were considered to be written by Thoth, the author and scribe viewed merely as the medium of Thoth. Thus the scribes paid homage to Thoth's gift of writing and acknowledged him as the source of their inspiration. Thoth was part of the daily life of many professionals. He was considered to be present in acts such as learning or writing; a force of god present in his gifts. By doing what Thoth does, albeit at a very minor and trivial level, you draw closer to him.

Amulets and Statues

Many amulets and statues of Thoth have been found, a few of which are described here. (See also chapter 3.) One is a faience piece, from the 22nd Dynasty, of a baboon holding a disc over the head of a cat which is seated between his knees. It appears to represent Thoth placing the solar disc either on the goddess Bastet (in cat form) or on the head of Ra (disguised as a male cat as in Spell 17 of the *Book of the Dead*).[684] From the Ptolemaic Period comes an elaborate bronze statuette of Thoth. He is enthroned with his feet resting on a footstool. Two depressions and holes before the god's footstool allowed for the attachment of another figure, most likely a small figure of a devotee. The inscription reads *"Words said by Thoth, Twice Great, Lord of Hermopolis; "May life, prosperity and health, a long life and a good and great old age be given (to) the doorkeeper of Thoth, Twice Great, Lord of Hermopolis, Djedhor, son of the Overseer of the Doors of the Third Phyle of Thoth, Twice Great, Lord of Hermopolis, Nesdjehuty, born of Itruri"*.[685]

On a votive stele from Hermopolis, dating to the 18th Dynasty, a man wearing an elaborate kilt adores the ibis of Thoth who wears a *menat* (a heavy necklace imbued with divine power). The text reads *"A royal offering (to the benefit of) Hesen; peace to the Lord of the Eight"*.[686]

---

[684] *Notes on Some Small Egyptian Figures of Cats*, Langton. 1936:117.
[685] *Two Objects Inscribed for Djedhor*, Teeter. 1990:203.
[686] *Stelae of the Middle and New Kingdoms in the Museum of Archaeology and Anthropology, University of Cambridge*, Dodson. 1992:278.

The heretic king, Akhenaten, tried to impose monotheism upon Egypt holding the sun god Aten to be the sole god. His new capital of Amarna was occupied for only about twenty years before it was abandoned after his death thus providing a wonderful snapshot of the period for archaeologists. It might be expected that the worship of any other deity was forbidden in Amarna of all places. Evidence from the excavations of private houses shows otherwise. Possibly the king considered that domestic worship was unimportant, it was the official cults that mattered, or maybe it was deemed impossible and unproductive to police an enforced monotheism on ordinary people. Most of the finds relating to deities other than Aten come from the Workman's Village which is not surprising. The king was likely to be uncaring of what his workers thought whereas his high level officials would have to be seen to follow the *'party line'* whatever their private beliefs. Many figurines, especially of anthropomorphic deities, were excavated in the Workman's Village. Taweret and Bes were common, not surprisingly as they were popular household deities. Thoth and Ptah were also well represented. The figurines ranged from unfired clay and pottery to faience and carved stone. Items of jewellery, images on ostraca, stelae and altars were also found. From the house of the sculptor Thutmose came a faience bead showing an ibis-headed Thoth striding forward with his hands clenched. Other sites yielded blue faience pendants and beads in the form of seated baboons. At least four stelae were found depicting Thoth. These are small domestic objects, the smallest being about 6cm by 4cm. One has a painted image, with traces of gilding, of a baboon wearing the lunar crown who is seated on an altar. The other stelae show baboons painted, or incised, on rough sandstone and chalk. One very detailed, but tiny, statue shows the baboon form of Thoth wearing a lunar disc and sitting on an altar. A scribe sits working below him, as if inspired by his god. There is also a fragment of painted wood with a cornice inscription to Thoth.[687]

Oracles and Letters

In the Late and Ptolemaic Period oracles became an important aspect of personal worship. The *Demotic Archive of Hor* explains how

---

[687] *The Material Evidence for Domestic Religion at Amarna and Preliminary Remarks on Its Interpretation*, Stevens. 2003:158-65.

Hor of Sebennytos became a follower of Thoth. His archive is on ostraca and dates to about 170 BCE. Originally a minor priest of Isis, Hor came from Pi-Thoth in the Delta region. In a dream he was told to go to the ibis shrine of Thoth near Saqqara. There he worked as a secretary and interpreter of dreams and oracles. Two further dreams provided the turning point in his life. The text gives details of a dream in which Hor is instructed to devote himself to the worship of Thoth. "*Go before Thoth and say, "come to me my great lord Thoth; beautiful is the lifetime long in festival."* At this time he acquired a new name, Horthoth - Hor of Thoth.[688]

From the ibis cemetery at Abydos large numbers of ostraca have been found, written in both Demotic and Greek, which are reports of dreams, questions about oracles and complaints or requests to Thoth. A number of the Greco-Roman ostraca refer to "*Thoth the thrice-great*".[689] These were all found close to his chapel. The receiving of oracles was closely related to the offering of mummified ibises and the practice became increasingly important in the Greco-Roman Period. This shrine must have been very important as oracles were given for the king. The earliest oracle dates to the late 20th early 21st Dynasty and is from the *Berlin papyrus*. One petition is addressed to Horus, but Thoth promises to keep the petitioner safe from the other deities. "*I shall propitiate for him...Amun...(and) Horus-the-Good.*" In another, Thoth promises to prevent any negative oracular decisions from the petitioned deities.[690]

Letters were also written to Thoth and placed with offerings. If any god is sympathetic towards written petitioning it must surely be the God of the Scribes. There are numerous Demotic documents from Tuna el-Gebel which were posted with the mummified ibis. They were often written on limestone and earthenware pots, rather than papyrus, which are not the easiest of materials to write on. Some were inside pottery bowls which will have contained food offerings. The earliest letter was from the Old Kingdom though most were from the Ptolemaic Period. A woman attendant of the ibises complains to Thoth about the seizure of her property by a man whom she names. One long detailed letter is written on behalf of a young boy and girl

---

[688] *Reflections of Osiris*, Ray. 2002:151.
[689] *An Oracle of Hermes Trismegistos at Saqqara*, Skeatt & Turner. 1968:199.
[690] *Two Oracle Petitions Addressed to Horus-khau with Some Notes on the Oracular Amuletic Decrees*, Hans & Fischer. 1996:139.

complaining about their father's treatment of them after their mother's death and his remarriage. There is a request by a son that his father be spared death from his illness. The son offers a monthly payment for ibis burials if his request is granted.[691]

In a letter from Nag el-Deir, in 502 BCE, the writer complains to Thoth about extreme persecution by a fellow worker. "*A communication of the humble servant Efou...unto Thoth, Twice Great, Lord of Hermopolis...Let me be protected from Psenteehe.*" Efou describes his work as "*for the Ibis*" and says "*if the heart be stout, one will be protected in the presence of Thoth*".[692]

The following is an extract of a petition from an old man, who begs Thoth to save him from his endless bad luck.

"*Calamity! O Thoth, Twice Great, Lord of Hermopolis!...*

It has befallen Esnekenbeo...from the hand of the Evil Genius....

Protect me from it!...

Our great Lord, I am too old for the troubles in which I am...

Propitiate for me the gods against whom I have committed wrongs and propitiate for me my Good Genius! Cause them to be gracious to me!

Save me from your destruction of wrongdoing! Protect me from the Evil Genius!

Save me from it! Do not give me to the Evil Genius! Take me for yourself; do not give me to it!

Save me from it from this day forward! Do not let it come near a person of mine! Do not let it come near a possession of mine! Do not let another have power over me except you (Thoth)!"[693]

Oaths

In common with all other deities, oaths were taken in Thoth's name. "*As the ka of Thoth endures, I did (it) by myself without my*

[691] *A Demotic Plea to Thoth in the Library of G. Michaelides,* Hughes. 1968:176-77
[692] *A Demotic Letter to Thoth,* Hughes. 1958:3-7.
[693] *A Demotic Plea to Thoth in the Library of G. Michaelides,* Hughes. 1968:178.

calling a scribe" and also "*I swear by the Lord of Hermopolis*".⁶⁹⁴ Swearing a false oath on the lover of Maat would have been particularly foolish, as the workman Huy discovered when he swore on Thoth's name regarding a lost or stolen scoop. "*By the servant of the Moon, Huy. He says, I am the man who falsely said 'As true as...' to the Moon concerning the scoop, and he caused me to see the greatness of his strength before the entire land. I will recount your manifestations to the fish in the river and to the birds in the sky, and they will say to their children's children, 'Beware of the Moon, the merciful, who knew how to avert this.*"⁶⁹⁵

Rewards

Like all deities it was expected that Thoth would reward his devoted followers. Ahmes governor of the Hare Nome says, on his statue at Karnak, "*I sailed up-stream to Hermopolis...I bent my arms to the prophets and their priests. I did good to their citizens. The reward thereof was that Tenen and Thoth caused me to arrive at Thebes as an honoured one.*"⁶⁹⁶ In a letter the scribe Meh enquires after the scribe Yey the younger "*here am I praying to Thoth and the gods, lords of Pi-Djehuty: May you be well! May you live! May you get credit for all you have done!*"⁶⁹⁷

Pentaweret had the following inscribed on a stele: "*Giving praise to your Spirit, O Thoth, Lord of hieroglyphs, the well-beloved god - that he may give L.P.H, alertness, favour and love, for the spirit of the sculpture Pentaweret.*"⁶⁹⁸ (L.P.H. was a common abbreviation for long life, prosperity and health.) The Royal Scribe Thuthirhesef inscribed the following in the temple of Sahure: "*[Prais]ing Thoth who determines the truth, that he may give a [happy?] lifetime [to] him who is in his favour.*"⁶⁹⁹

Through his guidance and grace the scribe advances in his career. "*O come to me that you may give me wisdom! I am a devotee of your*

---

⁶⁹⁴ *The Oath in Ancient Egypt*, Wilson. 1948:133-34.
⁶⁹⁵ *Village Life in Ancient Egypt: Laundry Lists and Love Songs*, McDowell. 1999:101-102.
⁶⁹⁶ *A Statue from the Karnak Cache*, Fairman. 1934:2.
⁶⁹⁷ *Three Hieratic Papyri in the Duke of Northumberland's Collection*, Barns. 1948:38.
⁶⁹⁸ *Ramesside Inscriptions Translated & Annotated. Vol III*. Kitchen. 2000:66.
⁶⁹⁹ *Ramesside Inscriptions Translated & Annotated. Vol III*. Kitchen. 2000:274.

domain."[700] Thoth *"made great him who was skilled in his employment"*.[701] A hymn to a baboon statue of Thoth, often copied by pupils, says *"My entranceway is sweet since the holy creature entered it. It has developed and is well furnished since my Lord set foot therein."*[702] Some prayers are less subtle than others, but probably more truthful. A hymn to Thoth inscribed on a writing board says *"Hail to you Thoth! I am the one who praises you, so may you give me house and property!"*[703]

An ostracan, from the 19th or 20th Dynasty, bears an invocation to Thoth from the scribe Amunhotep.[704] The scribe is shown kneeling with his arms upraised. The impression the drawing gives is one of joyful adoration. Amunhotep is almost smiling and is shown with a fat stomach, the sign of a life of affluence.

Help and Protection

Frequently the prayers were requests for help, many beg Thoth for relief from blindness. This was considered a divinely ordained punishment as were all natural disasters whether personal or national. Blindness was common amongst all Egyptians but the poor would have suffered most. It is also possible that *'darkness'* sometimes refers to other ailments such as depression. The following inscription, from the *Turin stele*, depicts Lunar Thoth in his barque worshipped by a baboon and the sculptor Neferronpet, his wife and daughter.

"Giving praise to Luna-Thoth:

Homage to the Merciful One.

I give him praise to the height of heaven:

I adore thy beauty.

Be thou merciful to me,

---

[700] *Hymns, Prayers and Songs*, Foster. 1995:148. *Prayer to Thoth for Wisdom in His Service.*
[701] *Ancient Egyptian Religion,* Cerny. 1952:60.
[702] *Hymns, Prayers and Songs*, Foster. 1995:146. *Hymn to Thoth.*
[703] *Cracking Codes: The Rosetta Stone and Decipherment*, Parkinson. 1999:148.
[704] *Egyptian Drawings*, Peck. 1978:118.

That I may see that thou art merciful:

That I may observe thy might.

Thou causest me to see a darkness of thy making;

Lighten me, that I may see thee.

For that health and life are in thine hand:

One liveth by thy gift of them."[705]

As well as being physically important the eye was a significant organ from the point of view of magic and religion. Eyes had special powers which could protect, as in the *wedjat* Eye, or harm through the 'evil eye'. "*O Thoth, thou shalt be my helper; so shall I not fear the eye.*"[706] Eyes and vision were also religiously significant. Many religions refer to vision and light and darkness when discussing spiritual enlightenment or confusion and doubt. Blindness in some of the texts may well refer to spiritual difficulties.

With an absence of negative and dangerous aspects, and given his devotion to Maat, Thoth is very approachable. People turned to him for help when they suffered injustice. As he resolved the problems of the deities Thoth can resolve the problems of ordinary people. "*I am guarded...just as Horus and Thoth guarded her who is with the Two Falcons.*"[707] Thoth is a protector both in life and after death, as he protects the barque of Ra so he will protect people and their property. "*I shall assume my form of the noble Ibis, to fly up over your head, and protect you with the plumes of (my) wings, that I may provide your (magical) protection like Re.*"[708]

Said to repel demons in the afterworld, the following spell is a short, panicking appeal to Thoth for protection. When faced with a terrifying and lethal enemy who has the time, or the presence of mind, to calmly recite a long spell? It was probably just as effective against the dangerous creatures in this life or even used to combat

705 *The Religion of the Poor in Ancient Egypt*, Gunn. 1916:92.
706 *Les Signes noir dans les rubriques*, Posener. 1949:81.
707 *The Ancient Egyptian Coffin Texts Vol 2*, Faulkner. 2007:184. Spell 581.
708 *Ramesside Inscriptions Translated & Annotated Vol IV*. Kitchen. 2003:23. *Festal Song of Thoth.*

nightmares. *"Get back, snake which attacks in the night...O Thoth, the night-snake! the night-snake!"*[709]

The worshipper need not fear for *"He is Thoth, who will make you safe"*.[710] Thoth was seen as a help and a refuge. In his letter to Thoth, Efou writes *"I have no human master to whom to turn to for help; I have only you, Thoth, a divine master"*. This phrasing is similar to a plea from a schoolboy letter to Thoth. *"It is thou that givest advice to him that has no mother."*[711] From the tomb of Amenwahsu, Thoth is described as *"Thoth who gives all protection"*.[712] The follower of Thoth was secure because *"The god Thoth is like a shield behind me"*.[713]

Love of Thoth

It is through hymns and prayers that we best understand the feelings of the worshippers towards their deities and the hymns to Thoth certainly reflect the worshippers' love. They are inspired by feelings of affection. *"Let us come and give thanks to Thoth, the God of Knowledge."*[714] Many other hymns praise the deities in general or recount myths. In hymns to Thoth we often find references to his relationship with people as individuals. *"Who recalls all that is forgotten; wise for him who is in error; the remembrancer of the moment and of infinity."*[715] This joyous adoration and love of the deities is more prevalent from the 18th Dynasty. Perhaps before then it wasn't considered seemly. *"My heart belongs to him."*[716]

Along with Ra, Horus, Amun and Hathor, Thoth was one of the few deities who were addressed as *'hearing'* deities; that is they responded to the petitioners' prayers and needs rather than just listening to them. Thoth is referred to as *"Dhwty-stm"* or *"Dhwty sdm"* - Thoth who hears.[717] Thoth never abandoned his followers. *"Heeding the supplications of him who calls to him. Who comes at the call of him*

---

[709] *The Ancient Egyptian Pyramid Texts,* Falkner. 2007:314. Utterance 733.
[710] *Traversing Eternity,* Smith. 2009:453.
[711] *A Demotic Letter to Thoth,* Hughes. 1958:9.
[712] *Ramesside Inscriptions Translated & Annotated. Vol III.* Kitchen. 2000:217.
[713] *Hathor and Thoth: Two Key Figures of the Ancient Egyptian Religion,* Bleeker. 1973:154.
[714] *The Living Wisdom of Ancient Egypt,* Jacq. 1999:68. *Statue of Horemheb.*
[715] *A Statue of Horemhab Before His Accession,* Winlock. 1924:3.
[716] *Hymns, Prayers and Songs,* Foster. 1995:146. *Hymn to Thoth.*
[717] *A God Who Hears,* Giveon. 1982:40-41.

who pronounces his name, who hears the prayers of him who sets him in his heart."[718]

Thoth's wisdom was available to those who were thoughtful, he was *"open for him who is silent"*.[719] Only the silent, that is the faithful and diligent, can find this source of divine love and sustenance.

In Summary

Despite his importance and status Thoth is still a personable god who will respond to an individual and protect them. *"I enter in before you in the form of the Baboon, twice-great, I am content, my step is steady (?) and pleasing. My countenance is kindly, gentle are my utterances, happy (enough) for laughter, when I see you as Re. Grace is with me, and peace is with me."*[720] From another hymn we have *"God of exceptional goodness among the gods"*.[721] Thoth is not to be feared by the honest and those in need for *"He is the lord of friendliness"* and *"God of incomparable goodness"*.[722]

As Petosiris concludes of Thoth *"You have made my heart walk upon your waters, he who walks on your road will never stumble"*.[723]

---

[718] *Ramesside Inscriptions Translated & Annotated. Vol III.* Kitchen. 2000:492.
[719] *Hathor and Thoth: Two Key Figures of the Ancient Egyptian Religion,* Bleeker. 1973:154.
[720] *Ramesside Inscriptions Translated & Annotated Vol IV.* Kitchen. 2003:24. *Festal Song of Thoth.*
[721] *Hathor and Thoth: Two Key Figures of the Ancient Egyptian Religion,* Bleeker. 1973:21.
[722] *Hathor and Thoth: Two Key Figures of the Ancient Egyptian Religion,* Bleeker. 1973:154.
[723] *The Living Wisdom of Ancient Egypt,* Jacq. 1999:42. *Petosiris.*

CHAPTER 14

HERMES TRISMEGISTUS AND BEYOND

"Where are Helius and Hephoestus, Gods of eldest eld? Where is Hermes Trismegistus, Who their secrets held?"[724]

Out of Egypt

Despite being *"lord of foreign lands"* Thoth did not often travel far beyond the Egyptian borders.[725]   Unlike some of their neighbouring cultures the Egyptians were not great travellers, or migrants, and were reluctant to leave their blessed land for long. Who would want to live away from the country which was the centre of the created world, and was an image of heaven, to live amongst foreigners who were inevitably described as miserable or wretched? *"The vile Asiatic is the pain of the place wherein he is."*[726] The worst fate was to die aboard *"what matters more than my being buried in the land where I was born?"*[727] Those Egyptians who settled outside their country will have worshipped, and built shrines to, their own deities but these would not necessarily have been adopted by the host population. Foreigners did settle in Egypt and some may well have incorporated the Egyptian

---

[724] *Hermes Trismegistus*, Longfellow. 2007:116.
[725] *Ancient Egyptian Religion*, Cerny. 1952:61.
[726] *The Tale of Sinuhe and Other Ancient Egyptian Poems*, Parkinson. 1997:223. *The Tale of Sinuhe*.
[727] *The Tale of Sinuhe and Other Ancient Egyptian Poems*, Parkinson. 1997:34.

deities into their pantheon and taken them back to their own countries but evidence is not easy to find.

Lands bordering Egypt, such as Sinai and Nubia, were settled by the Egyptians and they naturally brought their deities with them. Before the Ptolemaic Period there is little evidence for the worship of Thoth outside of Egypt except in these two countries. He wasn't the god of merchants, soldiers or adventurers so this is not surprising. Thoth was *"Lord of Iunut"*, the Iunut were the inhabitants of the Sinai Peninsula.[728] The *Sneferu texts* from Wadi Maghara, Sinai, refer to Thoth as one of the major deities alongside Hathor.[729] In the temple at Serabit el-Khadim, Ramesses VI is shown praying to *"Thoth of Mesdyt"*.[730]

Nubia had a close relationship with Egypt, and was considered a province of it at times, and a number of the Egyptian deities do appear in this country. Some temples were built by the Egyptian kings and could be considered part of the strategy for establishing a presence in the borderlands. Horemheb built a shrine to Thoth in Abahudeh, near Abu Simbel, and Ramesses II built a temple at Derr.[731] During the Late Period there was a growth in the cult of Thoth in Nubia. In the Ptolemaic Period the Nubian king Ergamenes built a major shrine of Thoth at Dakka and a Nubian ruler built the temple of Thoth at Debod. Some of Thoth's epithets were: *"Lord of Pnubs in Takens"* (the north of Nubia), *"Lord of Bigeh"* and *"Lord of the Southern Lands"*.[732]

Once outside Egypt the Egyptian deities did change, absorbing attributes of the local deities. The Thoth of Pnubs does have different traits to the Thoth of Hermopolis. No one was enforcing a strict religious dogma and deities developed to serve and reflect the needs of their communities. One example of this is the inclusion of Thoth of Pnubs in a triad with the goddess Tefnut and their son Arensnuphis. A shrine to this triad was built in Dakka, in the 3rd century BCE, by the Merotic king Arkamani II. Arensnuphis was originally a god from much further south in Africa who was absorbed into the local and

---

[728] *Thoth as Creator of Languages*, Cerny. 1948:122.
[729] *Thoth Or The Hermes Of Egypt*, Boylan. 1922:150.
[730] *The Routledge Dictionary of Egyptian Gods and Goddesses*, Hart. 2005:159.
[731] *Thoth Or The Hermes Of Egypt*, Boylan. 1922:161-62.
[732] *Thoth Or The Hermes Of Egypt*, Boylan. 1922:169-70.

Egyptian pantheons. The Egyptian Thoth was not part of any triad but this did not constrain the Nubians.[733]

In Philae Thoth is identified with Shu and Onuris (a local warrior god). As discussed in chapter 11, Shu and Thoth play similar roles in the Angry Eye and Distant Goddess myths and are easily assimilated into each other. Thoth is referred to as *"the mighty Shu, Lord of wine"* and *"the god of wine who drinks abundantly"*. Onuris was also referred to as the Lord of Wine. These epithets probably refer to Thoth's responsibility for the wine offering to pacify Hathor. (See chapter 11.) Onuris was originally the Lord of Pnubs, in the local myth it is Onuris who retrieves the Wandering Eye. Some of Thoth's epithets relate to the warrior aspect of Onuris such as *"Lion of the South"* and *"The living lion which overthrows the evil ones, mighty in strength, lord of victory"*. Thoth is also shown wearing a crown normally associated with Onuris.

In the Nubian depictions Thoth does not have his usual symbols of lunar crown or writing kit. In Dakka he is shown holding a snake entwined *was*-sceptre and in Debod he holds a *was*-sceptre with snake and scorpions. One text at Dendur reads *"the first serpent-form of Thoth"*. These emphasise his healing and magical aspects which were more important to the Nubians than his scribal and wisdom attributes.[734]

Beyond Nubia and Sinai there is virtually no evidence of the worship of Thoth. There was trade contact with Crete by the 3rd millennium BCE, with increasing contact by the time of the New Kingdom. It is believed that the baboon form of Thoth was imported into Crete at this time.[735]

In the Greco-Roman Period some Egyptian deities were adopted by other countries and cultures but Thoth was not one of them. The cult of Isis was widespread from the 4th century BCE and at one time was a rival to Christianity. For a number of reasons the Roman Empire was hungry for the Eastern mystery religions and the cult of Isis and Osiris found a welcome niche, alongside Mithraism and Christianity.

---

[733] *The British Museum Dictionary of Ancient Egypt,* Shaw & Nicholson. 2008:39,89.
[734] *Thoth Or The Hermes Of Egypt,* Boylan. 1922:169.
[735] *The British Museum Dictionary of Ancient Egypt,* Shaw & Nicholson. 2008:84.

The melodramatic resurrection rituals were more enticing than a god who liked hard work and adherence to *maat*.

Thoth, like many other major deities such as Hathor and Ra, was not particularly popular with the non-Egyptian cultures of the time. There seem to be two reasons for this. Thoth had a very *'close fit'* to Egyptian culture with its highly bureaucratic and centralised structure and all encompassing concept of *maat*. The Romans, for example, had bureaucracy and literacy but scribes were not highly regarded neither was *maat*. Secondly, these cultures already had wisdom and lunar deities, who were major players in their pantheons, so there was no divine vacancy for Thoth to fill.

The Egyptian Hermes

The Greeks called the Egyptian deities by the names of their own deities, choosing the nearest approximation. They equated Thoth with Hermes, their god of wisdom (the Roman god Mercury). Both gods later merged to become the hybrid, and eventually mortal, Hermes Trismegistus.

Hermes was the son of Zeus and the nymph Maia and was the *"swift messenger of all the gods"*.[736] He wore *"glittering golden sandals with which he could fly like the wind over land and sea"* and a winged hat. Hermes became the patron of travellers through his messenger role. The Egyptians weren't great travellers and don't appear to have had a deity with a specific travel aspect. Had they needed such protection Thoth would have been an obvious choice given his role as messenger.

Hermes' staff, the *caduceus*, is crowned with two snakes. Hermes was said to have laid his staff between two fighting serpents who ceased their battle and entwined themselves around his staff. This has parallels with Thoth pacifying the Two Combatants and reconciling opposites. Heralds carried a similar type of staff which was meant to guarantee their safe passage. Hermes' staff also had magical powers. He *"took the wand with which he seals men's eyes in sleep, or wakes them just as he pleases"*.[737]

---

[736] *Hesiod, the Homeric Hymns, and Homerica,* Homer. 2008:127. *XIX To Pan.* Trans. Evelyn-White.
[737] *The Iliad,* Homer. 2009:207. Trans. Butler.

The two gods are alike in that they act on behalf of, or assist, the other deities. Thoth though is more of a static maintainer. He acts to preserve the status quo unless it happens to be chaos or conflict in which case he restores order. Hermes represents movement. He introduces fluidity and brings new beginnings; because of this he can sometimes bring chaos and can be unpredictable. This aspect of his character gives us the term mercurial. The fluidity of Hermes also applies to possessions, which he 'liberates'. "*Born with the dawning, at mid-day he played on the lyre, and in the evening he stole the cattle of far-shooting Apollo.*" Hermes was also known as "*luck-bringing*", a god of coincidences and opportunities, and so was a popular patron of merchants, gamblers and thieves.[738]

Thoth and Hermes are both wisdom gods. Thoth personifies wisdom and understanding and Hermes was born precocious and knowledgeable. An inscription from the Ptolemaic Period was carved by a "*Servitor of the All-seeing Hermes*".[739] Naturally eloquent, Hermes was also credited with giving humanity language and speech. Both gods could be considered as "*him with the honeyed tongue, skilled in speech*".[740] Hermes had the ability to talk himself out of trouble. His charm and inventiveness reconciled him with Apollo, to compensate for the theft of the cattle Hermes gave Apollo a lyre. Hermes went to the underworld to negotiate with Hades for the release of Persephone and at times he played a peacekeeping role. Like Thoth, Hermes was always willing to help the other deities - when he wasn't tricking them. He protected the baby Dionysus, for example, and assisted Zeus on many occasions. Despite his mischievous ways Hermes was kind towards mortals and was well loved, as was Thoth. "*Hail, Hermes, giver of grace, guide, and giver of good things.*"[741]

Both gods are psychopomps and guide the dead in the afterlife. Hermes was known as the "*god of the gateway*" or "*the god dwelling at the gate*".[742] He was considered a guide of dreams and a teacher of the mysteries of the afterlife. Hermes also has magical aspects. He was

---

[738] *Hesiod, the Homeric Hymns, and Homerica,* Homer. 2008:110. *IV To Hermes.* Trans. Evelyn-White.
[739] *Men and Gods on the Roman Nile,* Lindsay. 1968:335.
[740] *The Myth of Horus at Edfu: II.C. (Continued),* Blackman & Fairman. 1943:3.
[741] *Hesiod, the Homeric Hymns, and Homerica,* Homer. 2008:127. *XVIII To Hermes.* Trans. Evelyn-White.
[742] *The Gods of Greece,* Stassinopoulos. 1983:193.

associated with divination and, as befits the god of transformations, he was the patron god of alchemists.

The gods are different in a number of ways. Hermes is no judge or creator and has little association with healing. As mentioned previously Thoth has no sexual aspects though he does have consorts. Hermes on the other hand had affairs with goddesses, Aphrodite in particular, and mortal women, by whom he fathered several children. Hermes has a much looser relationship with *maat* than Thoth and can sometimes appear as a rogue, albeit a very charming and lovable one. Hermes is associated with the planet Mercury which in Egyptian religion and astronomy was the planet of Seth. To the Greeks, and the Romans, the Moon was always a goddess whereas Thoth has a very strong lunar connection.

Hermes shared many attributes with Thoth but was not an exact fit; given the differences in the two cultures this is hardly unexpected. Mead, for one, was unimpressed. *"It was but a sorry equivalent that the Greeks could find in their own pantheon when, in the change of God-names, they were forced to 'translate' 'Thoth' by 'Hermes'."*[743] Once equated to Hermes, Thoth started to lose many of his Egyptian attributes as it was his magical aspects that attracted the most attention from the Greeks and later the Romans. The loss of his close relationship with Maat had a noticeable effect on the way Thoth was perceived during the Greco-Roman Period.

Morphing into Hermes Trismegistus

The Greek texts known as the *Corpus Hermetica* are a collection of writings all of which were attributed to Hermes Trismegistus. The appellation Trismegistus was based on one of Thoth's epithets *"Three Time Great"*. Given the importance of triads and trinities to religious symbolism, *'thrice great'* is a significant epithet as well as a phrase which means *'many times'*. The *Corpus Hermetica* was collated in Alexandria in the 2nd and 3rd centuries CE, which at the time was a great centre of learning and a rich source of religious, esoteric and other knowledge. Most of the writings are in the form of a narrative between the sage and his disciple. The wisdom of Hermes Trismegistus was also said to cover astrology, alchemy and the occult

---

[743] *Hymns of Hermes,* Mead. 2006:30.

arts. They incorporated much of the Egyptian traditions, particularly the *Book of Thoth* (see chapter 5), but are considered to be, in essence, a classical construct which included Persian, Gnostic and other influences. The *Hermetica* had a profound influence on the development of Western thought and philosophy. Hermeticism will not be discussed in this book as there are plenty of expert works available.

Hermes Trismegistus travelled far, in both distance and time, and was frequently referred to as *'the Egyptian'* and the god Thoth was overtaken by this projection. Hermes Trismegistus was eventually seen as the human founder of a religion and no trace of his divinity remained. This did help the hermetic writings to survive under the jurisdiction of a suspicious church. Many later books of alchemy cited the author as Hermes Trismegistus as it gave them more intellectual weight. The most famous of these texts is the Emerald Tablet allegedly found in the tomb of Hermes Trismegistus. It is now believed to be the work of an 8th century Arab alchemist. In the 18th century Antoine Court de Gebelin (1719-1784) published a book claiming that the Major Trumps (or Arcana) of the tarot cards formed the *Book of Thoth* which preserved esoteric Ancient Egyptian wisdom. This idea was developed in the 20th century by the magician Aleister Crowley (1875-1947).

Atlantis and Latter-day Interpretations

There is a tendency for some modern esoteric writers to view Thoth as a *'priest from Atlantis'* who was later deified. As Hermes Trismegistus was considered a mortal this is not a new theory. The origins of Egyptian culture are hard to establish as its great age has erased most of the early evidence. What there is indicates that their culture and civilization developed from native African sources, merging with those of migrating peoples from the Near East, rather than being implanted on backward locals by the superior Atlanteans. However, it is only fair to note what some Classical writers had to say on this subject. Cicero said that Thoth was *"worshipped by the people of Pheneus, is said to have killed Argus and consequently to have fled in exile to Egypt, where he gave the Egyptians their laws and letters. His Egyptian name is Theuth"*.[744] (Pheneus was in Greece and Argus

---

[744] *De Natura Deorum*, Cicero. 1951:341. Trans. Rackham.

was a giant slain by Hermes.) This appears to be the joining of the two gods together while claiming the superiority of the Greek Hermes. According to Strabo, "*Plato relates that Solon, having made inquiry of the Egyptian priests, reported that Atlantis did once exist*".[745]

The Greeks used myths to describe the deification of mortals and applied this reasoning, incorrectly, to the Egyptian myths. The Contendings of Horus and Seth may reflect political situations but the Egyptian deities were, and always had been, divine. Deification was extremely rare. Given their contempt towards foreigners the Egyptian theologians would never have given any credence to the theory that any part of their culture came from foreign lands, let alone one of their most important gods. They knew that Egypt was a reflection of Heaven.

We thus have a choice; either to attempt to understand the Egyptian deities as they did, or to base our understanding of them on the hellenocentric Greek interpretations.

---

[745] *Geography Vol I,* Strabo. 1932:391. Trans. James.

CHAPTER 15

CONCLUSION

"Thoth is my champion when it is dark, is dark."[746]

A conclusion should, in theory, summarise the findings and then answer the main question posed. This book's conception did not originate with a question but with a desire to get to know more about the God of the Scribes. It is true that a deity cannot be perceived of as a personality in human terms but most of us react best to a personality, real or perceived. My intention never was to write a biography about Thoth but to try and discover how the Egyptians perceived him and to delve beneath the general epithets of Lunar God and God of Wisdom and the accretions of Classical and later periods.

Thoth shows two faces to us. He is the creative and organising force of the universe and the laws that keep everything in motion. It is he *"who sets all things in their proper places"*.[747] He is the unbreakable laws of physics and the moral laws which all should aspire to. Budge was certainly impressed by Thoth. *"The character of Thoth is a lofty and a beautiful conception, and is, perhaps, the highest idea of deity ever fashioned in the Egyptian mind."*[748]

---

[746] *The Ancient Egyptian Pyramid Texts,* Faulkner. 2007:85. Utterance 279.
[747] *An Ancient Egyptian Book of Hours,* Faulkner. 1958:15.
[748] *The Gods of the Egyptians Vol 1,* Budge. 1969:415.

Despite such a cosmic and awe-inspiring role Thoth is not a remote or superior deity. He has not retreated in despair at human behaviour nor does he strike out in anger as some deities do. With his other face Thoth relates to the individual. He may have been the god of rulers and powerful men but he was also the hearing god who was approached by ordinary people seeking protection, reassurance, justice and healing. The hymns and prayers to Thoth show the warmth and affection in which he was held and his helpfulness is frequently remarked upon.

A key figure in the Egyptian pantheon and a mortal's guardian and guide Thoth's values and example continue to be relevant today. His cultural legacy of ritual, literacy, justice and peace-making form some of the best aspects of civilization. The gifts of writing and literature from the Lord of Writing still underpin and permeate our lives, only the technology has changed. If only his devotion to *Maat* and his peace-making abilities had found a similar home. We have a profound need for this tolerant God of Harmony who stands balanced where opposites clash.

The best conclusions and the answers to my questions about Thoth can be found, as ever, in the words of the Egyptians.

Who is he? "The glorious Ibis who came forth from the heart of the god."[749]

Where does he come from? "The Mansion of Books."

Where is he? "In every place where his ka desires to be."

What does he do? "Reckons all things."[750]

What is he like? "Of pleasing aspect, gentle, charming, loved by all."[751]

[749] *Thoth Or The Hermes Of Egypt*, Boylan. 1922:214.
[750] *An Ancient Egyptian Book of Hours*, Faulkner. 1958:14-15.
[751] *Hymns, Prayers and Songs*, Foster. 1995:146. *Hymn to Thoth*.

APPENDICES

1. SOME HYMNS & PRAYERS TO THOTH

This section gives a small selection of some of the many hymns and prayers to Thoth that have been found and translated. J.L. Foster in particular has translated many hymns and these can be found in his book *Hymns, Prayers and Songs*.

Hymns to Thoth from a Wooden Writing Board[752]

Praising Thoth in the course of every day:

O gods who are in heaven,

O gods who [are in earth]

[...] easterners,

come, that you may see Thoth crowned with his uraeus,

when the Two-Lords are established for him in Hermopolis,

that he may govern the people!

Rejoice in the Hall of Geb at what he has done!

Praise him, extol him, give him hymns!

- this god is the lord of kind-heartedness,

the governor of entire multitudes.

Now every god and every goddess,

who shall give praises to Thoth on this day -

he shall found their seats, and their offices in their temples

in the Island of Fire!

Hail to you Thoth!

I am the one who praises you,

---

[752] *Cracking Codes: The Rosetta Stone and Decipherment*, Parkinson. 1999:148-49.

so may you give me house and property!

May you establish me, create my livelihood,

in the land of the living,

as you have made them to live in the Island of Fire!

May you give me love, favours,

[...], sweetness, protection,

in the bodies, hearts, breasts of all mankind,

all patricians, all folk, all sunfolk!

Spell:

May you strike down my male and female enemies,

dead and living.

These are to be spoken by a man when he has offered to Thoth,

- justifying a man against my (sic) enemies

in the council of every god and every goddess!

For he is the chief of every god and every goddess,

this being what the great Company of gods has decreed for him.

Hymn to Thoth from a Stela from Deir el-Medina[753]

Giving praise to Moon-Thoth, great in strength for the Conclave of gods,

paying homage to the great god, Mighty one of the gods,

Great in dread power, kind and merciful,

in heeding the supplications of him who calls to him.

Who comes at the call of him who pronounces his name,

---

753 *Ramesside Inscriptions Translated & Annotated. Vol III.* Kitchen. 2000:492.

who hears the prayers of him who sets him in his heart.

I give you praise, [I exalt you]

(as) you please the gods daily.

Hymn to Thoth on a Statue of Khereuf[754]

Hail to you, lord of divine words (language)

Master of the mysteries which are in heaven and earth

Great God of primeval times, the primeval one who has given language and script.

Who hands over houses and establishes temples

who makes known the gods and what is theirs,

every craft and what belongs to it,

the lands and their boundaries and fields likewise.

The Threefold Gift of Thoth[755]

I am Thoth and I speak to you the language of Re as a herald. They spoke to you before my words were understood. I am Thoth, the lord of divine speech, who puts things in their right place. I give god's offerings to the gods and invocation-offerings to the blessed dead. I am Thoth who ascribes truth to the Ennead and all that comes from my mouth comes into being like (all that comes from the mouth) of Re.

---

[754] *Some Remarks on the Mysterious Language of the Baboons*, Velde. 1988:133.
[755] *Some Remarks on the Mysterious Language of the Baboons*, Velde. 1988:136.

2. CHRONOLOGY

Predynastic 5500-3100 BCE

Early Dynastic Period 1st - 2nd Dynasty 3100-2686 BCE

Old Kingdom 3rd - 6th Dynasty 2686-2181 BCE

First Intermediate Period 7th - 11th Dynasty (Thebes only) 2181-2055 BCE

Middle Kingdom 11th - 14th Dynasty 2055-1650 BCE

Second Intermediate Period 15th - 17th Dynasty 1650-1550 BCE

New Kingdom 18th - 20th Dynasty 1550-1069 BCE

Third Intermediate Period 21st - 24th Dynasty 1069-747 BCE

Late Period 25th - 31st Dynasty 747-332 BCE

Ptolemaic Period 332-30 BCE

Roman Period 30 BCE - 395 CE

3. PLACE NAMES

MODERN EGYPTIAN	ANCIENT EGYPTIAN	CLASSICAL
Abydos	Abdjw	
Abu Simbel		
Abahudeh (near Abu Simbel)		
Alexandria	Raqote	Alexandria
Bahariya (Oasis)		
Beni Hasan		
Cairo		
Dakka (Nubia)		
Dakhla (Oasis)		
Damanhur		Hermopolis Parva
Debod (Nubia)		
Deir el-Bahri (opposite Luxor)		
Deir el-Bersha (necropolis of Hermopolis Magna)		
Deir el-Hagar (Dakhla Oasis)		
Deir el-Medina (opposite Luxor)		
Dendera	Iunet (or Tanter)	Tentyris
Dendur (Nubia)		
Derr (Nubia)		
Edfu	Djeb	Apollonopolis
el-Amarna	Akhetaten	
el-Ashmunein	Khmun	Hermopolis Magna
el-Hibis (or el-Hiba)	Teudjoi	Ankyronpolis
el-Kab (or Elkab)	Nekheb	
el-Lisht (near Cairo)		

Elephantine	Abu	
Giza		
Ihnasya el-Medina	Henen-nesw	Herakleopolis Magna
Karnak	Ipet-isut	
Kom el-Ahmar	Nekhen	Hierakonpolis
Kom Ombo	Pa-Sebek	Ombus
Luxor	Waset	Thebes
Medinet Habu	Djamet (or Djeme)	
Memphis	Men-nefer	
Nag el-Deir		
Philae		
Qasr el-Agueze (near Luxor)		
Qift	Gebtu	Coptos (or Koptos)
Saqqara (necropolis of Memphis)		
Serabit el-Khadim (Sinai)		
Sesebi (Sudan)		
Speos Artemidos (near Beni Hasan)		
Tell el-Far'in	Pe and Dep	Buto
Tell Hisn	Iunu (or On)	Heliopolis
Tell om-Harb		
Tod	Djerty	Tuphium
Tuna el-Gebel (necropolis of Hermopolis Magna)		
Wadi Hammamat		
Wadi Kharig (Sinai, near Wadi Maghara)		
Wadi Maghara (Sinai)		

BIBLIOGRAPHY

Abt, T & Hornung, E (2003) *Knowledge for the Afterlife*. Zurich, Living Human Heritage Publications

Aelian & Scholfield A.F. (trans) (1957) *On the Characteristics of Animals Vol I*. London, William Heinemann Ltd

Aelian & Scholfield A.F. (trans) (1957) *On the Characteristics of Animals Vol II*. London, William Heinemann Ltd

Allen, T.A. (1974) *The Book of the Dead or Going Forth by Day*. Chicago, University of Chicago Press

Allen, T.G. (1949) *Some Egyptian Sun Hymns*. In *Journal of Near Eastern Studies*, Vol 8.4:349-55

Anthes, R. (1957) *The Legal Aspects of the Instructions of Amenemhet*. In *Journal of Near Eastern Studies*, Vol 16.3:176-190

Armour, R.A. (2001) *Gods and Myths of Ancient Egypt*. Cairo, American University in Cairo Press

Assmann, J. (1992) *When Justice Fails: Jurisdiction and Imprecation in Ancient Egypt and the Near East*. In *Journal of Egyptian Archaeology*, Vol 78:149-62

Barns, J. (1948) *Three Hieratic Papyri in the Duke of Northumberland's Collection*. In *Journal of Egyptian Archaeology*, Vol 34:35-46

Betro, M.C. (1996) *Hieroglyphics: The writings of Ancient Egypt*. New York, Abbeville Press

Blackman, A.M. (1921) *On the Position of Women in the Ancient Egyptian Hierarchy.* In *Journal of Egyptian Archaeology*, Vol 7.1/2:8-30

Blackman, A.M. (1937) *Preliminary Report on the Excavations at Sesebi, Northern Province, Anglo-Egyptian Sudan, 1936-37.* In *Journal of Egyptian Archaeology*, Vol 23.2:145-151

Blackman, A.M. (1945) *The King of Egypt's Grace before Meat.* In *Journal of Egyptian Archaeology*, Vol 31:57-73

Blackman, A.M. & Fairman, H.W. (1946) *The Consecration of an Egyptian Temple according to the Use of Edfu.* In *Journal of Egyptian Archaeology*, Vol 32:75-91

Blackman, A.M. & Fairman, H.W. (1943) *The Myth of Horus at Edfu (Continued): II.C.* In *Journal of Egyptian Archaeology*, Vol 29:2-36

Blackman, A.M. & Peet, T.E. (1925) *Papyrus Lansing: A Translation With Notes.* In *Journal of Egyptian Archaeology*, Vol 11.3/4:284-98

Bleeker, C.J. (1973) *Hathor and Thoth: Two Key Figures of the Ancient Egyptian Religion.* Leiden, E.J. Brill

Bleeker, C. J. (1975) *The Rainbow. A collection of Studies in the Science of Religion.* Leiden, E.J. Brill

Bomgioanni, A. & Croce, M.S. (ed) (2003) *The Treasures of Ancient Egypt from the Egyptian Museum in Cairo.* New York, Universe Publishing

Bomhard, A. S. (1999) *The Egyptian Calendar A Work For Eternity.* London, Periplus Publishing

Borghouts, J.F. (1978) *Ancient Egyptian Magical Texts.* Leiden, E.J. Brill

Boylan, P. (1922) *Thoth Or The Hermes Of Egypt.* Montana, Kessinger Publishing (Reprints)

Budge, E.A.W. (1971) *Egyptian Magic.* London, Dover Publications

Budge, E.A.W. (1969) *The Gods of the Egyptians Vol I.* London, Dover Publications

Buhl, M. (1947) *The Goddesses of the Egyptian Tree Cult.* In *Journal of Near Eastern Studies* Vol 6.2:80-97

Carter, H. (1917) *A Tomb Prepared for Queen Hatshepsuit and Other Recent Discoveries at Thebes*. In *Journal of Egyptian Archaeology*, Vol 4.2/3:107-118

Cerny, J. (1952) *Ancient Egyptian Religion*. London, Hutchinson's University Library

Cerny, J. (1948) *Thoth as Creator of Languages*. In *Journal of Egyptian Archaeology*, Vol 34:121-122

Cicero & Rackham (trans) (1951) *De Natura Deorum*. London, W Heinemann Ltd

Clagett, M. (1989) *Ancient Egyptian Science - A Source Book Vol I*. Philadelphia, American Philosophical Society

Clark, R.T. (1978) *Myth and Symbol in Ancient Egypt*. London, Thames & Hudson

David, R. (2002) *Religion and Magic in Ancient Egypt*. London, Penguin Books

Dawson, W.R. (1934) *Studies in the Egyptian Medical Texts: IV (Continued)*. In *Journal of Egyptian Archaeology*, Vol 20.3/4:185-188

Dennis, J.T. (1910) *The Burden of Isis*. London, John Murray

Dodson, A. (1992) *Stelae of the Middle and New Kingdoms in the Museum of Archaeology and Anthropology, University of Cambridge*. In *Journal of Egyptian Archaeology*, Vol 78:274-279

Dodson, A. (2001) *The Hieroglyphs of Ancient Egypt*. London, Connaught

El-Sabban (2000) *Temple Festival Calendars of Ancient Egypt*. Liverpool, Liverpool University Press

Emery, W.B. (1965) *Preliminary Report on the Excavations at North Saqqara 1964-5*. In *Journal of Egyptian Archaeology*, Vol 51:3-8

Fairman, H.W. (1934) *A Statue from the Karnak Cache*. In *Journal of Egyptian Archaeology*, Vol 20.1/2:1-4

Fairman, H.W. (1935) *The Myth of Horus at Edfu: I*. In *Journal of Egyptian Archaeology*, Vol 21.1:26-36

Faulkner, R.O. (1958) *An Ancient Egyptian Book of Hours*. Oxford, Griffith Institute

Faulkner, R.O. (1989) *The Ancient Egyptian Book of the Dead.* London, British Museum Publications

Faulkner, R.O. (2007) *The Ancient Egyptian Coffin Texts.* Oxford, Aris & Phillips

Faulkner, R.O. (2007) *The Ancient Egyptian Pyramid Texts.* Kansas, Digireads.com Publishing

Faulkner, R.O. (1937) *The Bremner-Rhind Papyrus: III: D. The Book of Overthrowing Apep.* In *Journal of Egyptian Archaeology,* Vol 23.2:166-185

Faulkner, R.O. (1938) *The Bremner-Rhind Papyrus: IV.* In *Journal of Egyptian Archaeology,* Vol 24.1:41-53

Faulkner, R.O. & Goelet, O. (2008) *The Egyptian Book of the Dead.* San Francisco, Chronicle Books

Fazzini, R. & van Dijk, J. (2007) *Recent Work in the Mut Precinct at South Karnak.* In *Egyptian Archaeology,* No. 31:10-13

Foreman, W. & Quirke, S. (1996) *Hieroglyphs and the Afterlife in Ancient Egypt.* London, British Museum Press

Foster, J.L. (1995) *Hymns, Prayers and Songs.* Atlanta, Scholars Press

Frankfort, H. (1948) *Kingship and the Gods.* Chicago, University of Chicago Press

Gardiner, A. (1953) *The Coronation of King Haremhab.* In *Journal of Egyptian Archaeology,* Vol 39:13-31

Gardiner, A.H. (1914) *New Literary Works from Ancient Egypt.* In Journal of Egyptian Archaeology, Vol 1.1:20-36

Gardiner, A.H. (1938) *The House of Life.* In *Journal of Egyptian Archaeology,* Vol 24.2:157-179

Gardiner, A.H. (1930) *The Origin of Certain Coptic Grammatical Elements.* In *Journal of Egyptian Archaeology,* Vol 16.3/4:220-234

Gibson, C. (2009) *The Hidden Life of Ancient Egypt.* Scotland, Saraband

Giveon, R. (1982) *A God Who Hears*. In van Voss, M.H., & Hoens, D.J., & Mussies, G., & van der Plas, D. & te Velde H. (eds.) *Studies in Egyptian Religion: Dedicated to Professor Jan Zandee*. Leiden, E.J. Brill

Glanville, S.R.K. (1926) *A New Duplicate of the Hood Papyrus*. In *Journal of Egyptian Archaeology*, Vol 12.3/4:171-175

Glanville, S.R.K. (1932) *Scribes' Palettes in the British Museum. Part I*. In *Journal of Egyptian Archaeology*, Vol 18.1/2:53-61

Griffith, F.L. (1917) *Bibliography 1916-1917: Ancient Egypt*. In *Journal of Egyptian Archaeology*, Vol 4.4:261-279

Griffith, F.L. (1927) *The Abydos Decree of Seti I at Nauri*. In *Journal of Egyptian Archaeology*, Vol 13.3/4:193-208

Griffith, F.L. (1926) *The Teaching of Amenophis the Son of Kanakht. Papyrus B.M. 10474*. In *Journal of Egyptian Archaeology*, Vol 12.34:191-231

Griffith, F.L. & Thompson, H. (1974) *The Leyden Papyrus*. London, Dover Publications

Gunn, B. (1916) *The Religion of the Poor in Ancient Egypt*. In *The Journal of Egyptian Archaeology*, Vol 3.2/3:81-94

Hans, W. & Fischer, E. (1996) *Two Oracle Petitions Addressed to Horus-khau with Some Notes on the Oracular Amuletic Decrees*. In *Journal of Egyptian Archaeology*, Vol 82:129-144

Hart, G. (2005) *The Routledge Dictionary of Egyptian Gods and Goddesses*. Abingdon, Routledge

Hart, G. (1990) *Egyptian Myths*. London, British Museum Publications

Hawass, Z. (2000) *Valley of the Golden Mummies*. New York, Harry N Abrams Inc

Herodotus & Selincourt, A. (trans) (2003) *The Histories*. London, Penguin Books

Homer & Evelyn-White (trans) (2008) *Hesiod, the Homeric Hymns, and Homerica*. Kansas, Digireads.com Publishing

Homer & Butler (trans) (2009) *The Iliad*. Kansas, Digireads.com Publishing

Hornung, E. (1996) *Conceptions of God in Ancient Egypt.* New York, Cornell University Press

Hornung, E. (2001) *The Secret Lore of Egypt and its Impact on the West.* New York, Cornell University Press

Houlihan, P.F. (1996) *The Animal World of the Pharaohs.* London, Thames & Hudson

Hoyo, J., Elliott, A. & Sargatal, J. (eds.) (1992) *Handbook of the Birds of the World Vol I.* Barcelona, Lynx Edicions

Hughes, G.R. (1958) *A Demotic Letter to Thoth.* In *Journal of Near Eastern Studies,* Vol 17.1:1-12

Hughes, G.R. (1968) *A Demotic Plea to Thoth in the Library of G. Michaelides.* In *Journal of Egyptian Archaeology,* Vol 54:176-182

Jacq, C. (1998) *Magic and Mystery in Ancient Egypt.* London, Souvenir Press

Jacq, C. (1999) *The Living Wisdom of Ancient Egypt.* London, Simon & Schuster

James, E.O. (1969) *Creation and Cosmology.* Leiden, E.J. Brill

James, E.O. (1958) *Myth and Ritual in the Ancient Near East.* London, Thames & Hudson

Jasnow, R. & Zauzich, K. (2005) *The Ancient Egyptian Book of Thoth.* Wiesbaden, Harrassowitz Verlag

Jauhiainen, H. (2009) *Do Not Celebrate Your Feast Without Your Neighbours Academic Dissertation.* Helsinki, University of Helsinki

Kamstra, J.H., Milde, H. & Wagtendank, K. (eds.) (1988) *Funerary Symbols and Religion. Essays dedicated to Professor MSHG Heerma Van Voss.* Kampen, J H. Kok

Kaper, O.E. (1995) *The Astronomical Ceiling of Deir el-Haggar in the Dakhleh Oasis.* In *Journal of Egyptian Archaeology,* Vol. 81:175-195

Karenga, M. (2004) *Maat, the Moral Ideal in Ancient Egypt.* London, Routledge

Kaster, J. (1993) *The Wisdom of Ancient Egypt.* America, Barnes & Noble Books

Keats, J. (1976) *Selected Poems.* London, Collins

Kemp, B. (1989) *Ancient Egypt: Anatomy of a Civilization.* London, Routledge

Kipling, R. (1976) *Just So Stories, The Crab That Played With the Sea.* London, Book Club Associates

Kitchen, K.A. (1993) *Ramesside Inscriptions Translated & Annotated. Volume I. Ramesses I, Sethos I and Contemporaries.* Oxford, Blackwell Publishers Ltd

Kitchen, K.A. (1996) *Ramesside Inscriptions Translated and Annotated. Volume II. Ramesses II, Royal Inscriptions.* Oxford, Blackwell Publishers Ltd

Kitchen, K.A. (2000) *Ramesside Inscriptions Translated and Annotated. Volume III. Ramesses II, his Contemporaries.* Oxford, Blackwell Publishers Ltd

Kitchen, K.A. (2003) *Ramesside Inscriptions Translated and Annotated Volume IV. Merenptah and the Late Nineteenth Dynasty.* Oxford, Blackwell Publishers Ltd

Klotz, D. (2010) *Two Overlooked Oracles.* In *Journal of Egyptian Archaeology*, Vol 96:247-254

Kurth, D. (2004) *The Temple of Edfu.* Cairo, The American University in Cairo Press

Langton, N. (1936) *Notes on Some Small Egyptian Figures of Cats.* In *Journal of Egyptian Archaeology*, Vol 22.2:115-120

Lawrence, D.H. (1994) *The Complete Poems of D H Lawrence.* London, Wordsworth Editions

Lesko, L.H (1991) *Ancient Egyptian Cosmogonies and Cosmology.* In Shafer, B.E. (ed.) (1991) *Religion in Ancient Egypt.* New York, Cornell University Press

Lesko, L.H. (1977) *The Ancient Egyptian Book of Two Ways*California, University of California Publications

Lewis, C.S. (1964) *Poems.* London, Geoffrey Bles

Lichtheim, M. (1988) *Ancient Egyptian Autobiographies.* Switzerland, Biblical Institute of the University of Fribourg

Lichtheim, M. (2006) *Ancient Egyptian Literature Volume II.* California, University of California Press

Lichtheim, M. (2006) *Ancient Egyptian Literature Volume III.* California, University of California Press

Lindsay, J. (1968) *Men and Gods on the Roman Nile.* London, Frederick Muller

Longfellow, H.W. (2007) *Hermes Trismegistus* from *A Shattered Visage Lies.* USA, Rutherford Press Limited

Manniche, L. (1999) *Sacred Luxuries.* New York, Cornell University Press

McDermott, B. (2001) *Decoding Egyptian Hieroglyphs.* London, Duncan Baird Publishers

McDowell, A.G. (1999) *Village Life in Ancient Egypt: Laundry Lists and Love Songs.* Oxford, Oxford University Press

Mead, G.R.S. (2006) *Hymns of Hermes.* Maine, Weiser Books

Mead, G.R.S. (2002) *Plutarch: Concerning The Mysteries Of Isis And Osiris.* Montana, Kessinger Publishing (Reprints)

Meyer, M. de (2004) *Some Ptolemaic Spielerei with scribal palettes.* In *Journal of Egyptian Archaeology,* Vol 90:221-223

Mosjov, B. (2005) *Osiris.* Oxford, Blackwell Publishing Ltd

Morenz, S. (1992) *Egyptian Religion.* New York, Cornell University Press

Mueller, D. (1972) *An Early Egyptian Guide to the Hereafter.* In *Journal of Egyptian Archaeology,* Vol 58:99-125

Nelson, H.H. (1949) *Certain Reliefs at Karnak and Medinet Habu and the Ritual of Amenophis I (Concluded).* In *Journal of Near Eastern Studies,* Vol 8.4:310-345

Nicholson, P.T. (2009) *Cults, Caches and Catacombs.* In *Current World Archaeology,* Issue 36:33-38

Oakes, L. & Gahlin, L. (2004) *Ancient Egypt.* London, Hermes House

Parkinson, R. (1999) *Cracking Codes: The Rosetta Stone and Decipherment.* London, British Museum Press

Parkinson, R.B. (1998) *The Tale of Sinuhe and Other Ancient Egyptian Poems*. Oxford, Oxford University Press.

Peck, W.H. (1978) *Egyptian Drawings*. New York, E.P. Dutton

Piankoff, A. (1972) *The Wandering of the Soul*. New Jersey, Princeton University Press

Pinch, G. (2002) *Egyptian Mythology*. Oxford, Oxford University Press

Pinch, G. (2006) *Magic in Ancient Egypt*. London, The British Museum Press

Poo, M. (1995) *Wine and Wine Offering in the Religion of Ancient Egypt*. London, Kegan Paul International

Posener, G. (1949) *Les Signes noir dans les rubriques*. In *Journal of Egyptian Archaeology*, Vol 35:77-81

Quirke, S. (1994) *Review: Translating Ma'at*. In *Journal of Egyptian Archaeology*, Vol 80:219-231

Quirke, S. & Spencer, J. (Eds.) (1992) *The British Museum Book of Ancient Egypt*. London, British Museum Press

Ray, J. (2002) *Reflections of Osiris*. London, Profile Books

Redford, D.B. (1971) *The Earliest Years of Ramesses II, and the Building of the Ramesside Court at Luxor*. In *Journal of Egyptian Archaeology*, Vol 57:110-119

Roth, A.M. & Roehrig, C.H. (2002) *Magical Bricks and the Bricks of Birth*. In *Journal of Egyptian Archaeology*, Vol 88:121-139

Ryholt, K. (1999) *The Carlsberg Papyri 4: The Story of Petese Son of Petetun*. Copenhagen, Museum Tusculanum Press

Sauneron, S. (2000) *The Priests of Ancient Egypt*. New York, Cornell University Press

Schorsch, D. (2001) *Precious-Metal Polychromy in Egypt in the Time of Tutankhamun*. In *Journal of Egyptian Archaeology*, Vol 87:55-57

Silverman, D.P. (1991) *Divinities and Deities in Ancient Egypt*. In Shafer, B.E. (ed.) (1991) *Religion in Ancient Egypt*. New York, Cornell University Press

Shakespeare, W. (1994) *The Tempest*. London, Wordsworth Classics

Shaw, I. & Nicholson, P. (2008) *The British Museum Dictionary of Ancient Egypt*. London, British Museum Press

Shorter, A.W. (1937) *The Papyrus of Khnememhab in University College, London*. In *Journal of Egyptian Archaeology*, Vol 23.1:34-38

Simpson, W.K. (1961) *An Additional Fragment of a 'Hatnub' stela*. In *Journal of Near Eastern Studies*, Vol 20.1:25-30

Simpson, W.K., & Ritner, R.K., & Tobin, V.A. & Wente, E.F. (2003) *The Literature of Ancient Egypt*. London, Yale University Press

Skeat, T.C. & Turner, E.G. (1968) *An Oracle of Hermes Trismegistos at Saqqara*. In *Journal of Egyptian Archaeology*, Vol 54:199-208

Sloley, R.W. (1931) *Primitive Methods of Measuring Time: With Special Reference to Egypt*. In *Journal of Egyptian Archaeology*, Vol 17.3/4:166-178

Smith, M. (1993) *The Liturgy of Opening the Mouth for Breathing*. Oxford, Griffith Institute

Smith, M. (2009) *Traversing Eternity*. Oxford, Oxford University Press

Stassinopoulos, A. & Beny R. (1983) *The Gods of Greece*. London, Weidenfield & Nicholson

Stevens, A. (2003) *The Material Evidence for Domestic Religion at Amarna and Preliminary Remarks on Its Interpretation*. In *Journal of Egyptian Archaeology*, Vol. 89:143-168

Strabo & Jones, H.L. (trans) (1932) *Geography Vol I*. New York, Cornell University Press

Strabo & Jones, H.L. (trans) (1932) *Geography Vol VIII*. New York, Cornell University Press

Strudwick, N. (2005) *Texts From the Pyramid Age*. Leiden, E.J. Brill

Taher, A.W. (2008) *News From Egypt*. In *Ancient Egypt*, Vol. 9.1 Issue 49

Taher, A.W. (2009) *News From Egypt.* In *Ancient Egypt,* Vol. 9.5 Issue 53

Taher, A.W. (2011) *News From Egypt.* In *Ancient Egypt* Vol. 11.4 Issue 64

Taylor, J.H. (Ed.) (2010) *Journey Through the Afterlife. Ancient Egyptian Book of the Dead.* London, The British Museum Press

Teeter, E. (1990) *Two Objects Inscribed for Djedhor.* In *Journal of Egyptian Archaeology* Vol 76:202-205

Teeter, E. & Johnson, J.H. (Eds.) (2009) *The Life of Meresamun.* Chicago, Oriental Institute Museum Publications No 29

Traunecker, C. (2001) *The Gods of Egypt.* New York, Cornell University Press

Tyldesley, J. (1995) *Daughters of Isis.* London, Penguin Books

Velde, H. (1988) *Some Remarks on the Mysterious Language of the Baboons.* In Kamstra, J.H., & Milde, H. & Wagtendank, K. (eds.) *Funerary Symbols and Religion. Essays dedicated to Professor MSHG Heerma Van Voss.* Hampden, J.H. Kok

Ward, W.A. (1961) *Comparative Studies in Egyptian and Ugaritic.* In *Journal of Near Eastern Studies* Vol 20.1:31-40

Ward, W.A. (1969) *The Semitic Root Hwy in Ugaritic and Derived Stems in Egyptian.* In *Journal of Near Eastern Studies,* Vol 28.4:265-267

Watterson, B. (1997) *Women in Ancient Egypt.* Stroud, Sutton Publishing Ltd

Wente, E.F. (1984) *Some Graffiti from the Reign of Hatshepsut.* In *Journal of Near Eastern Studies,* Vol 43.1:47-54

Wente, E.F. (1963) *Two Ramesside Stelas Pertaining to the Cult of Amenophis I.* In *Journal of Near Eastern Studies,* Vol 22.1:30-36

Wernick, N. (2009) *Timekeeping in Ancient Egypt.* In *Ancient Egypt* Vol 9.3 Issue 51:29-32

Wilkinson, R.H. (1994) *Symbol and Magic in Egyptian Art.* London, Thames & Hudson

Wilkinson, R.H. (2003) *The Complete Gods and Goddesses of Ancient Egypt.* London, Thames & Hudson

Wilkinson, R.H. (2000) *The Complete Temples of Ancient Egypt.* London, Thames & Hudson

Wilson, H. (1993) *Understanding Hieroglyphics: a Quick and Simple Guide.* London, Michael O'Mara Books Ltd

Wilson, J.A. (1935) *The Libyans and the End of the Egyptian Empire.* In *The American Journal of Semitic Languages and Literature,* Vol 51.2:73-82

Wilson, J.A. (1948) *The Oath in Ancient Egypt.* In *Journal of Near Eastern Studies,* Vol 7.3:129-156

Winlock, H.E. (1924) *A Statue of Horemhab Before His Accession.* In *Journal of Egyptian Archaeology,* Vol 10.1:1-5

Zabkar, L.V. (1988) *Hymns to Isis in Her Temple at Philae.* New England, University Press of New England

INDEX

CPSIA information can be obtained at www.ICGtesting.com
Printed in the USA
LVOW03s0421270614

391995LV00005B/38/P